REASON
and
HUMAN GOVERNMENT

Alan E. Johnson

Philosophia Publications
Pittsburgh, Pennsylvania

For permissions or other information,
contact Alan E. Johnson at
https://alanjohnson.academia.edu/contact.

Print ISBN: 978-0-9701055-8-5
Digital ISBN: 978-0-9701055-9-2
Library of Congress Control Number: 2026900234

Cover image

Photograph of President John F. Kennedy as he signed, on
October 23, 1962, the proclamation for the interdiction of
the delivery of offensive missiles to Cuba during the Cuban
Missile Crisis (public domain; photographic image courtesy
of the John F. Kennedy Presidential Library)

Published by

Philosophia Publications
301 South Hills Village Drive
Suite LL200-112
Pittsburgh, Pennsylvania 15241
USA
http://www.PhilosophiaPublications.com

To the Memory of John F. Kennedy

For his example of rational political leadership

But what is government itself but the greatest of all reflections on human nature? If men were angels, no government would be necessary. If angels were to govern men, neither external nor internal controls on government would be necessary. In framing a government which is to be administered by men over men, the great difficulty lies in this: You must first enable the government to control the governed; and in the next place, oblige it to control itself. A dependence on the people is no doubt the primary control on the government; but experience has taught mankind the necessity of auxiliary precautions.

—James Madison, Federalist Number 51

[The scenes of the American Revolution] *were* the pillars of the temple of liberty; and now, that they have crumbled away, that temple must fall, unless we, their descendants, supply their places with other pillars, hewn from the solid quarry of sober reason. Passion has helped us; but can do so no more. It will in future be our enemy. Reason, cold, calculating, unimpassioned reason, must furnish all the materials for our future support and defence. — Let those materials be moulded into *general intelligence, sound morality*, and in particular, *a reverence for the constitution and laws* . . . .

—Abraham Lincoln, Address Before the Young Men's Lyceum of Springfield, Illinois, January 27, 1838 (emphasis in the original)

CONTENTS

Preface.. vi

Introduction 1

Chapter 1. Is Government Necessary?................................7

Chapter 2. Governmental Recognition and Protection of
  Individual Rights 23

Chapter 3. Legitimate Affirmative Powers of Government
 50

Chapter 4. Forms of Government 74

Chapter 5. Case Study: Political Leadership in the Cuban
  Missile Crisis..106

Epilogue 176

Appendix. The Historical Background of the 1962 Cuban
  Missile Crisis..182

Notes 218

Selected Bibliography......................................252

Index 264

About the Author 268

PREFACE

Confucius said, "To take what you know for what you know, and what you do not know for what you do not know, that is knowledge indeed."[1] This statement epitomizes the challenges I have experienced in writing the present book.

This is the concluding volume of my philosophical trilogy on free will, ethics, and political philosophy. The first book, *Free Will and Human Life* (2021),[2] necessitated my study of some scientific fields in which I was not an expert. Although I still cannot call myself a scientist, I acquired sufficient knowledge in science and other relevant fields to discuss the major arguments for and against free will and to conclude that free will, properly understood, exists and is beneficial to human life.

The second book in this trilogy, *Reason and Human Ethics* (2022),[3] was more than six decades in the making, going back to questions I pondered as early as age fifteen. It replaced an earlier book, published in 2000, which amounted to a first—but unsatisfactory—draft on issues of ethics, metaphysics, and religion. The 2022 book included portions of the 2000 book that survived my subsequent critical scrutiny; I deliberately consigned the remainder of the 2000 book to publishing (out-of-print) oblivion. The analysis and conclusions in the 2022 book constitute my final statement on ethics and related questions of metaphysics and religion.

Preface

The present third book of this philosophical trilogy addresses difficult questions of political philosophy. I have been studying and thinking about political philosophy since the 1960s. Some of my tentative views on aspects of this subject have changed a number of times over the decades. This book represents my final conclusions. With regard to questions about which I still entertain doubts, I adumbrate the major alternatives and cite references on all sides of the issues for the reader's further study and reflection. There are, however, important matters about which my views are sufficiently formed and ready for presentation to the public. This is why I have written this book and why it has taken me so long to complete it.

These three books may be considered as three parts of an overall work titled *The Philosophy of Human Life*. Each of these volumes can be read separately and independently of the others, but the entire expanse of my thought on human philosophy can be found in this trilogy along with my earlier books on Roger Williams and the Electoral College.[4]

This work sets forth my own political philosophy. For my remarks over the years on the history of political philosophy, see my papers posted on Academia.edu[5] and my numerous comments in "Political Philosophy and Ethics," the online Goodreads.com discussion group that I founded in 2014.[6]

As in all my books and essays, when I discuss or cite other writers in the present book, my agreement or disagreement with them should not be construed to extend to issues other than those being immediately addressed. I often agree with other thinkers on some matters and disagree with them on others.

The page numbers of the print edition of this book are inserted in italicized braces (*{}*) at the appropriate locations of the ebook edition. The page numbers identified in the index of the ebook refer to these italicized page numbers, and that index is accordingly identical to the index in the printed book.

I will post any errata and supplemental comments at https://chicago.academia.edu/AlanJohnson/Books,-Book-Excerpts,-and-Errata-Supp-Comments.

Reason and Human Government follows logically from *Free Will and Human Life* and *Reason and Human Ethics*. A premise of *Free Will and Human Life* is that human beings have some free will in both their individual and collective lives. Another premise is that they have some ability to exercise their reasoning abilities in a correct manner. Although humans are not perfect, they can use their free will and reason to improve their individual, social, and political lives.

Examples of political progress in the United States include the abolition of slavery in the nineteenth century, the substantial (though not yet complete) abolition of Jim Crow legislation and related practices in the twentieth century, and the legal gender equality that became a part of US constitutional, statutory, administrative, and judicial law during the twentieth and twenty-first centuries.

Progress in political matters is not, however, inevitable. Indeed, there are setbacks. Human beings in each generation should exercise their free will and reason to ascertain proper political objectives and to facilitate the achievement of those ends by voting, public advocacy, and/or direct political action. As elaborated in *Reason and Human Ethics*, correct reasoning about both ends and means is important for all people at all times. This is especially true in a political context.

I wish to thank my wife, Miriam (Mimi) Lindauer, for our frequent discussions relevant to ethical and political philosophy over the decades. I dedicated my first postretirement book, *The First American Founder: Roger Williams and Freedom of Conscience* (2015), to her. Mimi has been one of my major interlocutors on these subjects since we first met some decades ago.

My intention during college and graduate school was to become a professor of political philosophy. For a number of reasons, this plan did not come to fruition. Instead, I began my professional career as a writer and editor of government and history textbooks for high school students. Thereafter, I became an attorney, focusing primarily, though not exclusively, on constitutional, governmental, employment, and land use litigation. Since retiring from law practice in 2012, I have written and published books and essays on philosophy, history, political science, and law.

This book reflects all of these experiences as well as my introduction to critical thinking about political issues as a high school debater. In this regard, I owe a great deal to my high school debate coach, the late David Kanellis. I also express my gratitude to other instructors in high school, college, graduate school, and law school who facilitated my intellectual development. While it is unlikely that any of them would agree with all of the views expressed in my books, these teachers were nonetheless an inspiration to me and other of their students.

The photograph on the cover of the present book was taken of President John F. Kennedy as he signed, on October 23, 1962, the proclamation for the interdiction of the delivery of offensive missiles to Cuba during the Cuban Missile Crisis. As explained in chapter 5 of this book, I regard President Kennedy's handling of this crisis as a model of astute political leadership.

Alan E. Johnson
January 8, 2026

INTRODUCTION

This is a work of political philosophy. Political philosophy is, in my view, the search for knowledge, as distinguished from opinion, regarding the nature of human government.[1] Chapter 1 addresses the fundamental questions of what government is, its consistency with human ethics, and its necessity and desirability for human life as we know it. Chapter 2 proceeds with a discussion of governmental recognition and protection of individual rights. Chapter 3 considers the legitimate affirmative powers of government. Chapter 4 delineates and evaluates different forms of government, both philosophical and historical. Chapter 5 is a case study of political leadership in the 1962 Cuban Missile Crisis. An epilogue states overall conclusions of this work. The appendix provides an account of the historical background of the Cuban Missile Crisis, including the Marxist roots of international Communism, the 1917 Bolshevik revolution in Russia, the historical development of the Marxist-Leninist regime in the Soviet Union, Fidel Castro's successful 1959 revolution in Cuba, and the US-instigated 1961 invasion at the Bay of Pigs in Cuba.

This book attempts to identify and elaborate basic principles of political philosophy. Although these principles might be understood to transcend any particular time and place, it must be acknowledged that we live in an age (the twentieth and twenty-first centuries) that differs, in significant respects, from earlier epochs. Many of us live in political societies with widespread literacy, an industrial or postindustrial economic base, instant communication with others all over the world, universal media, constantly evolving technology, and many other unprecedented phenomena.

Accordingly, the present work attempts not only to identify enduring principles of government but also to discuss how they would apply to our contemporary circumstances.

IMPORTANT TERMS

The terms used in political philosophy and general political discourse are often confusing and ambiguous, because different people mean different things by them. Thus, it makes sense at the start of the present discussion to explain how this book uses certain critical words and phrases.

Constitution and **form of government** and **polity** refer to the governmental organization of an actual or projected political society. The word **regime** is sometimes used in this sense, but "regime" is often associated in the English language with an authoritarian or totalitarian system. Thus, we speak of the Nazi regime or the Stalinist regime but do not, in ordinary speech, characterize democratic-republican political societies as "regimes."

When capitalized, **Constitution** means a specific written document—such as the United States Constitution–that provides an overall set of rules for a particular political society. When not capitalized, **constitution** refers to a type of polity that does not have a single, formal, written document as its basic law but may, or may not, have a series of historical documents that operate as guiding principles for its form of government, as in the United Kingdom. The lowercase plural word **constitutions** refers to both written and unwritten forms of government.

Government means something different in parliamentary systems like the United Kingdom than in presidential democratic republics like the United States. "Government" in the UK refers to the executive department headed by a prime minister, as distinguished from the legislature or the judiciary. In polities like the United States, "government" refers to all three branches of government—executive, legislative, and judicial—and associated administrative agencies. The present book uses the latter definition of "government." For an expanded definition of "government" (the "state"), see the beginning of Chapter 1 of this book.

Direct democracy is a system of government in which adult citizens vote on all or most governmental laws and decisions without representatives, separation of powers, checks and balances, and constitutional protections of individual rights. The classic example is Athens from about 460 BCE to about 320 BCE. However, only male citizens could vote in Athenian direct democracy. Women, metics (noncitizens), and slaves (of whom there were many) had no political power.

A **democratic republic** or **constitutional democracy** or **representative democracy** has a democratic base that usually elects the legislature and, directly or indirectly, the executive. Indirect methods of electing the president or prime minister include the Electoral College in the United States and the legislature in parliamentary and some other systems. Democratic republics also typically have written or unwritten constitutional protections of individual rights, often enforced by the judiciary. The adjective "democratic-republican" refers to this type of government.

Democracy includes any of the foregoing types of democracy. However, at least in the United States, the words "democracy" or "democratic" usually are understood to include the constitutional features of a democratic republic, as distinguished from a direct democracy. Accordingly, when American politicians and others use the terms "democratic" or "undemocratic," they normally include the separation of powers, checks and balances, and protections of individual rights in the US Constitution, as amended.

OVERVIEW OF THIS BOOK

Chapter 1 ("Is Government Necessary?") addresses the apparent contradiction of political life. If the initiation of physical force is wrong when committed by an individual human being against another, why is it morally acceptable for governments to initiate physical coercion in the form of taxes, laws, regulations, and so forth? This chapter discusses the philosophical challenge of anarchism. It demonstrates that the abolition of government is simply impossible in our present-day complex societies. Although this fact would appear to incorporate a contradiction, it is, in the last analysis, not a contradiction, because minimalist or perhaps even nonexistent government might be possible **after** the ethical reformation of humanity. Ethical reformation includes correct reasoning about both ends and means (see my book *Reason and Human Ethics*[2]). Although we should work for such an ethical reformation, it will not occur in our lifetimes and, probably, not for many centuries or millennia, if at all. In the meantime, humans should strive to improve their individual, social, and political lives by promoting rational and ethical thinking and behavior.

Chapter 2 ("Governmental Recognition and Protection of Individual Rights") discusses the first duty of government: to recognize and enforce individual rights, i.e., those rights that an individual human being possesses to be free from governmental coercion as well as rights that a person has to be protected by government against the coercion or fraud of others. The question of positive socioeconomic rights is deferred to Chapter 3.

Chapter 3 ("Legitimate Affirmative Powers of Government") discusses my disagreement with the minarchist views of Ayn Rand and others that government should be limited to the police, the armed forces, and the law courts. Although these are legitimate functions of government, there are many others, which Chapter 3 elaborates at some length.

Chapter 4 ("Forms of Government") discusses the various types of polities and concludes that a democratic republic with constitutional separation of powers, checks and balances, and recognition of individual rights is the best model.

Chapter 5 ("Political Leadership in the 1962 Cuban Missile Crisis") analyzes the decision-making of Soviet Premier Nikita Khrushchev and President John F. Kennedy in the 1962 Cuban missile crisis.

An epilogue summarizes and elaborates upon the book's general conclusions.

Introduction

The Appendix ("Historical Background of the 1962 Cuban Missile Crisis") addresses, in some depth, the writings of Karl Marx, Friedrich Engels, and Vladimir Lenin; the history of the 1917 Bolshevik revolution and its aftermath in the Soviet Union; the successful revolution of Fidel Castro and his followers in 1959 and the subsequent transformation of Cuba into an authoritarian or totalitarian Communist regime; US planning of what became the Bay of Pigs invasion in Cuba during the presidential administrations of Dwight D. Eisenhower and John F. Kennedy; and the events and outcome of the actual Bay of Pigs invasion in 1961.

CHAPTER ONE
IS GOVERNMENT NECESSARY?

THE PROBLEM

Sociologist Max Weber famously defined the "state" (government) as follows:

> In the past the use of physical violence by widely differing organizations—starting with the clan—was completely normal. Nowadays, in contrast, we must say that the state is the form of human community that (successfully) lays claim to the *monopoly of legitimate physical violence* within a particular territory—and this idea of "territory" is an essential defining feature. For what is specific to the present is that all other organizations or individuals can assert the right to use physical violence only insofar as the *state* permits them to do so. The state is regarded as the sole source of the "right" to use violence.[1]

The first question about human government is whether it is necessary.

Merriam-Webster defines "anarchism" as "a political theory holding all forms of governmental authority to be unnecessary and undesirable and advocating a society based on voluntary cooperation and free association of individuals and groups."[2]

Various forms of anarchism have been proposed throughout the millennia. The present chapter discusses whether anarchism is desirable or even possible in advanced communities. It concludes that some kind of government is necessary for the foreseeable future. Chapters 2 and 3 address the functions of government that are appropriate in today's complex societies.

The question of the necessity of government arises from a fundamental perplexity at the root of political philosophy. It is axiomatic that an individual human does not have a moral right (at least absent extremely unusual circumstances) to initiate physical force against other humans. Anarchists extrapolate this principle to society at large. Government, in their view, has no moral right to initiate physical coercion against others by way of taxation, conscription, regulation, or other uses of explicit or implicit force. Anarchists consider all such practices as ultimately initiating physical force, because, if one refuses to comply with governmental directives, government will, ultimately, send its police officers to arrest the dissenter. Thus, anarchists reject all governmental laws and, indeed, the institution of government itself.

Some anarchists are fond of pointing out that primitive societies such as hunter-gatherer tribes have gotten along just fine without government.[3] But what if anarchism is impossible in complex societies such as exist in the present century? We cannot go back to a hunter-gatherer existence. What then?

The present chapter addresses such questions. I focus on contemporary anarchocapitalism, because anarchocapitalist writings attempt to answer the question of how voluntary associations might totally replace government. I have been unable to find similar projections for the abolition of government in other forms of anarchism. But my basic arguments against anarchocapitalism would also apply to other anarchist theories insofar as they advocate the complete abolition of government.

CONTEMPORARY ANARCHOCAPITALISM

Murray N. Rothard (1926–95) was the major twentieth-century proponent of anarchocapitalism. He elaborated its principles in his book *For a New Liberty: A Libertarian Manifesto*, originally published in 1973, with a second edition in 1978 and a further publication of the second edition by the Ludwig von Mises Institute in 2006.[4] He also discussed his anarchocapitalist theory in *Power and Market: Government and the Economy*[5] and *The Ethics of Liberty*.[6]

Rothbard proceeded on the basis of what he called the nonaggression axiom, which he described as followed:

> The libertarian creed rests upon one central axiom: that no man or group of men may aggress against the person or property of anyone else. This may be called the "nonaggression axiom." "Aggression" is defined as the initiation of the use or threat of physical violence against the person or property of anyone else. . . .
>
> While opposing any and all private or group aggression against the rights of person and property, the libertarian sees that throughout history and into the present day, there has been one central, dominant, and

overriding aggressor upon all of these rights:
the State.[7]

Rothbard famously broke with Ayn Rand, who
supported the concept of a minimalist government
limited to police, defense against foreign aggressors,
and courts. I discuss Rand's political philosophy in the
section on minarchism in Chapter 3 of this book.
Rothbard rejected Rand's objections to anarchism, as
did another proponent of anarchocapitalism, J. Michael
Oliver, in his book *The New Libertarianism: Anarcho-
Capitalism*.[8] However, Oliver, unlike Rothbard,
substantially agreed with some other aspects of Rand's
philosophy. In the present discussion, we will focus
mainly on Rothbard's *For a New Liberty*, which, to my
knowledge, sets forth the anarchocapitalist alternative
in clearest detail.

CRITIQUE OF ROTHBARD'S ANARCHOCAPITALISM

Rothbard often avoided using the term
"anarchocapitalism" or "anarcho-capitalism," because
the various historical uses of the term "anarchism"
departed significantly from its etymological meaning.[9]
Nevertheless, he wrote in *The Ethics of Liberty* that he
was "able to expound and defend the 'anarchocapitalist' political creed" in his book *For a New
Liberty*.[10] Furthermore, his disciples and others have
often applied the "anarchocapitalist" label to him in the
sense that he did, indeed, advocate the abolition of all
government and its replacement by capitalistic
institutions.

In case there is any doubt about Rothbard's
ownership of the term "anarchocapitalism," he railed

against government (what he called "the State") at every opportunity in his writings. In *The Ethics of Liberty*, for example, he argued:

> The State may therefore be defined as that organization which possesses either or both (in actual fact, almost always both) of the following characteristics: (a) it acquires its revenue by physical coercion (taxation); and (b) it achieves a compulsory monopoly of force and of ultimate decision-making power over a given territorial area. Both of these essential activities of the State necessarily constitute criminal aggression and depredation of the just rights of private property of its subjects (including self-ownership). For the first constitutes and establishes theft on a grand scale; while the second prohibits the free competition of defense and decision-making agencies within a given territorial area—prohibiting the voluntary purchase and sale of defense and judicial services.[11]

Accordingly, Rothbard proceeded on the basis of two basic postulates: (1) government is irredeemably evil and must be totally abolished, and (2) "the free competition of defense and decision-making agencies within a given territorial area" is both desirable and workable. This is why his doctrine is called "anarchocapitalism."

Rothbard's reductive premise that all government is evil ignores the fact that different kinds of governments exist and that some are better than others. Chapters 2, 3, and 4 of the present book explain how democratic republics with constitutional protections of individual rights, separations of powers, checks and balances, and (in countries with large territories) federalism help guard against authoritarianism.

Moreover, Rothbard's argument that all government should be eradicated depends on his implicit premise that a desirable and workable alternative exists. Anarchists have criticized government as such for millennia. Rothbard's unique contribution appears to be his position that private, capitalistic associations can and should totally replace government. The following discussion will examine his specific proposals and compare them to the laws and procedures of democratic-republican governments.

Private Defense Agencies: Criminals

We define "criminals" as those individuals or private organizations that initiate force or fraud against other individuals or against private or public organizations. Democratic-republican governments address such phenomena by enacting written criminal laws and by enforcing such laws by means of governmental police and courts.

In the United States and similar democratic republics, a person accused of committing a criminal offense is arrested, on the basis of an arrest warrant or other probable cause determination, by federal, state, or local law enforcement officers and is tried in an official governmental proceeding with a right to trial by jury in felony and significant misdemeanor cases. Established criminal procedure affords the accused certain constitutional and legal protections. See, for example, Article I, Section 9, Clause 2 (habeas corpus) and the Fourth, Fifth, Sixth, Eighth, and Fourteenth

Amendments to the United States Constitution as well as the Federal Rules of Criminal Procedure, the Federal Rules of Evidence, and state constitutional, procedural, and evidentiary law. Upon conviction, the defendant has a right to appeal pursuant to the Federal Rules of Appellate Procedure and analogous state appellate rules. These constitutional and legal protections are well established in US law. Other democratic republics have similar, though not identical, criminal procedures.

Rothbard rejects all of this. He argues that all governmental laws and institutions (here, governmental law enforcement and courts) should be abolished and replaced by competitive nongovernmental capitalistic organizations.

Anarchocapitalism rests on the fundamental fallacies of false analogy and category error. To use Rothbard's analogy, capitalistic competition works in the realm of the manufacture and sale of shoes; ergo, nongovernmental capitalistic competition would also work to provide free-market substitutes for police and courts.[12] This analogy, false as it is, is a substitute for proof in Rothbard's visionary world.

How, then, would it work? Rothbard initially refuses to answer, suggesting, instead, that we just have to have faith in the market:

> The point is that the advocate of a free market in *anything* cannot provide a "constructive" blueprint of such a market in advance. The essence and **the glory of the free market** is that individual firms and businesses, competing on the market, provide an ever-changing orchestration of efficient and progressive goods and services:

continually improving products and markets, advancing technology, cutting costs, and meeting changing consumer demands as swiftly and as efficiently as possible. The libertarian economist can try to offer a few guidelines on how markets *might* develop where they are now prevented or restricted from developing; but he can do little more than point the way toward freedom, to call for government to get out of the way of the productive and ever-inventive energies of the public as expressed in voluntary market activity. No one can predict the number of firms, the size of each firm, the pricing policies, etc., of any future market in any service or commodity. **We just know**—by **economic theory** and by **historical insight**—that such a free market will do the job infinitely better than the compulsory monopoly of bureaucratic government.[13]

"We just know," says Rothbard, that the market is always right. Allegedly infallible "economic theory" tells us so, as does subjective "historical insight." Never mind that most economists do not accept anarchocapitalist "theory" and have different "historical insights" than Rothbard. All we need is Faith in the Market. Rothbard's book is filled with questionable factual interpretations of the past and rosy predictions about the future. But suppose we do not blindly accept these sanguine assumptions. What if we critically examined Rothbard's speculations about how his glorified market might deal with the very important question of criminal justice?

14

Rothbard argued that all land (including streets, roads, and highways), water (lakes, rivers, and oceans), and air should be privately owned. This would, he suggested, enable the owners of such real estate to hire private security forces to prevent or stop criminal activity on their land.[14] Rothbard admitted that his system could lead to discrimination against perceived undesirables who wish to use the streets or access housing: "It might be charged that all this will allow freedom 'to discriminate' in housing or use of the streets. There is no question about that. Fundamental to the libertarian creed is every man's right to choose who shall enter or use his own property. . . ."[15]

In other words, owners of housing could discriminate against racial or other minorities by refusing to allow them to purchase or rent houses. Owners of streets could even refuse entry to their streets. Such a system could easily degenerate into the kind of racial housing and neighborhood segregation that characterized much of the United States before enactment of the US Fair Housing Act of 1968. This Act was later amended to also protect people with disabilities and families with children. All such laws would be eradicated, along with government, in Rothbard's new feudal order of local capitalistic overlords. It would be a case of "back to the future."

Although private security forces are permitted in the United States today, they must be in compliance with governmental legal requirements.[16] A private security officer is not a governmental police officer and generally has no powers other than those of an ordinary citizen. Specifically, unless private officers have a specialized police officer certification, they cannot use force, let alone excessive force, and they may not detain anyone except where permitted under citizen arrest laws.[17] With the abolition of government and governmental law enforcement, all such protections would disappear. Private security officers would be able to act without legal constraint. One could expect the rampant use of excessive force, for example, especially against minorities. This has been a continuing problem in the United States for a long time, but it would only worsen with the abolition of governmental law enforcement subject to legal constraints under (but not limited to) the Fourth and Fourteenth Amendments to the United States Constitution and enforced by the federal and state judiciaries.

Chapter 12 of *For a New Liberty* discusses further the questions of private police and private defense agencies. Private companies and individual people could retain private defense agencies, by analogy to their retention of private insurance companies. There would be many such agencies, and disagreements between them would be possible, if not frequent.

Rothbard does not consider this a problem. First, he says there would be a libertarian legal code, to which all private defense agencies, private courts, and private arbitrators would agree.[18] But how, in the absence of government, could it be certain that they would all agree on a legal code? Is it not more likely that some private agencies (for example, those specializing in representing criminals or perhaps even organized crime) would refuse assent to a legal code promulgated by other private actors?

This is further complicated by Rothbard's insistence on the proportionality principle for criminal punishment. Under that principle, restitution is often appropriate for monetary offenses like theft. What about physical assault? Here, the punishment can be more extreme. According to Rothbard,

> In the question of bodily assault, where restitution does not even apply, we can again employ our criterion of proportionate punishment; so that if A has beaten up B in a certain way, then B has the right to beat up A (or have him beaten up by judicial employees) to rather more than the same extent.
>
> Here allowing the criminal to buy his way out of this punishment could indeed enter in, but only as a voluntary contract with the plaintiff. For example, suppose that A has severely beaten B; B now has the right to beat up A as severely, or a bit more, or to hire someone or some organization to do the beating for him (who in a libertarian society, could be marshals hired by privately competitive courts). But A, of course, is free to try to buy his way out, to pay B for waiving his right to have his aggressor beaten up.[19]

This raises the interesting question whether all private courts in a nongovernmental society would agree on a legal code written by Rothbard and his libertarian followers. I think not.

But how would this work in practice? If Person A (who was "insured" by Company A) beat up Person B (who was "insured" by Company B), Person B could file a legal action with Company B against Person A. If

Person A refused to settle the case with Person B, a "trial" would be conducted in a private court (or arbitration) selected by Company B (or by agreement between Company A and Company B). In this proceeding, nobody would have the power to subpoena witnesses, because Rothbard considers the subpoena power (as well as compulsory jury service) to be a violation of individual rights.[20]

Now, suppose the "trial" results in a judgment in favor of Person B against Person A (who would be represented by Company A's "lawyers"). The judgment would specify that Person B "has the right to beat up A (or have him beaten up by judicial employees) to rather more than the same extent" that A beat up B. Person A could now either accept and submit to the punishment or could appeal to another company that provides appellate services. What if Person A then loses that appeal and still refuses to submit to the punishment of being beaten up by Person B? The libertarian legal code would specify how many appeals would be permitted. In such case, after the exhaustion of all available appeals, if Person A still refused to accept the final judgment, Company B would resort to force against Person A. Would Company A then defend Person A against such force?

The criminal justice system proposed by Rothbard raises many questions. It points to the possibility that such an anarchocapitalist society would devolve into a Hobbesian "war of all against all," as history has evidenced in many instances of "failed states." I think the chances of such a catastrophe are better than even. Indeed, I am reminded of a statement made long ago in a much different context: "he that out of a desire to

18

repaire his house, shall move all the foundations, will sooner be buried in the ruines of the old, then live to see the erection of a new structure."[21]

Defense Against Foreign Aggression

Rothbard wrote *For a New Liberty* during the Cold War, and that book addressed the concern that the anarchocapitalist society he proposed for the United States would leave the country exposed to an invasion from the Soviet Union. He initially responded as follows: "The Russian question . . . assumes, *not* that libertarianism has been established everywhere throughout the globe, but that for some reason it has been established *only* in America and nowhere else. But why assume this? Why not first assume that it has been established *everywhere* and see whether we like it?"[22] This answer proves the utter unreality of what Rothbard was proposing. It shows that Rothbard was suggesting only a presumably perfect society in speech—one that could not be accomplished on the ground in any foreseeable century. About fifty years after he wrote this statement, neither the United States nor Russia is anything close to an anarchocapitalist society, not to mention the remainder of the entire world.

Rothbard next considered the possibility that the Soviet Union might actually attempt to conquer the United States:

> Let us assume that the Soviet Union would really be hell-bent on attacking a libertarian population within the present boundaries of the United States (clearly, there would no longer be a United States government to form a single nation-state). In the first place, the form and quantity of defense

expenditures would be decided upon by the American consumers themselves. Those Americans who favor Polaris submarines, and fear a Soviet threat, would subscribe toward the financing of such vessels. Those who prefer an ABM system would invest in such defensive missiles. Those who laugh at such a threat or those who are committed pacifists would not contribute to any "national" defense service at all. Different defense theories would be applied in proportion to those who agree with, and support, the various theories being offered. Given the enormous waste in all wars and defense preparations in all countries throughout history, it is certainly not beyond the bounds of reason to propose that private, voluntary defense efforts would be far more efficient than government boondoggles. Certainly these efforts would be infinitely more moral.[23]

This argument of Rothbard is even more risible than the earlier one. Instead of a unified, national defense strategy, Rothbard proposed that everyone who wants to could choose their own favorite defense system and voluntarily contribute what they wished to such a defense without taxation and with no understanding of whether such a scattered approach would have any chance against a military attack such as Hitler achieved in Western Europe and elsewhere during World War II.

Finally, Rothbard argued that an anarchocapitalist society would be able to defeat any invaders, because orders could not be transmitted to an existing government and because the people would resist with guerrilla warfare.[24] However, Nazi Germany ruled northern and western France (the "occupied zone") directly, without any French government, after the German conquest in 1940.[25] Moreover, internal guerrilla resistance by French people was unsuccessful in dislodging Hitler's armies; it took the massive Allied Normandy invasion of 1944 to finally remove German troops from France and other countries in Western Europe.

The Soviet Union disintegrated in 1991 and was eventually replaced by the authoritarian government of Vladimir Putin in the first decade of the twenty-first-century. There is no likelihood that the Putin regime will invade the United States, though it has had no hesitation in attempting to conquer Ukraine by military force.

Other questions regarding foreign policy will be addressed in chapters 3 and 5.

CONCLUSION

Murray Rothbard's presentation of anarchocapitalism raises many additional questions, but the foregoing are the most fundamental. His panacea for societal problems is the abolition of government: "The ultimate libertarian program may be summed up in one phrase: the abolition of the public sector, the conversion of all operations and services performed by the government into activities performed voluntarily by the private-enterprise economy."[26]

As established above, anarchocapitalism (or other forms of anarchism) would not work, and any attempt to implement such a system under conditions existing in the twenty-first century would likely have disastrous consequences.

We remain with the contradiction between individual ethics and political ethics discussed at the beginning of this chapter. That contradiction will disappear, if ever, only when the vast majority of people are ethical and rational. Even then, some minimal government may be necessary for administrative purposes. However this may be, the disappearance or severe minimization of government will not be accomplished in the present century or even in foreseeable future centuries.

Some government is necessary. The next two chapters address what kind of government is appropriate under current circumstances.

CHAPTER TWO
GOVERNMENTAL RECOGNITION AND
PROTECTION OF INDIVIDUAL RIGHTS

INTRODUCTION

The term "individual rights" is, absent definition, exceedingly ambiguous. In this book, "individual rights" are those rights that an individual human being has to be free from governmental coercion as well as rights that a person has to be protected by government against the coercion or fraud of others. The question of positive socioeconomic rights is deferred to the next chapter.

"Individual rights," as thus defined for present purposes, are of two kinds: (1) natural rights, i.e., rights that an individual possesses by virtue of the fact of being human,[1] and (2) legal rights, which an individual human being has as a result of constitutional, judicial, or legislative pronouncements. This chapter addresses both kinds of individual rights.

The present chapter also discusses whether a government should employ the doctrine of judicial review to protect such rights. Judicial review, in the present context, is "a constitutional doctrine that gives to a court system and especially to a supreme court the power to annul legislative or executive acts which the judges declare are contrary to the provisions of the constitution."[2]

We consider these questions primarily in the light of three documents: (1) the United Nations Universal Declaration of Human Rights,[3] (2) the Declaration of Independence of the United States of America,[4] and (3) the United States Constitution[5] and its interpretation and application by the US judiciary. Similar provisions are contained in the written or unwritten constitutions of some other countries as well as the European Union.[6]

INDIVIDUAL RIGHTS

General Principles

The United Nations Universal Declaration of Human Rights (UDHR) states, in the first clause of its preamble, that "recognition of the inherent dignity and of the equal and inalienable rights of all members of the human family is the foundation of freedom, justice and peace in the world . . . ." Article 1 of the UDHR reads: "All human beings are born free and equal in dignity and rights. They are endowed with reason and conscience and should act towards one another in a spirit of brotherhood." Article 2 states that "[e]veryone is entitled to all the rights and freedoms set forth in this Declaration, without distinction of any kind, such as race, colour, sex, language, religion, political or other opinion, national or social origin, property, birth or other status."

The above-quoted UDHR language is clearly based on an understanding of human nature, i.e., on what are called "natural rights." It refers to the "the equal and inalienable rights of all members of the human family." All people, by nature, are "born free and equal in dignity and rights." In other words, notwithstanding many factual differences among human beings as they exist in their various cultures, they all are, by human nature, equal in individual rights vis-à-vis government. These natural rights are "inalienable": They cannot be alienated to government in any social or political compact.

The UDHR does not say that all humans are, or should necessarily be, equal in the property they do in fact possess. It also does not assert that all human beings equally exercise their reason and conscience. Humans, by their nature, are "endowed with reason and conscience" and are, accordingly, **capable** of exercising reason and conscience, whether or not they factually do so. Of course, those humans who suffer from the more serious forms of brain injury or psychosis may be limited in their ability to use reason or to think and act in an ethical manner.

This UDHR language reminds Americans of their Declaration of Independence, which, among other things, famously proclaims: "We hold these truths to be self-evident, that all men [human beings] are created equal, that they are endowed by their Creator with certain unalienable Rights, that among these are Life, Liberty and the pursuit of Happiness." Thomas Jefferson was the principal architect of the Declaration of Independence. However, his draft did not include the word "Creator"; that term was added by another, perhaps Benjamin Franklin. In the context of the Deistic Enlightenment views prevalent among the intellectual elite at that time, "Creator" could refer to a nonpersonal God of science and philosophy rather than a God of revelation. None of the principal drafters (Jefferson,

Franklin, John Adams) of the Declaration was a conventional Christian.[7]

Similarly, Article 1 of the UDHR states: "All human beings are born free and equal in dignity and rights. They are **endowed** with reason and conscience and should act towards one another in a spirit of brotherhood" (emphasis added). This language appears to have been influenced by the US Declaration of Independence (1776). It speaks of humans being "endowed" but does not use the Declaration's phrase "endowed by their Creator . . . ." The UDHR was written for the United Nations, to which nations all over the world belonged. Their various peoples had many different religions, and the UDHR made an effort not to discriminate among them.

The second paragraph of Article 29 of the UDHR indicates how individual rights are qualified by the following general principle: "In the exercise of his [or her] rights and freedoms, everyone shall be subject only to such limitations as are determined by law solely for the purpose of securing due recognition and respect for the rights and freedoms of others and of meeting the just requirements of morality, public order and the general welfare in a democratic society." Of course, these are broad concepts that would require greater specificity when applied to concrete situations. For example, a concern for "morality" would not justify laws enforcing religious taboos that do not involve using force or fraud against others.

The 1787 Constitutional Convention formulated the text of the original United States Constitution. The requisite number of states ratified the Constitution during 1787 and 1788. The new government established

26

by the Constitution went into effect in early 1779. This initial version of the Constitution was concerned with the organization of the national government, not (with a few exceptions) with the identification of individual rights. However, the Congress adopted in 1789 what became known as the Bill of Rights (the first ten constitutional amendments), and the requisite number of states ratified these ten amendments on December 15, 1791. These and some later constitutional amendments listed certain individual rights. In some cases, these rights can be understood as natural rights. In other cases, they can be construed as simply legal rights. Additionally, some of these rights could be considered both natural and legal. Although the following analysis is not exhaustive, it addresses some specific rights and discusses whether they are natural rights or legal rights or both.

Specific Individual Rights

Life

Article 3 of the UDHR states in relevant part: "Everyone has the right to life . . . ." The US Declaration of Independence recognizes "life" as a natural and "unalienable" right. The US Constitution provides that neither the federal (Fifth Amendment) nor the state (Fourteenth Amendment) governments may deprive any person of life without due process of law.

The US Constitution, but not the UDHR, seems to recognize the possibility of a criminal judgment of capital punishment provided that the requirements of procedural due process are satisfied. Accordingly, in US courts, capital cases are often analyzed under the Eighth

27

Amendment's prohibition of cruel and unusual punishments. My own view is that capital punishment should be abolished in the United States (as it has in many other countries) for the reason that courts and juries are not infallible no matter how much due process has been afforded the defendant. Innocent people have been wrongfully convicted and executed under capital punishment regimes.[8] Other arguments for the abolition of capital punishment exist, but I think this one is the strongest. I am, however, undecided whether capital punishment is appropriate for the most heinous crimes against humanity, for example, the death by hanging administered as the judgment in the trial at Nuremberg of leading Nazi officials for genocide and similar crimes. But, even in such extreme cases, it can be argued that the worst punishment of all is life in prison without parole. And there is a legitimate question whether government ever has an ultimate right to execute convicted criminals.

Constitutional, legal, and political battles over the question of abortion have raged for many decades in the United States. Different religions have different positions on this issue. Evangelical Christians and Roman Catholics usually oppose abortion, though the Bible does not directly address the practice.[9] Scientists have been unable to give a definitive answer of when, if at all, human life begins in the womb. Many people say that the government should not interfere with a woman's body by forcing her to bear an unwanted child, especially when the mother's life or health are threatened or when the fetus suffers from a serious medical defect. It appears impossible to answer such questions from a purely philosophical or scientific perspective.

Under such circumstances, the compromise set forth in the US Supreme Court decision in *Roe v. Wade*, 410 U.S. 113 (1973),[10] appears reasonable. The Court held that, during the first trimester after conception, the abortion decision and its effectuation should be left to the medical judgment of the pregnant person's attending physician. In the second trimester, a state may, in promoting its interest in the health of the mother, regulate the abortion procedure in ways that are reasonably related to maternal health. Viability of the fetus occurs sometime between twenty-four and twenty-eight weeks after conception. For the stage subsequent to viability (the third trimester), the state, in promoting its interest in the potentiality of human life, may, if it chooses, regulate, and even proscribe, abortion except where necessary, in appropriate medical judgment, for the preservation of the life or health of the mother. However, on June 24, 2022, the US Supreme Court overruled *Roe v. Wade* and its progeny and held that each state should determine its own abortion regime. *Dobbs v. Jackson Women's Health Organization*, 597 U.S. 215 (2022).[11]

No universal consensus exists regarding the issue of abortion. Moreover, as indicated above, philosophers and scientists cannot provide a definitive answer to this question. Theologians often express one view or another, but government should not be in the business of enforcing any particular religious doctrine. Under these circumstances, the Supreme Court's analysis in *Roe v. Wade* makes some sense. Government should not force women to obtain abortions, but women should be free to decide whether they should have an abortion within the framework of *Roe v. Wade* or a similar paradigm.

The right to life is also at issue in the case of conscription. Should government have power to conscript people into military service and force them to kill people or be killed by them? It is my view that governments should avoid conscription whenever possible. In the case of an existential threat, such as the situation confronting the United Kingdom and the United States in the Second World War or of Ukraine when faced with Russian imperialistic aggression in the twenty-first century, it may be a necessary evil. As to whether governments should ever have the power to wage war, see chapters 1 and 3 and the epilogue of this book; cf. chapter 5 and the appendix.

Liberty

Article 3 of the UDHR states that "[e]veryone has the right to ... liberty ...." The US Declaration of Independence recognizes "liberty" as a natural and "unalienable" right. The US Constitution provides that neither the federal government (Fifth Amendment) nor the state governments (Fourteenth Amendment) may deprive any "person" (not just citizens) of liberty without due process of law. Law professors John E. Nowak and Donald D. Rotunda have described the general contours of the liberty interest recognized in the due process clauses as follows:

> There are two distinct ways in which a person may be deprived of liberty. First, the government might deprive the person of his [or her] freedom of action by physically

restraining him [or her]. Second, the government might limit someone's freedom of choice and action by making it impossible or illegal for that person to engage in certain types of activity. This last category can also be subdivided into two parts. The government might deny a person the ability to exercise a right with special constitutional protection (such as the right to free speech or the right to privacy); this restraint would constitute a clear deprivation of liberty. There are also cases where the government forecloses a form of freedom of action to an individual which does not have special constitutional status (such as the freedom to engage in a particular business activity). Thus we may subdivide "liberty" into three headings involving governmental restraints on (1) physical freedom, (2) the exercise of fundamental constitutional rights and (3) other forms of freedom of choice or action.[12]

Article 4 of the UDHR states: "No one shall be held in slavery or servitude; slavery and the slave trade shall be prohibited in all their forms." The Thirteenth Amendment to the US Constitution provides: "Neither slavery nor involuntary servitude, except as a punishment for crime whereof the party shall have been duly convicted, shall exist within the United States, or any place subject to their jurisdiction." After the Civil War, some Southern states circumvented the Thirteenth Amendment by wrongfully convicting African Americans and farming them out as slave labor for business corporations.[13]

Needless to say, freedom from slavery is a natural right and, properly, a constitutional or legal right. It is a right not only against government but also against individuals or institutions. Government is properly expected to enforce this right. But many Southern state governments, before and after the Thirteenth Amendment, were complicit, through legislation and otherwise, in perpetrating a slavery regime.

As noted above, the Fifth and Fourteenth Amendments to the US Constitution state that neither the federal nor the state governments may deprive any person of liberty without due process of law. A vast case law interpreting and applying these due process clauses exists, and the present discussion can only touch on some of its holdings. Most essentially, the courts must afford procedural due process to parties in both criminal and civil cases.[14] Liberty is certainly at stake in criminal proceedings. But the US Supreme Court has also recognized liberty interests in, for example, cases involving freedom of association, the right to interstate travel, the right to privacy, and the right to vote. Although the Supreme Court seems to prefer what courts call a "substantive due process" analysis in such "unenumerated rights" cases, it should be noted that the Ninth Amendment to the Constitution explicitly provides that "[t]he enumeration in the Constitution, of certain rights, shall not be construed to deny or disparage others retained by the people."[15]

The liberty interest recognized by the US Constitution also involves the natural and "unalienable" right listed in the Declaration of Independence to the "pursuit of Happiness." As Supreme Court Justice Potter Stewart stated in his opinion of the court in *Board of Regents v. Roth*:

> "While this Court has not attempted to define with exactness the liberty . . . guaranteed [by the Fourteenth Amendment], the term has received much consideration and some of the included things have been definitely stated. Without doubt, it denotes not merely freedom from bodily restraint but also the right of the individual to contract, to engage in any of the common occupations of life, to acquire useful knowledge, to marry, establish a home and bring up children, to worship God according to the dictates of his own conscience, and generally to enjoy those privileges long recognized . . . **as essential to the orderly pursuit of happiness** by free men." *Meyer v. Nebraska*, 262 U. S. 390, 399. In a Constitution for a free people, there can be no doubt that the meaning of "liberty" must be broad indeed. See, e. g., *Bolling v. Sharpe*, 347 U. S. 497, 499-500; *Stanley v. Illinois*, 405 U. S. 645.[16]

In his judicial opinion, Justice Stewart seemed to focus on what used to be called the "common man." I would define the Declaration's "pursuit of Happiness" even more broadly to include theoretical pursuits, including unpopular views about metaphysics and religion and other philosophical and scientific interests. The Declaration's phrase "the pursuit of Happiness" initially meant, of course, the actions of people in pursuing financial well-being as well as other forms of material happiness. But Thomas Jefferson, the author of that phrase, considered John Locke to be one of "the three greatest men that have ever lived, without any exception . . . ."[17] And Jefferson had read Locke's *Essay Concerning Human Understanding*,[18] which extolled "an unalterable **pursuit of happiness** in general," which Locke described as "preferring and pursuing true happiness as our greatest good" while being "obliged to suspend the satisfaction of our desire in particular cases." In other words, Locke pointed to a philosophical kind of happiness, as distinguished from the quotidian and ephemeral happiness attending such things as money and property.[19]

Property

Article 17 of the UDHR states: "Everyone has the right to own property alone as well as in association with others" and "[n]o one shall be arbitrarily deprived of his property."

The Due Process Clauses of the Fifth and Fourteenth Amendments to the US Constitution provide that no person shall be deprived of property without due process of law. The Takings Clause of the Fifth Amendment (which has been applied to state and local government by way of the Fourteenth Amendment) states that property shall not be taken for public use without just compensation. Furthermore, Article I, Section 10, Clause 1 (the Contract Clause) of the Constitution reads, in pertinent part: "No State shall . . . pass any . . . Law impairing the Obligation of Contracts." Many thousands of federal and state court cases have interpreted and applied these various provisions, and it is impossible in the present book to summarize the holdings of these cases throughout the complicated constitutional history of the United States.[20]

Is property a natural right? This is a very difficult question that has perplexed many philosophers, scholars, and general commentators.

At some level, the right to be free from governmental interference with one's property is a natural right. Subject to reasonable taxation and regulation for the common good, government should not confiscate money and property that one acquires by one's own efforts.

When individuals form a business corporation or limited liability company (LLC), the income and property of such artificial entity does not inure to it as a matter of natural right. A corporation or limited liability company does not exist in nature. It is created and regulated by government, with laws granting limited liability to its investors. Limited liability means that the individual investors are (with rare exceptions) not personally liable for the contract or tort liabilities of the company in any amount exceeding their own personal investment. Such limited liability does not exist without governmental laws; individuals in an ordinary partnership do not have any such limitation on their personal liability for the partnership's contract and tort liabilities. However, in limited liability partnerships (LLPs)—another creation of government—the limited partners (but not the general partners) enjoy limited liability.

The fact that private business corporations, limited liability companies, and limited partnerships do not trigger natural right does not mean that they are helpless against governmental power. To the contrary, governmental laws properly define the legal rights and responsibilities of these organizations.

Freedom of Thought

Freedom of thought is one of the most important rights of human beings. It is a natural right because it is essential to our humanity. Historically, it has often been called "freedom of conscience."

Article 18 of the UDHR states: "Everyone has the right to freedom of thought, conscience and religion; this right includes freedom to change his [or her] religion or belief, and freedom, either alone or in community with others and in public or private, to manifest his [or her] religion or belief in teaching, practice, worship and observance."

The First Amendment to the US Constitution states in relevant part: "Congress shall make no law respecting an establishment of religion, or prohibiting the free exercise thereof . . . ." The US Supreme Court has applied these constitutional protections to state and local governments by way of the Fourteenth Amendment, and state constitutions have similar provisions.

These written formulations are somewhat narrower than what, in my view, this right involves. Freedom of thought means that government has no right to compel anyone to adopt a particular view of religion or, indeed, any religion at all. Religionists, atheists, and agnostics all are, or should be, protected by this right. Moreover, freedom of thought means that government cannot forbid philosophical, political, or any other kind of thought.

History is full of examples of violations of freedom of thought. Theocracies of every kind routinely violate it.[21] Totalitarian regimes attempt to brainwash and control the minds of people within their territory. All such governments persecute and prosecute people who disagree with the officially approved religion or ideology.

Freedom of Speech

Freedom of speech is intimately related to freedom of thought. Freedom of speech allows individuals to express their thoughts and views. This, too, is a natural right because it is an integral part of being human. Governments have, however, recognized certain exceptions to the right of free speech in statutory or decisional law applicable to defamation, incitement to immediate unlawful action, fraud, threats, and so forth. But the default rule in democratic republics is that speech, whether oral or written, should be free from governmental censorship or control.

Accordingly, Article 19 of the UDHR provides: "Everyone has the right to freedom of opinion and expression; this right includes freedom to hold opinions without interference and to seek, receive and impart information and ideas through any media and regardless of frontiers."

The First Amendment to the US Constitution states, in relevant part, that "Congress shall make no law . . . abridging the freedom of speech, or of the press . . . ." A large number of court cases in the United States have interpreted and applied this constitutional command in many different factual circumstances. The US Supreme Court has also applied these provisions to state and local governments, and state constitutions contain similar protections for speech.

Freedom of Association and Assembly

Article 20 of the UDHR states that "[e]veryone has the right to freedom of peaceful assembly and association" and that "[n]o one may be compelled to belong to an association."

The First Amendment to the US Constitution provides that "Congress shall make no law . . . abridging . . . the right of the people peaceably to assemble, and to petition the Government for a redress of grievances." US case law protects freedom of association.

These are also natural rights belonging to human beings as such. Again, there are obvious exceptions to freedom of association and assembly, for example, engaging in a criminal conspiracy and incitement to riot. Additionally, the right to assembly is qualified, in the case of the First Amendment, by the requirement to assemble "peaceably." Thus, the January 6, 2021 mass attack on the US Capitol building, resulting in many injuries to defending police officers and interrupting a congressional proceeding mandated by the Constitution, would not fall under the protection of this constitutional right.

Freedom from Torture or Other Inhumane Punishment

Article 5 of the UDHR states: "No one shall be subjected to torture or to cruel, inhuman or degrading treatment or punishment." The Eighth Amendment to the US Constitution prohibits the infliction of "cruel and unusual punishments. . . . ." These are natural rights, and they are, in the United States and some other countries, also legal rights. Nevertheless, the presidential administration of George W. Bush blatantly committed torture in its treatment of prisoners captured during the Afghanistan and Iraq wars.[22]

Equal Protection of the Law

Article 7 of the UDHR states: "All are equal before the law and are entitled without any discrimination to equal protection of the law. All are entitled to equal protection against any discrimination in violation of this Declaration and against any incitement to such discrimination."

The Fourteenth Amendment to the US Constitution provides that no state shall "deny to any person within its jurisdiction the equal protection of the laws." The Fourteenth Amendment was ratified after the Civil War on July 9, 1868. There was no explicit constitutional guarantee of equal protection of the laws before this amendment. However, the Supreme Court later held that the Fifth Amendment Due Process Clause, applicable to the federal government, had an implicit equal protection component analogous to the Fourteenth Amendment Equal Protection Clause.[23]

Equality before the law has not always existed. Before the Civil War, slaves did not have legal equality with free persons in the United States. After the Civil War and even after the ratification of the Thirteenth, Fourteenth, and Fifteenth Amendments, Southern governments in the United States turned a blind eye to lynching, and they conspired with private corporations in order to, effectually, re-enslave Blacks. Women did not have legal equality with men until relatively recently. Historically, in monarchies and feudal states, monarchs and nobles had more legal rights than peasants, serfs, or even the emerging bourgeoisie. Today, a vast case law exists regarding what equal protection of the law means and how it should be applied.

JUDICIAL REVIEW

The United States has had a tradition of judicial review since the US Supreme Court's 1803 decision in *Marbury v. Madison*. Judicial review in this sense is the constitutional or legal power of a federal (national) or state court to declare a legislative or executive act of the national or state governments unconstitutional and unenforceable.[24]

In the United States, judicial review operates within the regular US court system. Some other countries have constitutional courts, outside their regular judicial systems, that address constitutional issues.[25]

The Judicial Branch of the US Government

The US Constitutional Convention, after several months of deliberation, formally adopted the text of the original Constitution of the United States on September 17, 1787. Copies of the proposed Constitution were then sent to each of the thirteen states for ratification. The requisite number of states ratified the Constitution on June 21, 1788, and the new government became operative in 1789.

During the state ratification debates of 1787–88, Alexander Hamilton, John Jay, and James Madison authored, under the pseudonym "Publius," their famous explanation and defense of the 1787 US Constitution in a series of newspaper articles, which were collected and published in book form as *The Federalist*.[26]

The original public explanation and defense of the judicial branch of the US government was contained in numbers 78–83 of *The Federalist*, authored by Alexander Hamilton, a lawyer in New York state. In these essays, Hamilton addressed several issues that were discussed in the ratification debates.[27]

In *Federalist* number 78, Hamilton outlined his theory of judicial review in the context of supporting the Constitution's lifetime tenure of federal judges, subject to "good behavior." Under the Constitution, "civil Officers of the United States" (which, pursuant to historical practice, include judges) "shall be removed from Office on Impeachment for, and Conviction of, Treason, Bribery, or other high Crimes and Misdemeanors."[28] Hamilton argued that such lifelong tenure would prevent presidents and legislators from removing judges for political reasons. A constitution is higher law than ordinary statutes or common law. A court is tasked with determining what the law is, especially when two laws conflict. This requires the famous separation of the three branches of government (executive, legislative, judicial) in the US Constitution: The judiciary is separate from the executive and legislative branches and must be independent of either of these two political branches. Hamilton wrote:

> The complete independence of the courts of justice is peculiarly essential in a limited constitution. By a limited constitution I understand one which contains certain specified exceptions to the legislative

authority; such for instance as that it shall pass no bills of attainder, no ex post facto laws, and the like. Limitations of this kind can be preserved in practice no other way than through the medium of the courts of justice; whose duty it must be to declare all acts contrary to the manifest tenor of the constitution void. Without this, all the reservations of particular rights or privileges would amount to nothing.

Hamilton was referring to the text of Constitution proposed by the 1787 Constitutional Convention. After this original Constitution went into effect in 1789, the ten amendments constituting what became known as the Bill of Rights were ratified in 1791. As we have seen, the Bill of Rights and several later amendments added other individual constitutional rights to the very few recognized by the 1787 Constitution. Hamilton's reasoning applies with even greater force to the individual rights recognized in certain amendments to the Constitution. This includes the Ninth Amendment proviso that "[t]he enumeration in the Constitution, of certain rights, shall not be construed to deny or disparage others retained by the people."

Marbury v. Madison and Judicial Review

Hamilton's argument for judicial review was later echoed by Chief Justice John Marshall in the famous case of *Marbury v. Madison*.[29] Although Hamilton's *Federalist* number 78 as well as scattered early court decisions in the United States supported a concept of judicial review, the 1803 decision of the US Supreme Court in *Marbury v. Madison* established that doctrine for the remainder (to date) of US constitutional history.

Chief Justice John Marshall's opinion of the court in that case analyzed the concept of judicial review as follows.

The case came to the Supreme Court on the alleged basis of its original jurisdiction. The U.S. Constitution states that the Supreme Court has original jurisdiction in "all Cases affecting Ambassadors, other Public Ministers, and Consuls, and those in which a State shall be a Party...."[30] Otherwise, it has only appellate jurisdiction.

William Marbury and others "severally moved the [Supreme Court] for a rule to James Madison, secretary of state of the United States, to show cause why a mandamus should not issue commanding him to cause to be delivered to them respectively their several commissions as justices of the peace in the district of Columbia."[31] In contradiction to the above-quoted constitutional command, Congress had enacted a law that would have permitted Marbury and the others to file an action directly in the Supreme Court under its original jurisdiction. The Supreme Court held that the constitutional provision must prevail over the congressional legislation and therefore dismissed the case on the ground of lack of jurisdiction.[32]

In reaching this conclusion, Chief Justice Marshall's opinion of the court made some famous statements, of which the following are a sample:

> The question, whether an act, repugnant to the constitution, can become the law of the land, is a question deeply interesting to the United States; but, happily, not of an intricacy proportioned to its interest. It seems only necessary to recognise certain

principles, supposed to have been long and well established, to decide it. . . .

It is emphatically the province and duty of the judicial department to say what the law is. Those who apply the rule to particular cases, must of necessity expound and interpret that rule. If two laws conflict with each other, the courts must decide on the operation of each. . . .

Thus, the particular phraseology of the constitution of the United States confirms and strengthens the principle, supposed to be essential to all written constitutions, that a law repugnant to the constitution is void; and that *courts*, as well as other departments, are bound by that instrument.[33]

In the course of his opinion, Marshall discussed some individual constitutional rights in the original Constitution that would be protected by this principle (later called "judicial review"): the prohibition of bills of attainder and ex post facto laws and the requirements in the Constitution for conviction of treason. "From these, and many other selections which might be made, it is apparent that the framers of the constitution contemplated that instrument as a rule for the government of *courts*, as well as of the legislature."[34]

During the twentieth century, the Supreme Court employed judicial review in articulating and applying several individual rights protected by the explicit and sometimes implicit language of the Constitution. Some of those rights are discussed above in the section titled "Individual Rights" of this chapter.

Attacks on Judicial Review in the United States

Both the political left and the political right have attacked judicial review, often with the complaint of "unelected judges" determining governmental policy. Of course, not all judges are unelected. Although the US Constitution provides that Article 3 federal judges are appointed, not elected, some state constitutions provide for the popular election of state court judges.

The opposition of the political left to judicial review was prevalent during the era of the late nineteenth and early twentieth centuries, when the US Supreme Court held, in various cases, that federal, state, and local economic and social regulation of business violated the Due Process Clauses or the Contract Clause of the US Constitution. Such opposition has been revived, to an extent, with Supreme Court decisions in recent decades invalidating or limiting some federal, state, and local economic and social regulations.

The opposition of the political right to judicial review emerged strongly in the last half of the twentieth century in fierce opposition to US Supreme Court decisions that recognized and expanded individual rights in such areas as school desegregation, the rights of criminal defendants, separation of religion and government, contraception, and abortion. Although such conservative opposition to "unelected judges" remains today, the right-wing attacks on the Supreme Court have moderated to some extent with the Court's exercising judicial review to invalidate or limit progressive economic and social legislation and to overrule earlier precedents favoring a constitutional right to an abortion. Next on the Supreme Court's

45

chopping block may be earlier Supreme Court decisions recognizing constitutional rights to contraception and same-sex marriage. The current tendency of the Supreme Court under the judicial appointments by conservative presidents (chosen in 2000 and 2016 by the Electoral College in opposition to the national popular vote) with the consent of the Senate (which is based on the concept of two votes per state) appears to be in a conservative direction. This may or may not change, depending on the results of future presidential elections and appointments to the Supreme Court.

A NEW (YET OLD) APPROACH TO INDIVIDUAL RIGHTS AND JUDICIAL REVIEW

Summary (with Some Elaboration) of the Previous Discussion

"Individual rights" are (1) natural rights, i.e., those rights belonging to an individual human being as a result of human nature, against governmental coercion or against the force or fraud of others (understood as the first duty of government under any express or implied social or political contract), and (2) those rights belonging to an individual as a result of constitutional or other legal protections. Individual rights, in the present context, are not socioeconomic entitlements that may impinge upon the rights of others by way of taxation or otherwise. The present discussion defers to chapter 3 the difficult subject of socioeconomic legislation and regulation.

Individual natural rights against governmental coercion, properly identified, are inalienable, because they cannot, philosophically, be given up to government in any social or political contract. It is a difficult task of political and legal philosophy to identify the contours of such natural rights. Among other things, as discussed in chapter 1, this does not necessitate or imply anarchism. Government is necessary for certain legitimate functions, including, but not limited to, the protection of individual rights against the depredations of others.

An entity created by government, such as a corporation or limited liability company, which affords its shareholders or owners limited contract, tort, or other liability, is not a natural human being. As such, it has legal but not natural rights.

The United States, under its written Constitution, has a separation of powers of the three branches of the federal government. The two political branches consist of the president and the Congress, which are both subject to forms of democratic election. The third branch is the judiciary. US Supreme Court justices as well as federal appellate and trial court judges are appointed for life ("good behavior") by the president with the consent of the Senate, subject to being removed only by constitutional impeachment provisions. The Founders intended the federal judiciary to be above politics.

The judiciary is the appropriate institution for protecting the natural and legal rights of individual humans. In addition to the list of specific natural and legal rights in the US Constitution, the Ninth Amendment affords federal justices and judges the power to protect unenumerated natural rights by stipulating that "[t]he enumeration in the Constitution, of certain rights, shall not be construed to deny or disparage others retained by the people."

A New (Yet Old) Approach

Conservatives love to say that the United States is a republic, not a democracy. At the same time, they criticize the "unelected judges" of the federal judiciary, arguing that that their use of judicial review to expand individual rights is undemocratic. In short, they try to have it both ways.

It is true that the United States is not a "democracy" in the ancient Greek definition of that term—the direct, in-person voting of all male citizens on legislation and the seating of hundreds of such citizens as both judge and jury in criminal cases without any right of appeal. Such a democratic Athenian jury convicted Socrates in 399 BCE of impiety (not believing in the gods in which the city believed) and corrupting the young through his impiety; they sentenced him to death by ingestion of hemlock, which penalty was effectuated. It is also true that the United States is not a democracy in the sense that the will of citizens expressed through their elected representatives in Congress is the final word on individual rights and other constitutional issues.

History, including American history, is replete with examples of factions of people violating, either directly or through their political leaders, the natural rights of individual human beings to freedom of thought, freedom of speech, freedom of association, privacy, liberty, and so forth. As discussed above, Alexander Hamilton and Chief Justice John Marshall celebrated an independent branch of the federal government—the judiciary—that safeguards, by way of judicial review, individual humans from such violations. During the late nineteenth and early twentieth centuries, however, the Supreme Court twisted the Fourteenth Amendment's language in order to bring corporations (which the Court now defined as "persons"[35]) within the purview of that amendment while refusing to recognize the Fourteenth Amendment's core design of protecting human beings. Later, the Warren Court (1953–69) was, for the most part, the first Supreme Court majority to vindicate individual human rights. Hopefully, it will not be the last.

The US Supreme Court and lower courts have properly employed judicial review to invalidate legislative and executive acts that deprive individual human beings of their natural and analogous legal rights. Opponents of judicial review argue that the "unelected" judiciary should not countermand legislation enacted by Congress (which is directly elected by citizens, though often with gerrymandered electoral districts in the House of Representatives and a limitation of two senators per state in the Senate) or executive actions by the president (chosen by the Electoral College). However, the Declaration of Independence recognized that certain individual rights are "unalienable," i.e., that they are not given up to legislative or executive abridgment. The individual natural rights discussed in this chapter were never alienated to government and should remain sacrosanct. As such, the judicial branch of the federal government, which is appointed by the president in conjunction with the Senate, properly protects them.

CHAPTER THREE
LEGITIMATE AFFIRMATIVE
POWERS OF GOVERNMENT

INTRODUCTION

Chapter 1 of this book addressed the question whether government is necessary. It discussed anarchism in general and anarchocapitalism in particular, concluding that some kind of government is necessary in complex societies existing in the present and foreseeable centuries.

Chapter 2 considered individual rights, both those that exist by nature (individual natural rights) and those that exist by law. However, the question of socioeconomic rights or entitlements was deferred to the present chapter.

This chapter discusses legitimate affirmative governmental powers, including the general contours of criminal and noncriminal law.[1]

Chapters 2 and 3 are, in a sense, independent of the form of government that a society possesses. Chapter 4 analyzes different forms of government and concludes that a regime ruled by a philosophical elite (as in Plato's *Republic*) is not practically possible and would probably not be desirable in any event. The best type of government is a democratic republic, though every democratic republic that has ever existed has left considerable room for improvement. Perfection does not exist in this world, but improvement is always possible. Improvement depends on the ethical and rational faculties of both political leaders and of the populace at large.

GOVERNMENT AND CRIMINAL LAW

As chapters 1 and 2 explained, the first duty of government is to protect individuals and private organizations from criminal activity. Philosopher John Locke explained the rationale for governmental criminal law in his *Second Treatise of Government* (1690). Before the formation of government, in what Locke called the "state of nature," each person had the right to forcibly resist or punish those who used force against that person's (or others') life, liberty, or possessions.

Locke defined "property" as "Life, Liberty, and Estate." In a parenthetical, Locke also stated: "By *Property* I must be understood here, as in other places, to mean that Property which Men have in their Persons as well as Goods." "Property," for Locke, began with a property right to one's person (right to life and liberty in a broad sense), which also entailed one's material goods and lands.[2]

Locke explained the origin of government as follows:

> The great and *chief end* therefore, of Mens uniting into Commonwealths, and putting themselves under Government, *is the Preservation of their Property.* **To which in the state of Nature there are many things wanting."**

First, **There wants an *establish'd*, settled, known *Law*, received and allowed by common consent to be the Standard of Right and Wrong, and the common measure to decide all Controversies between them.** For though the Law of Nature be plain and intelligible to all rational Creatures; yet Men being biassed by their Interest, as well as ignorant for want of Study of it, are not apt to allow of it as a Law binding to them in the application of it to their particular Cases.

Secondly, **In the State of Nature there wants *a known and indifferent Judge*, with Authority to determine all differences according to the established Law.** For every one in that State being both Judge and Executioner of the Law of Nature, Men being partial to themselves, Passion and Revenge is very apt to carry them too far, and with too much heat, in their own Cases; as well as negligence, and unconcernedness, to make them too remiss, in other Mens.

Thirdly, **In the State of Nature there often wants *Power* to back and support the Sentence when right, and to *give* it due *Execution*.** They who by any Injustice offended, will seldom fail, where they are able, by force to make good their Injustice: such resistance many times makes the punishment dangerous, and frequently destructive, to those who attempt it.

Thus Mankind, notwithstanding all the Priviledges of the state of Nature, being but in an ill condition, while they remain in it, are quickly driven into Society. Hence it comes to pass, that we seldom find any number of Men live any time together in this State. The inconveniencies, that they are therein exposed to, by the irregular and uncertain exercise of the Power every Man has of punishing the transgressions of others, make them take Sanctuary under the establish'd Laws of Government, and therein seek *the preservation of their Property*. **'Tis this makes them so willingly give up every one his single power of punishing to be exercised by such alone as shall be appointed to it amongst them; and by such Rules as the Community, or those authorised by them to that purpose, shall agree on. And in this we have the original *right and rise* of both the *Legislative and Executive Power*, as well as of the Governments and Societies themselves.**[3]

Centuries of legal evolution have resulted in the criminal law we have today. As discussed in chapter 2, criminal law includes, in the United States and elsewhere, the constitutional, statutory, and rule-based procedural protections upon which criminal defendants can rely to ensure that they will not be convicted without due process of law. This system does not always produce a just result, but it is preferable to the alternative of every person being judge, jury, and executioner of subjective justice.

Criminal law, in the United States and elsewhere addresses, among other things, homicide, assault, robbery, theft, fraud, embezzlement, and insider trading.

GOVERNMENT AND NONCRIMINAL LAW

Government also provides various kinds of law applicable in a noncriminal context. The following discussion addresses some of the main types of noncriminal law. The focus here is on law as it developed in Great Britain and in countries influenced by British law, including the United States. Continental Europe and some other countries have been influenced by the Napoleonic Code, which has similar, though not identical, concepts and procedures. Law in still other countries has had different origins.

Property Law

Real estate law in Britain and the United States developed over many centuries, going back to the feudal order in medieval Europe. As a result of its antique origins, real property law in these countries has many unique concepts and terms, originally deriving from medieval legal estates, that endlessly perplex first-year law students (of which I was once one). These notions developed both through common (judge-made) and statutory law.

Today, the main principles of Anglo-American real estate law are sufficiently well established that purchasers and sellers of real estate can usually rely on firm legal principles in their transactions. Additionally, government records titles to real estate such that each parcel of land has defined and legally enforceable boundaries and other characteristics.

In chapter 2 of this book, we inquired whether someone has a natural right to property acquired by inheritance or purchase. In his *Second Treatise of Government*, philosopher John Locke argued that natural rights to real estate (including the fruits, vegetables, and animals on that real estate) arose in the "state of nature," before government and before the invention of money, as a result of the abundance of available land and the fact that any individual's possession of land was naturally limited by the amount that could be used without spoilage. But the invention of money (typically, nonperishable metal) totally changed that dynamic, permitting unlimited acquisition (resulting in the reduction of the amount of free land), and leading to the rise of government. From that point on, one could say that the title to property was conventional rather than natural.[4] Today, government defines property rights without attempting the impossible task of ascertaining whether a particular piece of real or personal property has passed from one owner to another in a just succession of owners over many centuries or, even, millennia.

For example, most real estate today in the United States was originally acquired by the forced dispossession of Indigenous peoples from their lands. Moreover, the wealth of many people has been inherited from ancestors who were involved, directly or indirectly, with the long and brutal history of slavery in the United States and its subsequent reappearance in the

Jim Crow laws and practices of the Southern states. There would be a natural right to ownership and possession of such property only if there were a natural right to forcible dispossession of the Indigenous occupants of their land as well as to the historical development of the land by the institution of slavery.

A somewhat similar phenomenon occurred in Britain. The Norman Conquest (1066 CE) resulted in the Norman conquerors dispossessing Anglo-Saxon landowners and imposing on them a medieval feudal system. Of course, the Anglo-Saxons had themselves earlier conquered the same territory from the Celts, and the Romans had even earlier controlled much of England.

In the early twentieth century, a distinguished legal scholar remarked on the parallels between the Norman Conquest and the appropriation by the United States government of Native lands:

> Into this condition of Anglo-Saxon law were suddenly introduced Norman rulers with their Norman organization. **William the Conqueror dispossessed every Anglo-Saxon landholder who had been in arms with Harold. . . . William's first insistence was that he was a true conqueror; all the land of England belonged to him because he had gained it by a conquest title. This was a current legal conception of barbarian origin, but it has remained in our conception that the United States has title to all the Indian land, subject to an Indian right of occupation. Every title to land in England must come from the**

Conqueror because he had become the owner of it all. This was the cardinal principle, and he and his successors made the claim good by law.[5]

Thus, property rights today are not natural rights. They are conventional rights—rights established by law. This does not necessitate a radical redistribution of lands and wealth (likely another impossible task), but it does mean that government has some legitimate power, if exercised carefully and rationally, to regulate property.

Statutory or common law in democratic republics normally protects a person's legal rights in real and personal property vis-à-vis other people and private entities. For example, in the United States, private landowners can file lawsuits against others sounding in trespass, encroachment, quiet title, nondisclosure of hidden defects in property sales, misrepresentation or fraud in real estate transactions, nuisance, easement disputes, and so forth.

Lawsuits regarding personal property can be brought for conversion (deprivation of personal property), negligent or intentional damage to personal property, bailment issues (when personal property is entrusted to another for safekeeping), and other such issues.

Litigation between government and individual landowners can involve such matters as zoning disputes, takings claims, regulatory issues, and government permits. Although such disputes are often based on state statutes or local ordinances, they sometimes have constitutional ramifications.

Constitutional issues arise when government allegedly "takes" private property in violation of the Fifth Amendment Takings Clause of the United States Constitution (applied to state and municipal governments by way of the Fourteenth Amendment and by cognate state constitutions and laws) or when government deprives someone of property in violation of the Fifth or Fourteenth Amendment Due Process Clauses.

Accordingly, property rights in the United States are rooted in constitutional, statutory, or common law.

Contract Law

Traditional contract law as it arose in England and the United States goes back many centuries. It was developed in the English courts by a progression of case law precedent called the common law. Occasionally, a statute intervened, but it was mostly a judicial phenomenon. This also remained true after its transposition to the American colonies, which later became the United States. Today, there are unofficial "Restatements" of the laws of contract and other common law areas such as torts. Although these are not legally binding on courts, they nevertheless are frequently cited in the case law and, in that manner, often become precedential. But contract law in the United States remains, mainly, judge-made law.

That is not, however, the situation with commercial law. Since the 1950s, all individual states in the United States have adopted by statute, in whole or in part, a model law called the Uniform Commercial Code. These statutes address the complicated transactions involved in commerce. Subjects include the sale of goods, negotiable instruments, commercial paper, and secured transactions.

Space does not permit a more detailed treatment here. Interested readers can easily research the various aspects of commercial law on the internet or otherwise.

Tort Law

Tort law has been defined as "[a]n area of law that deals with the wrongful actions of an individual or entity, which cause injury to another individual's or entity's person, property, or reputation, and which entitle the injured party to compensation."[6]

Tort law includes, among other causes of action, claims for wrongful death, assault, battery, false imprisonment, defamation, fraud, negligence (automobile accidents etc.), professional malpractice, premises liability, and product liability (as to which strict liability applies).

Tort law developed over centuries in Britain and the United States through common law precedent. In recent times, however, some aspects of tort law have been codified in statutes.

GOVERNMENT AND THE ECONOMY

One of the most difficult questions of political philosophy and political economy is the issue of the extent, if any, to which government should exert control over the economy.

A few things are clear. A command economy, such as existed in the Soviet Union during the twentieth century, does not work. Extensive governmental ownership and control over the economy led to negative results and, arguably, to the eventual disintegration of the Soviet Union.

At the other extreme, an economy totally free of governmental regulation also does not work. Contrary to some economic theories, people do not always make rational economic (or other) decisions. Moreover, unfettered economic freedom leads to what are called "externalities." The profit motive of laissez-faire capitalism is focused on short-term financial gains for corporate shareholders and other investors. Long-term maladies like air pollution and climate change are ignored to the detriment of society and, indeed, the globe. Governmental regulation is necessary to protect the common good as distinguished from those focused only on short-term profit.[7]

Government creates an overall legal structure for corporations, limited liability companies, not-for-profit organizations, and similar entities. Laws prohibit fraudulent practices and insider stock trading. Antitrust legislation has been a part of the US economic system for well over a century. People may—and do—debate the details of such legislation, but these kinds of measures are generally legitimate governmental actions.

Additionally, as discussed more fully in chapter 2, governments grant limited liability to corporate shareholders and limited partners: their personal assets normally cannot be accessed in contract and tort judgments. This special governmental dispensation is all the more reason that government should regulate business practices with a view to the common good.

Some kind of regulated market economy—avoiding both totalitarian government economic control and unrestrained capitalistic profitmaking at the expense of humanity—is therefore appropriate. I am not an economist, and the economists, in fact, differ among themselves on such matters. But it is important for government leaders, as well as their voting constituents, to seek a rational balance between individual greed and the common good. Moreover, it is an ethical obligation of every human being to consider and act upon a rational appraisal of not only their short-term financial interest but also the welfare of the society at large.

As I write this book, a relatively new problem is confronting the United States and the world at large. This is the challenge of artificial intelligence (AI). Apart from the ethical and practical issue of students using AI to cheat on papers, AI presents a possible threat to the employment of middle-class workers, adding to the ongoing trend of automation replacing working-class employees. Although it is possible that the economy will adjust to AI without causing massive unemployment, we must consider the possibility that AI and automation will result in the permanent unemployment of large masses of people. In such event, it will be necessary to reexamine our cherished assumptions about political economy. Considering my advanced age, this problem will likely not become a crisis in my lifetime. However, it may be a matter that later generations will have to address.

What would such a solution involve? Perhaps the entire concept of an economy based on full or almost full employment would turn out to be impossible. Perhaps a universal basic income (UBI) scheme would have to be adopted. But where would the money come from? Many assumptions we have taken for granted for centuries might have to be revisited. I don't have the answers, but I wish succeeding generations the best of luck in figuring them out, if, indeed, such a task becomes necessary.

GOVERNMENT AND SOCIOECONOMIC LEGISLATION

Are Socioeconomic Rights Natural Rights?

We often hear politicians and others claiming that people have a "right" to various desiderata, meaning not merely a legal right but a "human right."

What is a "human right"? To speak correctly, a "human right" would be what was historically called a "natural right," i.e., a right that a person has by virtue of being a human being to be free from unjustified governmental coercion. The individual natural rights discussed in chapter 2 qualify as "human rights" in this sense.

But some people mean something more in their use of the term "human rights." They argue that individual humans have certain socioeconomic "human rights" to health care, education, minimum basic income, and so on. I agree that many, if not all, of such measures are legitimate objects of government. However, they are not, strictly speaking, natural rights or human rights. The reason is that they require the taxation or regulation of others in order to achieve their objectives. It may very well be the case that such socioeconomic legislation is justified on rational grounds, but such benefits constitute legal rights or entitlements rather than natural or human rights as such.

Socioeconomic Legislation

Socioeconomic legislation covers a broad range of social services. In the United States, it might be said to have begun, on the national level, with the New Deal legislation of the 1930s; state and local governmental socioeconomic measures began earlier. Examples of federal socioeconomic legislation include Social Security (which involves individual employee contributions over a lifetime of work), Medicare (same), Medicaid, Supplemental Security Income (SSI), Supplemental Nutrition Assistance Program (SNAP), public housing, and many other social welfare programs on the national, state, and local levels.

The objectives of such programs are legitimate. In ascertaining the wisdom of such governmental measures, however, it is important for governmental leaders and their voting constituents to use reason and evidence to ascertain whether such programs accomplish their intended purposes or whether an alternative method is more appropriate. Unfortunately, instead of such rational analysis, these kinds of issues often instead become subjects of political demagoguery.

As I write the present chapter in 2025, US President Donald Trump and his administration are making radical efforts to undermine such programs. Time will tell whether, or to what extent, they will be successful.

GOVERNMENT AND DISEASE PREVENTION

The US government has long been involved in efforts to combat disease, both in the United States and in other countries. These efforts are a legitimate objective of government and have often been successful, mostly through vaccinations, in preventing or ameliorating the outbreak of deadly diseases such as polio, smallpox, diphtheria, rubella, measles, and COVID-19.

Unfortunately, anti-vaccination campaigns, based on misinformation or disinformation, have opposed such efforts, leading, for example, to a resurgence of measles in the United States and an only partially successful response to COVID-19 during the 2020s. As a result of the emergency situation arising in the early 2020s in the United States, governmental authorities made some mistakes, but the vaccinations made possible by quick pharmaceutical development (aided, financially and otherwise, by government) probably prevented millions of additional deaths over the more than one million people who have perished from the disease to date.

In the present era of "America First" nationalism, it is often questioned why the United States provides assistance to people in other countries for disease prevention and mitigation. The answer is obvious. In today's interdependent world, diseases originating elsewhere on the planet can quickly migrate to the United States. For example, COVID-19 originated in China, not in the United States. Making the United States a walled fortress against immigration does not prevent infectious diseases from being rapidly transmitted to this country.

GOVERNMENT AND RELIGION

Government and religion should remain separate. I discuss this at length in my book *The First American Founder: Roger Williams and Freedom of Conscience.*[8]

GOVERNMENT AND ETHICS/MORALITY

As I explained in my book *Reason and Human Ethics*, individual human beings should strive to achieve, in both understanding and practice, an ethical and rational perspective with regard to both ends and means.[9] This includes, among other things, moderation regarding the acquisition of wealth. People rightfully attempt to obtain a financially comfortable situation for themselves and their families. But greed, in and of itself, is not good, notwithstanding the popular slogan of yesteryear. Greed is not good for an individual and is not good for a society. Materialism, beyond what one reasonably needs for oneself and one's family, is not ethically appropriate. Ultimately, the common good, as well as the good for individuals, will be achieved only when people abandon their irrational lust for excessive wealth and needless material trinkets.

I believe in some degree of free will.[10] Accordingly, I generally think that government should not legislate religious or other concepts of morality in matters involving mutually consenting adults. This includes, but is not limited to, sexual/gender preferences and conduct. However, the question of legalizing prostitution is difficult for reasons of public health and human trafficking, and I do not currently take a position on that question. And, although I consider alcoholism and drug addiction to be a threat to one's mental and physical health, I do not support governmental laws against alcohol and marijuana. I tend, however, to think that "hard drugs" should be prohibited or otherwise regulated. But these are difficult questions.

I discuss the issue of abortion in chapter 2.

GOVERNMENT AND DISCRIMINATION

Governmental discrimination against people on the basis of such classifications as race, national origin, sex, and religion is rightly prohibited in the United States by the equal protection provisions of federal and state constitutions. During the last many decades, federal and state legislation and regulations have also prohibited private individuals from discriminating against other private individuals with regard to such categories. A watershed moment was the enactment of the national Civil Rights Act of 1964. This statute and its legislative and administrative progeny prohibited such private discrimination in, for example, employment, public transportation, hotels, restaurants, and housing.

Should government have the power to enact and enforce such antidiscrimination legislation? Yes. The United States, for example, has a long history of racial, gender, and religious discrimination. One of the legitimate purposes of government is to promote the common good. These measures facilitate the achievement of a good society.

GOVERNMENT AND EDUCATION

Different people have different abilities, aptitudes, and interests. Accordingly, people pursue different paths in life, including different career/occupational paths. Many find that the remunerative work they are able to secure does not correspond to their actual interests. Others are able to find some degree of satisfaction with their remunerative employment or self-employment. Still others decide to focus on parenting while their spouses provide the necessary economic base for their families.

To the extent that people are, or will become, voting citizens in a democracy, they all have one common need and responsibility: sufficient education in civics (government) and history to vote rationally on political issues. They do not need to become experts on political matters, and, indeed, most do not have time, even if they have the interest, to become experts. But they require a basic education on political and historical matters, as well as informal logic and critical thinking, so that they know how to avoid misinformation and disinformation. Above all, they need to recognize the telling marks of would-be authoritarian political leaders so that they know to reject them at the polls. History education should include objective facts regarding the rise of authoritarianism or totalitarianism throughout history, including identification of the demagogic lies of Hitler, Mussolini, Stalin, and other infamous tyrants. As the saying goes, an ounce of prevention is worth a pound of cure.[11]

It is also appropriate for public (tax-supported) schools to teach other standard skills and knowledge that every person should possess to lead a good life— for example, reading, writing, basic mathematics, basic science, and so forth. Again, this is conducive to the common good, and it is a legitimate object of government. The large majority of people cannot afford private schools. Public elementary and secondary schools are their only salvation.

To the extent that people live in wealthy families, they may be able to afford to educate their children in private primary and secondary schools. Most families, however, cannot afford to send their children to private schools. Accordingly, it is necessary and important for government to provide public schools for elementary and secondary education. This education should be secular, not religious, in nature; taxpayers should not be required to subsidize religious schools, especially in situations in which tax revenues for public schools are diverted to religious institutions.[12]

FOREIGN POLICY: INTERNATIONAL POLITICS AND WAR

Questions of foreign and defense policy are among the most difficult subjects of political philosophy and political science. To simplify matters, I approach this issue solely from the perspective of the United States, which has the unique and perhaps unenviable position of having been one of the great world powers since at least World War II. Until the recent radical foreign policy pivot of the second presidential administration of Donald J. Trump, it was also called "the leader of the free world."

During the last one hundred years, there have been some extreme positions that I regard as hopelessly irrational or misguided. One is the pre–World War II policy of "America First" isolationism, which has now been revived by Donald Trump, at least with regard to Europe. If the United States had followed such a policy in the 1940s, Hitler would have conquered all of Europe, Great Britain, and perhaps the Soviet Union and other areas to the east and south of Germany. The Nazi regime would have totally eliminated Jewish people and other perceived undesirables.

Isolationism was a viable option in the nineteenth century, when the United States was young and not a major power. It has not been a real option since the 1930s.

The opposite of isolationism is the view that the United States should become the "Rome" of the world, interfering, whenever it deems appropriate, in international conflicts. Such notions led to the fiascos in Vietnam, Afghanistan, and Iraq.

Proper foreign policy requires very careful reasoning, with evidence, about both ends and means.

What are the appropriate ends of US foreign policy? First, of course, is the protection of the United States. At this time, there is very little prospect of any attempt by another nation to invade this country. However, several countries possess nuclear weapons, and the US government should maintain a nuclear deterrent. The Cold War doctrine of "mutually assured destruction" (MAD) is still the best way to prevent a nuclear war, short of disarmament, with adequate inspection, of all nuclear powers. Unilateral disarmament has never been a rational policy for any but the naive and ignorant.

The second objective of US foreign policy ought to be to encourage democratic-republican states whenever possible. During the last few years, Ukraine has made a valiant attempt to defend itself against Russian invasion and bombardment. Ukraine is, essentially, a democratic-republican state, whereas Russia is a corrupt authoritarian regime under the control of Vladimir Putin. Putin's dream is to reestablish the pre-Soviet Russian empire, permeated by reactionary values and controlled by himself and, presumably, his successors. He has specialized in bombing civilians in order to terrorize Ukraine. After Trump took office for his second presidential administration, he repeated Putin's talking points and excoriated Ukraine President Volodymyr Zelenskyy, blaming him for the war and humiliating him in a February 28, 2025 televised conference at the White House.[13]

The Ukrainian people have demonstrated their determination to resist Putin during (as of the present writing) more than three years of war, which started with a massive Russian invasion on February 24, 2022. Unlike the local populations of Vietnam, Afghanistan, and Iraq, the Ukrainian people have a strong commitment to constitutional democracy. Before Trump assumed office for the second time (January 20, 2025), the administration of US President Joe Biden, along with several countries in Europe, strongly supported Ukraine, providing that country with substantial military assistance. The Trump administration has, however, seemed willing to abandon Ukraine under the "America First" mantra. Trump, however, is extremely variable, and it is impossible to know which side he will be on in the future.

Ukraine is a rare example of a fight that is worth making, as contrasted with many previous episodes of US alliances with authoritarian or semi-authoritarian regimes. Moreover, Ukraine does not demand—and the US would not accept—a presence of US troops on the ground in that country except, possibly, as peacekeepers following a final deal between Putin and Ukraine.

Are there any other types of objectives that would justify US military involvement in a foreign war? Probably not. Our interventions in the Middle East have been prompted, at least in part, by a need for Middle East oil. With the increasing success and affordability of renewable energy, that need has substantially diminished in recent times, though Trump has done everything he possibly could do to destroy US renewable energy and promote fossil fuels. One is reminded of Walt Kelly's depiction in a 1970 Earth Day poster of his cartoon character Pogo saying, "WE HAVE MET THE ENEMY AND HE IS US."[14]

Nonmilitary foreign aid is also an important component of US foreign policy. Instead of using the hard power of military might, foreign aid attempts to alleviate suffering in other countries and thereby encourage them, through such soft power, to adopt or strengthen constitutional democracy. Nevertheless, this has been another area of government that President Trump has attempted to eviscerate during the first year of his second term of office. The chief beneficiary of this "America First" policy will be China, which has an extensive soft power program of foreign aid throughout much of the world.

US foreign and defense policy will present many conundrums to future presidents. In each case, they and their advisers should use reason and evidence to carefully evaluate both ends and means before making a decision about the correct course of action. Chapter 5 of the present book discusses a real-life example of such deliberation in the 1962 Cuban Missile Crisis.

TAXATION

In the preceding sections of this chapter, I have discussed the legitimate and necessary powers of government in a complex society such as the United

States. It is obvious that such governmental functions cannot be exercised without taxation. Voluntary contributions would be totally insufficient.

The tax system should reflect the diverse economic situations of the people being taxed. Wealthy people should be taxed more, and at a higher rate, than poorer people. US tax laws and regulations currently enable rich people to manipulate the system in order to protect their wealth from regular tax rates.[15] Such preferential treatment should be changed so that wealthy people are, in fact, paying more and at higher rates than others.

The reader might ask how all this is justified from the point of view of natural right or natural law. In ancient and medieval political philosophy, not to mention biblical injunctions, it was held that the desire for more and more wealth was a violation of ethics or morality. Although every person and family should have adequate wealth to live—and even live comfortably—rich people should pay not only the same percentage of their real income as poorer people but, in fact, more. This meets the ethical standard as well as providing sufficient financing of government.

A CRITIQUE OF MINARCHISM

Chapter 1 addressed the theory of anarchocapitalism, as set forth in the writings of Murray Rothbard. Rothbard frequently used the word "libertarian" to describe his teachings, but many right-libertarians do not accept anarchism. Rather, they support a severely limited type of government that was historically called the "night-watchman state."

In recent times, this view of extremely limited government is called "minarchism." Perhaps its most famous exponent was Ayn Rand (1905–82). She articulated this political philosophy in her book *The Virtue of Selfishness*.[16] Rand's basic principle was as follows: "The proper functions of a government fall into three broad categories, all of them involving the issues of physical force and the protection of men's rights: *the police*, to protect men from criminals—*the armed services*, to protect men from foreign invaders—*the law courts*, to settle disputes among men according to objective laws."[17] Government should have no other function, and these limited functions should be financed by voluntary means.[18]

The previous sections of this chapter constitute my answer to minarchism.

CONCLUSION

This chapter has discussed certain affirmative powers of government that are legitimate and often necessary. This is not an exhaustive list, and many more functions could be identified. But the present account has demonstrated that minarchism is not a realistic limitation of government in today's complex societies.

CHAPTER FOUR
FORMS OF GOVERNMENT

Is there no virtue among us? — If there be
not, we are in a wretched situation. No
theoretical checks — no form of
Government, can render us secure. To
suppose that any form of Government will
secure liberty or happiness without any virtue
in the people, is a chimerical idea.

James Madison in the Virginia Ratifying
Convention, June 20, 1788[1]

INTRODUCTION

In his above-quoted remarks regarding the
then-proposed United States Constitution, James
Madison observed that no form of government can
secure liberty or happiness unless there is virtue among
the people. He was referring especially to the
democratic republic envisioned by the Constitution. By
"virtue," I understand (or reinterpret) Madison to mean
a devotion to the common good, proper reasoning about
both ends and means, and an ethical perspective
generally.[2] Socrates famously said that virtue is
knowledge. In the case of a citizen exercising the right
to vote, some knowledge of how government works and
of the constitutional and political history of the country

is important, though some citizens will, of course, be better informed about such matters than others.

Political philosophers throughout the millennia have described and evaluated various forms of government. The present chapter discusses the main types of government that have occurred or been proposed in recent times, with references back, when appropriate, to earlier historical developments.

THE PURPOSES OF THIS CHAPTER

This chapter considers various types of historical and projected political societies with two objectives in mind: (1) to understand such polities on their own terms, and (2) to distinguish between better and worse forms of government with a view to outlining the best possible form of government given the human condition in the present epoch.

Such words as "better," "worse," and "best" have often been dismissed by academic political and social scientists as inadmissible "value judgments" expressing merely subjective "personal preferences" not subject to rational analysis. In this view, reason can only be applied to means, not ends. As I have explained elsewhere, I reject this approach. Reason can and should be applied to both ends and means.[3]

How, then, should types of polities be evaluated? The goal is good government—government that promotes good ends while using good means, with both its ends and means determined by reason and evidence. The discussion in the present chapter addresses individual polities with reference to the rationality of both their ends and means.

HISTORICAL BACKGROUND

One might write an exhaustive account of all the types of political entities that have existed around the world throughout human history. Such a prodigious endeavor would be far beyond the scope of the present book; this author simply has neither the time nor the space to prepare it.

Instead, the present work focuses on the kinds of polities that exist, have existed, or could exist in the present age of advanced technology and commercial exchange in mostly industrial or postindustrial societies.

But these commercial societies have a historical background, and the relevant history often goes back to the peculiar way political societies developed in Europe. There may be some parallels in Asian or other non-European history, but I do not have the expertise to address them.

It is commonly understood that European history developed in three stages: ancient, medieval, and modern.

Ancient European polities involved city-states in Greece and elsewhere. There were also imperial entities such as the Roman empire.

The European Middle Ages were dominated by the Roman Catholic Church and by various relatively weak nation-states or other political entities. A military, political, and economic system called "feudalism" was widespread throughout Europe during this era.[4]

The modern age began, more or less, with the Italian Renaissance, which involved city-states in Italy. Gradually, powerful nation-states developed in continental Europe and the British Isles. The major class divisions in these countries were the monarchy, the

76

aristocracy, the peasantry, and an emerging bourgeois class that focused on economic production and exchange.

The dominant economic system in early modernity was mercantilism, which Merriam-Webster defines as follows:

> an economic system developing during the decay of feudalism to unify and increase the power and especially the monetary wealth of a nation by a strict governmental regulation of the entire national economy usually through policies designed to secure an accumulation of bullion . . . , a favorable balance of trade, the development of agriculture and manufactures, and the establishment of foreign trading monopolies. . . .[5]

Ecclesiastical establishments, with the assistance of allied governments, strictly enforced religious doctrines during the medieval and early modern eras. Religious dissenters were burned at the stake or otherwise tortured and executed in the Catholic and Protestant mergers of church and state.

The European Enlightenment advocated liberation from the religious and economic constraints of medieval and early modern political society. In 1776, Adam Smith published what became the most famous treatise supporting laissez-faire economics, *An Inquiry into the Nature and Causes of the Wealth of Nations* (frequently referred to as *The Wealth of Nations*). This work became the bible of free-market economic theory.

Gradually, free-market economics replaced mercantilism as the dominant economic ideology. This revolution entailed the view that a free market should supersede governmental control of the economy: economics should be separate from government, just as Enlightenment thinkers advocated freedom of conscience with regard to religious matters. Modern philosophers, starting with Machiavelli, criticized ancient and medieval philosophy for aiming too high in matters of ethics and politics. Some of these philosophers taught that a commercial republic should replace monarchy, aristocracy, theocracy, and mercantilism. As Ralph Lerner has explained:

> The old order was preoccupied with intangible goods to an extent we now hardly ever see. The king had his glory, the nobles their honor, the Christians their salvation, the citizens of pagan antiquity their ambition to outdo others in serving the public good. To thinkers like [Charles Secondat, Baron de] Montesquieu, [David] Hume, and [Adam] Smith, those earlier pretensions evinced a state of mind in some respects admirable, in other respects astonishing, in most respects consequential, but at bottom absurd. A good part of the political program of these commercial republicans was getting other men to judge likewise. . . .
>
> Eighteenth-century men had to be brought to see how fanciful those noncommercial notions were. To the commercial republicans, aristocratic imagination and pretension were not totally devoid of social value. Honor could be specious and yet politically useful; pride

could engender politesse and delicacy of taste, graces that make life easy. The weightier truth, however, was that concern with these fancies skewed public policy and public budgets, sacrificing the real needs of the people to the petty desires of their governors. As Montesquieu put it, these "imaginary needs are what the passions and foibles of those who govern ask for: the charm of an extraordinary project, the sick desire for a vain glory, and a certain impotence of mind against fantasies."[6]

These modern political philosophers aspired to replace theocracy, mercantilism, and other aspects of the early modern order with a focus on economic gain. They succeeded in liberating the passion for moneymaking from traditional ethics. They were not so successful in suppressing religion. Indeed, some Christian sects adopted a prosperity gospel at odds with the Sermon on the Mount and an eschatological vision in conflict with democratic republicanism.[7]

DEMOCRATIC REPUBLICS

Democratic republics in the world today differ from each other in the details of their forms. I am most familiar with the US democratic republic, having lived in the United States all my life and studied and written about American political history and government. Accordingly, this section begins with an analysis of the form of government that exists in the USA. Subsequent subsections will address other types of democratic republics, especially parliamentary democracies.

Chapter 4. Forms of Government

The United States of America

The constitutional history of the United States could be said to have begun with the July 4, 1776 Declaration of Independence,[8] which transformed the Revolutionary War against Great Britain (commenced in 1775) into a War for Independence. The 1783 Treaty of Paris ended this war, with Great Britain recognizing the independence of the United States of America.

The famous second paragraph of the Declaration of Independence stated:

> We hold these truths to be self-evident, that all men are created equal, that they are endowed by their Creator with certain unalienable Rights, that among these are Life, Liberty and the pursuit of Happiness. —That to secure these rights, Governments are instituted among Men, deriving their just powers from the consent of the governed, — That whenever any Form of Government becomes destructive of these ends, it is the Right of the People to alter or to abolish it, and to institute new Government, laying its foundation on such principles and organizing its powers in such form, as to them shall seem most likely to effect their Safety and Happiness.

These words were largely adopted, with some modifications, from John Locke's *Second Treatise of Government*, originally published anonymously in 1689 (dated 1690). Thomas Jefferson was the principal author of the Declaration of Independence, but his draft was revised by others in some respects. For example, Jefferson's language for the first sentence of the above

80

quotation did not use the word "Creator"; instead, he wrote: "We hold these Truths to be sacred & undeniable; that all Men are created equal and independent; that from that equal Creation they derive Rights inherent and unalienable; among which are the Preservation of Life, and Liberty, and the Pursuit of Happiness . . . ."[9]

The Second Continental Congress governed the US central government from the date of the Declaration of Independence until the Articles of Confederation became effective on March 1, 1781. The US achieved independence from Great Britain in 1783. As a result of dissatisfaction with the Articles of Confederation, a Constitutional Convention was conducted in the summer of 1787.

The Convention proposed a new Constitution, which was ratified by the requisite number of states in 1788, and went into effect in 1789. Portions of Sections 8 and 9 of Article I of the Constitution set forth some individual rights, and the first ten amendments (later collectively known as the Bill of Rights) thereto referenced additional rights, as did the Thirteenth, Fourteenth, Fifteenth, Nineteenth, Twenty-Fourth, and Twenty-Sixth Amendments. The Ninth Amendment explicitly recognizes unenumerated rights: "The enumeration in the Constitution, of certain rights, shall not be construed to deny or disparage others retained by the people."

The federal (national) government of the United States is not a direct democracy, because the people at large do not vote directly on legislation or other governmental actions.[10] Additionally, the US Constitution[11] provides for a separation of powers (not always complete) among the executive, legislative, and judicial branches of the federal government, checks and balances between the branches, and individual rights that must be recognized by government (see chapters 2 and 3, above, for details).

The Preamble to the Constitution states:

> **We the People of the United States**, in Order to form a more perfect Union, establish Justice, insure domestic Tranquility, provide for the common defence, promote the general Welfare, and secure the Blessings of Liberty to ourselves and our Posterity, **do ordain and establish this Constitution for the United States of America.**[12]

This sentence recognizes that sovereignty reposes in the people, and not in a king or in the state governments that had existed since the Declaration of Independence. The Framers of the Constitution rejected the view held by most nations for millennia that sovereignty resided in a monarch, in some group of oligarchs or nobles, or in any political entity.[13]

Under the Constitution, the national government has limited powers; the residue of legitimate political power rests in the state governments. The state governments create local governments, for example, counties, townships, and municipalities.

Under Article IV, Section 4 of the US Constitution, "The United States [government] shall guarantee to every State in this Union a Republican Form of Government. . . ." In *Federalist* No. 39,[14] James Madison observed that "the republican complexion of this system" could be found "in its absolute prohibition of titles of nobility" (Article I, Section 10, Clause 8). In other words, the Constitution rejected the entire system of landed aristocracy in Great Britain and continental Europe, whereby monarchs granted land and special legal privileges to nobles that were not afforded to the people at large. The term "republican" was understood to be a form of government that was neither monarchical nor aristocratic.

It is interesting that state and local governments in the United States have sometimes incorporated elements of direct democracy that are not present in the national government. Thus, town meetings wherein residents in attendance vote directly on legislation have long been a practice in some New England states and, more recently, in some western states. Additionally, some states have adopted procedures whereby voters can initiate or reject legislation independently of their elected representatives.

James Madison has long been called the "Father of the Constitution." He certainly was one of the most influential delegates at the Constitutional Convention, and the *Federalist* papers that he authored contain some of the most cogent discussions of the Constitution that have ever been written. However, the notes that Madison took at the Convention (not published until decades later) show that the document that eventually emerged differed in some important respects from his own vision. Many weeks were occupied during the Convention with debates between Madison and his group of nationalist delegates, on the one hand, and delegates supporting more involvement of the state governments in the structure and operation of the new US government, on the other.[15]

The founding era of the United States was marred by two major flaws: the institution of slavery and the geographical expansion of White settlers at the expense of Indigenous peoples. These two evils had commenced during the seventeenth century with the initial settlements by European immigrants of Virginia and New England.

Slavery was abolished only with the victory (1865) of the North against the South in the very bloody Civil War, followed by the nationwide constitutional abolition of slavery by the Thirteenth Amendment (ratified December 6, 1865). The Fourteenth Amendment (ratified July 9, 1868) stated that "[a]ll persons born or naturalized in the United States and subject to the jurisdiction thereof, are citizens of the United States and of the State wherein they reside. No State shall make or enforce any law which shall abridge the privileges or immunities of citizens of the United States; nor shall any State deprive any person of life, liberty, or property, without due process of law; nor deny to any person within its jurisdiction the equal protection of the laws." The Fifteenth Amendment provided: "The right of citizens of the United States to vote shall not be denied or abridged by the United States or by any State on account of race, color or previous condition of servitude." As discussed in chapter 2, the South managed to circumvent these constitutional commands by various "Jim Crow" laws until this discriminatory regime was outlawed by the Civil Rights Acts of 1964 and 1965.

While slavery was largely (but not entirely) a Southern phenomenon, the forced removal of Indigenous peoples from their lands occurred in both the North and the South during and after the seventeenth century. Additionally, from 1860 to 1978, Native children were often separated from their parents and imprisoned in boarding schools, usually operated by religious orders, where they were forced to renounce their traditional culture and religion and to adopt White culture and religion. The federal government supported this compulsory assimilation project.[16]

At the time of its founding as a nation, the United States was a predominantly agrarian country. Although the Industrial Revolution in the United States began in the late eighteenth century, it did not become widespread until the second half of the nineteenth century. From that time until the present, large metropolitan areas have become increasingly prevalent.

The Industrial Revolution resulted in more and more people becoming employees rather than, as in the past, small farmers or independent artisans. Huge business corporations came to dominate the US economy. Their leaders inaugurated the first Gilded Age (the last three decades of the nineteenth century and the first few years of the twentieth century), exhibiting huge disparities in wealth between corporate leaders and working people. This was followed by the Progressive Era, in which political leaders such as Theodore Roosevelt and Woodrow Wilson advocated breaking up large business conglomerates called "trusts" and reformers obtained the passage of such social and economic legislation as child labor laws and food safety measures.

During the late nineteenth and early twentieth centuries, the US Supreme Court was hostile to governmental economic and social reform efforts. A majority on the Court adhered to the notion that laissez-faire economics was dictated by the US Constitution (which it was not) and that Social Darwinism should prevail. This all came to a head with the stock market crash of 1929 and the ensuing Great Depression—the most devastating economic collapse in American history.

As a result of the election of 1932, Franklin D. Roosevelt became president in 1933, and the various components of Roosevelt's New Deal were promptly enacted by Congress. This program included the Social Security Act, public works projects, banking and security reforms, governmental assistance to farmers, and many other measures. When the Supreme Court began striking down this legislation on the professed ground that it was unconstitutional, President Roosevelt asked Congress to increase the number of justices on the Court so as to allow the appointment of new, pro-New Deal justices. Although Congress rejected this request, the Court soon changed its stance on the New Deal, and most of its programs eventually passed constitutional muster.

The dispute over how to interpret and apply the US Constitution began in the famous conflict between Secretary of State Thomas Jefferson and Secretary of the Treasury Alexander Hamilton during the 1790s and has reappeared, in different forms, throughout US history. Today, the debate is largely between those supporting some version of "original intent" and those advocating a "living Constitution." The problem is exacerbated by the extreme difficulty of passing amendments to the Constitution under Article V of that document. Under such circumstances, I endorse the analysis in the opinion of the Court authored by Chief Justice John Marshall in the famous case of *McCulloch v. Maryland*, 17 U.S. 316 (1819):

> A constitution, to contain an accurate detail of all the subdivisions of which its great powers will admit, and of all the means by which they may be carried into execution, would partake of the prolixity of a legal code, and could scarcely be embraced by the human mind. It would probably never be understood by the public. Its nature, therefore, requires, that only its great outlines should be marked, its important objects designated, and the minor ingredients which compose those objects be deduced from the nature of the objects themselves. . . . In considering this question, then, we must never forget, that it is a constitution we are expounding. . . .
>
> This provision is made in a constitution intended to endure for ages to come, and, consequently, to be adapted to the various crises of human affairs. To have prescribed the means by which government should, in all future time, execute its powers, would have been to change, entirely, the character of the instrument, and give it the properties of a legal code. It would have been an unwise attempt to provide, by immutable rules, for exigencies which, if foreseen at all, must have been seen dimly, and which can be best provided for as they occur . . . .

> . . . Let the end be legitimate, let it be within the scope of the constitution, and all means which are appropriate, which are plainly adapted to that end, which are not prohibited, but consist with the letter and spirit of the constitution, are constitutional.[17]

As for legitimate ends, the Supreme Court has held that Congress may constitutionally pass a law providing for spending in order to advance the "general welfare" pursuant to Article I, Section 8, Clause 1 of the Constitution, subject to express constitutional limitations, if any.[18]

The foregoing discussion addresses some of the main features of the US democratic republic. We now turn to other forms of democratic government.

Presidential Executives in Other Countries

Several other countries have a presidential executive, but many of these do not have the same kinds of separation of powers, checks and balances, and individual rights guarantees as are found in the US constitutional system. France qualifies as a democratic republic, though it has a unique semi-presidential system with both an elected president and a prime minister.[19]

Parliamentary Democracy

In the typical parliamentary system, a prime minister is elected by a legislature to undertake executive responsibilities along with a cabinet. The most famous example of a parliamentary democracy is the United Kingdom, but many European and other countries also have parliamentary systems. Although the UK and some other parliamentary democracies are technically governed by monarchs, these monarch have been essentially figureheads in modern times.

Because a prime minister is directly responsible to the legislature, separations of powers between the executive and the legislature do not exist in a parliamentary democracy. However, most parliamentary democracies retain important features of individual rights and rule of law.[20]

European Union

The European Union is an interesting supranational organization with a complicated history and structure. It currently has twenty-seven member states. Each member nation has given up some aspects of its sovereignty to the EU. Although space does not permit an extensive discussion here, additional information can be easily located online as well as in books about its nature and organization.[21]

DIRECT DEMOCRACY

In contrast to representative democracy, direct democracy is rule by citizens casting votes on routine legislation directly, without representation. Republican institutions such as bills of rights, separation of powers, federalism, and rule of law are (or are often) absent.

The most famous example of direct democracy was ancient Athens, where citizens voted in person on routine legislation and on many executive decisions. Athens was famous for recognizing freedom of speech. However, like other Greek cities, the Athenian government controlled religion and religious practices. In 399 BCE, Socrates was formally indicted for not believing in the gods in which the city believed, for allegedly bringing in new divinities, and for corrupting the young with his religious impiety. A jury of about 500 male Athenian citizens, chosen by lot, found him guilty of these offenses and sentenced him to execution by ingestion of hemlock, which was subsequently conducted.[22]

Thus, the direct democracy of Athens, by way of a jury of several hundred citizen jurors, with no separate, professional judge to rule on such issues as the admissibility of evidence and with no right of appeal to a higher court, tried Socrates for impiety and condemned him to death. Direct democracy involves, almost by definition, tyranny of the majority, and the framers of the United States Constitution deliberately designed that fundamental law in a way that precluded majority tyranny.

Direct democracy has been present in some form at the famous New England town meetings. Direct democracy in the traditional New England town meeting setting is perhaps workable to some extent because residents of small towns presumably have familiarity with the issues affecting their communities. However, some people have recently proposed adopting direct democracy for larger governmental entities by utilizing internet technology. Citizens would vote online on individual items of proposed legislation. They would vote directly on legislation instead of voting for representatives.

Extending direct democracy to a large political entity would be problematic. National and even state/regional or large municipal governments have to decide many exceedingly difficult questions, including, on the national level, complicated foreign policy issues.

Voters generally do not have time to acquaint themselves with the kinds of knowledge that are necessary for informed decision-making on important national issues; they are too busy with their jobs and families. Additionally, such voters do not have the expertise in constitutional and other law that is important for the protection of individual rights.

Thus, democracies in our era are representative rather than direct democracies. The ideal form of representative democracy is that people will elect candidates who can devote full time to understanding—with the help of expert advice in legislative committees and similar expert assistance in the executive department—the very difficult and complicated issues confronting government in our time. This system is, of course, far from perfect. History shows that citizens are often motivated by demagoguery and other irrationality to choose authoritarian or incompetent leaders. But, absent an ethical and rational transformation of humanity, representative democracy, with constitutional protections of individual rights, is preferable to the available alternatives.

EPISTOCRACY (RULE OF THE KNOWLEDGEABLE) AND MERITOCRACY

The term "epistocracy" is a recent neologism derived from the Greek words for knowledge (ἐπιστήμη, *epistēmē*) and rule (κράτος, *kratos*). The original concept of epistocracy was elaborated in Plato's *Republic*. The following discussion addresses that ancient dialogue as well as recent epistocratic proposals. The word "meritocracy," as applied to government, has a similar meaning.

Plato's *Republic*

Plato (427–347), a philosopher in classical Athens, wrote many dialogues and a number of letters. His most famous dialogue is the *Republic*, which addresses the question "what is justice" for both an individual and a *polis*. A Greek polis consisted of a city and its surrounding area. Each polis had a πολιτεία (*politeia*), a form of government. The word *"Republic"* is the historical, though somewhat inaccurate, English translation of the Greek title (*Πολιτεία, Politeia*) of Plato's great work.

The *Republic* articulated a "city in speech," which its principal interlocutor, the fictional Socrates, called "a beautiful city" or, in other words, the best thinkable polis. Socrates formulated a thought experiment in which philosophers, with their superior knowledge and wisdom, ruled the city, with the aid of a military class. The third, and lowest, class consisted of the moneymakers, those whose principal interest was to acquire money and associated goods and services. The moneymaking class had nothing to do with government.

The city in speech proved to be practically impossible, because it required the expulsion of all residents (other than the philosophic ruling class and perhaps the military class) over ten years old as well as the communism of women, children, and property in the philosophic and soldier classes. "In the *Republic* Socrates founds a city in speech, i.e., not in deed; accordingly the *Republic* does not in fact present the best political order but rather brings to light the limitations, the limits, and therewith the nature of politics (Cicero, *Republic* II 52)."[23] In the last analysis, the *Republic* is more about ethical principles and the nature of political life than a serious proposal for political reformation.[24] Additionally, it is questionable whether Plato's utopian political order is consonant with human nature.[25]

Recent Epistocratic/Meritocratic Proposals

Various forms of epistocracy or meritocracy have been proposed by various authors in recent times.

Perhaps the most radical of these schemes is by an author who goes by the apparent pseudonym of Jaqueisse. His book is titled *The Philosopher Kingdom*.[26] This book consciously imitates Plato's *Republic* without recognizing that Plato never intended that work to be a practical proposition. Although Jaqueisse has some ethical views in common with Plato, his explicitly totalitarian regime is entirely inconsistent with individual liberty and rather assumes that government should be in the business of forcing people to be virtuous cogs in a coercive governmental machine. This is, quite simply, contrary to human nature. Force and virtue are antithetical. The result would be a totalitarian state rivaling that of Stalin's Soviet Union and Mao's People's Republic of China. I have critiqued this book at greater length elsewhere.[27]

Jason Brennan is perhaps the foremost contemporary exponent of epistocracy, which he defines as follows: "Epistocracy means the rule of the knowledgeable. More precisely, a political regime is epistocratic to the extent that political power is formally distributed according to competence, skill, and the good faith to act on that skill."[28] He discusses various epistocratic proposals, for example, values-only voting, restrictions on suffrage (voter qualification exams), and universal suffrage with an epistocratic veto. The latter appears to be his favorite form of epistocracy. A close analysis of his book *Against Democracy* establishes that Brennan's real aim is to substitute an economic libertarian elite for democracy. I have critically examined his diagnosis and proposed solution(s) elsewhere.[29]

Another epistocratic scheme is to weight votes by educational level or other standard: People who have more education would receive more votes than those with lesser education.[30] This, in effect, would create an electoral caste system. Educational level is often correlated with class. Governmental policies already often work to the advantage of the upper economic classes over the lower economic classes. This kind of system would exacerbate and institutionalize such inequality by making it much more difficult for working class voters to oppose elites who have no interest in the lower classes or who think low socioeconomic status is somehow a badge of personal inferiority.

OLIGARCHY AND PLUTOCRACY

"Oligarchy" (in classical Greek) means "rule of a few," and "plutocracy" is "rule of the wealthy." In historical practice, these two regimes have often combined: oligarchy often (but not always) includes plutocracy. Property qualifications for voting have been used to achieve these kinds of systems.

Oligarchy and plutocracy can also result from other kinds of laws. For example, in France, before the 1789 Revolution, the landed aristocrats, who had been given their estates by the monarchs, paid no taxes. Only the Third Estate (the peasants and the emerging bourgeois class) paid taxes. A similar phenomenon may be developing in the United States today, where conservative legislators attempt to reduce or eliminate taxes on the wealthy while purporting to pay for these tax reductions by gutting long-established safety net and social welfare programs for the less fortunate.

As this book is being prepared, President Donald J. Trump, himself a billionaire, has stuffed his cabinet and other high governmental offices with other billionaires. Trump loves the Gilded Age and is trying to resurrect it. Gold is his favorite color.

AUTHORITARIAN REGIMES

Authoritarian regimes have been the default type of government for millennia. Even today, about one-third of the governments throughout the world are authoritarian.[31] There are four types of authoritarian political orders: standard authoritarianism, totalitarianism, theocracy, and Erastianism.

Standard authoritarianism is a political system in which a monarch, dictator, or elite group effectively controls the entire government, without separation of powers, checks and balances, or individual rights. Although popular elections may exist, the political leader or leaders control the results—either directly through electoral manipulation or indirectly through populist demagoguery. The judiciary is not independent but is rather controlled, directly or indirectly, by the leader or leaders. Corruption is often rampant.[32]

Totalitarianism is the "most absolute form of government, based around a supreme leader, a single guiding ideology, and total political control over all aspects of public and private life."[33] One could add that a committee of political leaders might serve the same

95

function as a supreme leader, though a popular cult of personality surrounding a singular totalitarian ruler is the norm. Fascist Italy, Nazi Germany, the Soviet Union (especially under Joseph Stalin), the People's Republic of China (especially under Mao Zedong), and North Korea were examples of totalitarian political societies in the twentieth century. Perhaps the only current example of a totalitarian polity is North Korea, though China and Russia both retain many characteristics of their totalitarian past.[34] The classic fictional portrayal of a totalitarian regime is George Orwell's novel *1984*.[35]

Theocracy ("rule of god" in Greek) is an authoritarian or totalitarian religious regime controlled, directly or indirectly, by religious leaders or alleged religious prophets. Such governments promulgate and enforce strict religious laws and persecute religious dissenters. Historical examples include sixteenth-century Geneva, seventeenth-century Massachusetts Bay, and present-day Iran and Saudi Arabia.[36] The novel (and later television series) titled *The Handmaid's Tale* graphically illustrates a theocracy in a contemporary context.[37]

Erastianism is the doctrine that government should dictate religion and control the church in ecclesiastical and other matters. (The term "Erastianism" is actually a misnomer, but it has come to have this meaning.) The philosopher Thomas Hobbes, who was affected by the violent conflicts between Puritans and Anglicans in the English Civil Wars, set forth a theoretical argument for such a doctrine in his famous work *Leviathan or The Matter, Forme and Power of a Commonwealth Ecclesiasticall and Civil* (1651). State control of religion was a policy of several English monarchs, including, especially, Henry VIII, Elizabeth I, James I, and Charles I.

There are, of course, fundamental differences between every kind of authoritarianism and democratic republicanism. A democratic republic is more consonant with human nature than authoritarian regimes. But what are the outlines of a good democratic republic? The next section addresses that question.

OUTLINE OF A MODEL DEMOCRATIC REPUBLIC

The United States and all other actual nations (except any that are newly created) have a history. That history would have to be taken into account in any transition to a more perfect system. Article V of the United States Constitution has a very difficult procedure for amendment. It would probably be impossible to make significant changes to the US Constitution in a short period of time. Accordingly, the following proposed model of a democratic republic is, like Plato's *Republic*, a polity in speech. Since I do not propose to adopt the unserious proposal of the Platonic Socrates to deport everyone over ten years old, the best that could be hoped for is that some of the model's provisions might be adopted by one or more democratic republics.

The following model is an overall guide, not a detailed blueprint. It does not claim perfection, and modification of its details might be necessary in any case of actual implementation. Furthermore, this outline lacks many details that would have to be carefully considered in any constitutional reform.

The principles set forth in chapters 2 and 3 of this book are incorporated by reference as the basic framework of this model democratic republic. Chapter 2 discusses how governments should, and can, protect individual rights. Chapter 3 addresses the legitimate powers of government.

Bill of Rights

A new constitution should include a bill of rights in accordance with chapter 2 of the present book. The enumeration of rights should be more clearly elaborated than in the present US Constitution, and there should be a provision for unenumerated rights as in the current Ninth Amendment.

Federalism

Perhaps the first thing to consider is the extent of the polity's territory and population. A polity such as the United States has a very large territory and a very large population. For such countries, it makes sense to have what has been historically called a "federal" system. There is a central government with constitutional authority over the entire nation. Regional (provincial, state) governments provide an intermediate level of government, limited to the territory and population of their particular region or state. Finally, governments at the county and municipal levels address local concerns.

The Branches of the National Government

The branches of the national government would consist of an executive, a bicameral legislature, and a judiciary. The following discussion generally, but not entirely, tracks the organization of the United States Constitution, as amended. To the extent not countermanded by the following remarks, that document may be consulted for details not discussed here.

Citizenship would be defined as in the Fourteenth Amendment to the US Constitution. All adult citizens would be entitled to vote in all executive and (to the extent they are residents of the applicable legislative district) legislative elections.

The Executive Branch

The executive branch would be headed by a president and vice president, both of whom would run for election on a single ballot elected by the majority of all popular votes cast nationwide, with each voter (adult citizen) having one vote and one vote only. The election for president and vice president would be every four years. No person could be president for a total of more than eight years.

No electoral college or similar filtering mechanism would exist.[38] A system of instant runoff voting would be operative such that, in the event the initial round of vote counting did not produce a majority winner, successive rounds of vote counting would be conducted under the principles of ranked-choice voting.[39] Alternatively, if ranked-choice voting were deemed not desirable, then there would be a physical runoff election between the two presidential candidates receiving the highest numbers of votes in the first round of ballots.

The president's powers and duties would generally be the same as in Article II of the US Constitution, subject to the checks and balances outlined in those provisions. It may be important to specify such powers and duties in somewhat greater detail as a result of the historical experience of the United States, especially in light of the presidential administrations of Donald J.

Trump, which have reminded Americans that their country was founded in explicit opposition to monarchy and tyranny.

The impeachment provisions in the US Constitution are also incorporated by reference, though some fine-tuning of them may be appropriate. It may also be important to spell out the circumstances in which a former president could be criminally prosecuted for actions taken during that person's presidency.

The Legislative Branch

The structure of a bicameral legislature would be similar but not identical to that outlined in Article I of the United States Constitution, as amended. A house of representatives would be elected by citizen voters every two years on the basis of legislative districts. There would be national prohibitions against gerrymandering of congressional districts, though the details of such prohibitions would be difficult to formulate. State governments would still exist, but each state would have a number of senators proportionate to that state's population. Senators would be elected by citizen voters of the state every six years. Senate elections would be staggered in a manner analogous to the current system in the United States.

The powers and duties of the national bicameral legislature would be consistent with the principles of chapters 2 and 3, above.

The Judicial Branch

There would be a supreme court and lower federal courts generally consistent with Article III of the United States Constitution, as amended. The supreme court and lower federal courts would have the explicit power of judicial review, as discussed in chapters 2 and 3 of this book. Terms of justices on the US Supreme Court would be limited to twenty years. After retirement, they would continue to receive the judicial salaries and benefits they would have received if they had remained on the Supreme Court. Although they could do volunteer work, they would not be allowed any employment with, or representation of, a for-profit business, and they would be prohibited from taking any remuneration from any for-profit entity that has appeared, or may appear, before the federal courts. However, such retired justices could give speeches and write books and articles for reasonable compensation. The code of ethics for sitting US Supreme Court justices would be essentially the same as that applicable to lower-court federal judges, and enforcement mechanisms should be formulated in light of the unique situations of supreme court justices.

Administrative Agencies

A national government governing a large and complex society must have administrative agencies to carry out legislative and executive directives. In the United States, the Congress normally establishes such agencies, and many of the rank-and-file administrative employees have been civil servants entitled to civil service legal protections against being fired at will by the president.

The president of the United States has constitutional power to appoint, subject to the consent of the Senate, the heads of the executive departments. These are called "political appointees" or "political employees," and they can be summarily dismissed by the president. Congress also has established "independent agencies" that are intended to be beyond the reach of presidential power and often perform a regulatory, quasi-prosecutorial, or quasi-judicial function.[40]

President Donald J. Trump has advocated a "unitary executive" theory that seeks to abolish independent and other agencies and to destroy the civil service protections that civil servants have enjoyed since the 1883 Pendleton Act. If successful, such actions would give immense power to the president by restoring the "spoils system" that existed more than 140 years ago and, with Trump's other aggrandizement of legislative and judicial power, tending toward absolute monarchy. As of the time of final publication of the present book (early January 2026), the Supreme Court had not definitively weighed in on these issues, though the majority of the justices appear to be favorable disposed to the unitary executive theory.

The US Supreme Court will likely soon resolve these controversies. But one of the issues that should be addressed in any constitutional reformation is the proper status and independence of governmental administrative agencies and their personnel as well as civil service protections for administrative employees generally.

Sovereignty and the Electoral Franchise

"Sovereignty," in the constitutional sense, means the ultimate authority in a political order.[41] Sovereignty in a democratic republic, often called "popular sovereignty," is understood to rest in its citizens. If something like Plato's *Republic* were possible and desirable, one could argue that sovereignty would reside in those who are most rational and knowledgeable about political philosophy, constitutional law, economics, and so forth. However, as explained above, Plato's *Republic* is impossible and, even if possible, undesirable; similar epistocratic or meritocratic devices would also lead to negative consequences.

Citizens generally do not have sufficient leisure to become experts on political and economic matters. Moreover, citizens are occasionally, though not always, swayed by demagogues whose interest is merely to have power for its power's sake or to push through a narrow, irrational, ideological agenda. The experience of our epoch shows that a considerable portion of a democratic electorate can be misguided by misinformation and disinformation perpetrated by dishonest media and politicians.

Additionally, experts frequently disagree among themselves on important political and economic questions. Because a political order ruled by experts is impossible in both theory and practice, and because historical experience shows that rule by a monarch, an oligarchy, or some other privileged person or group usually leads to some kind of tyranny, the doctrine that sovereignty resides in the people remains an important concept; it is the least bad option. But this doctrine has rightly been tempered in the United States and other democratic republics by constitutional protections for individual rights as well as by an independent judiciary, appointed directly or indirectly by the citizens, to enforce such individual rights (see chapter 2). As discussed above, representative democracy—with constitutional rights, separation of powers, and checks and balances—is better than direct democracy.

Chapter 5 of my book *Reason and Human Ethics* specifically addresses the question of citizen and media ethics. Because sovereignty resides in the citizens of a democratic republic, it is very important that citizens be properly educated in ethics, constitutional government, and relevant constitutional and political history. More generally, *Reason and Human Ethics* addresses the proper ethical education and habituation of all people within a country. As Confucius said,

> From the emperor down to the mass of the people, all must consider the cultivation of the person the root of everything besides.
>
> It cannot be, when the root is neglected, that what should spring from it will be well ordered. [42]

The difference between a direct democracy and a democratic republic is that the latter has governmental institutions, directly or indirectly responsible to the citizens, that constitute the actual, day-to-day government of the country. These institutions include elected representatives to the legislature, an elected president, and a judiciary that adheres to and enforces constitutional principles and the rule of law.

In a model democratic republic, the citizens would be prepared for their electoral duties by education in ethics, critical thinking, government, and history, together with basic science. They would exercise their ethical understanding and basic political and historical knowledge and rationality in electing a president and legislators who would then carry forward these principles in governing the country. In making decisions about proper governance of the nation, the elected officials would consult experts of various points of view. From this information they would formulate and apply political and economic measures conducive to the common good (see chapter 3). In the background, the supreme court or constitutional court would protect the individual rights (see chapter 2) of the people living in the polity.

The executive and legislative leaders of such a model democratic republic would have sufficient knowledge, combined with an ethical foundation, to govern wisely. Perfection does not exist in the human world, but such leadership would be much more beneficial than demagogic rule by those who lust for power or have ideological desiderata that are inconsistent with the common good. Occasionally, in human history, we see a political leader that approaches the ideal, though each actual, historical leader has had some imperfections. In the next and final chapter of this book, we consider the thinking and actions of a US president who just might have saved humankind from a nuclear war with his rational decision-making in the 1962 Cuban Missile Crisis.

CHAPTER FIVE

CASE STUDY: POLITICAL LEADERSHIP IN THE 1962 CUBAN MISSILE CRISIS

> Fifty years ago [October 1962], the Cuban missile crisis brought the world to the brink of nuclear disaster. During the standoff, U.S. President John F. Kennedy thought the chance of escalation to war was "between 1 in 3 and even," and what we have learned in later decades has done nothing to lengthen those odds. We now know, for example, that in addition to nuclear–armed ballistic missiles, the Soviet Union had deployed 100 tactical nuclear weapons to Cuba, and the local Soviet commander there could have launched these weapons without additional codes or commands from Moscow. The U.S. air strike and invasion that were scheduled for the third week of the confrontation would likely have triggered a nuclear response against American ships and troops, and perhaps even Miami. The resulting war might have led to the deaths of 100 million Americans and over 100 million Russians.
>
> Graham Allison, "The Cuban Missile Crisis at 50" [1]

The preceding epigraph delineates the high stakes of the October 1962 Cuban Missile Crisis. President John F. Kennedy (sometimes hereafter referred to as "JFK") and his advisers faced a potentially calamitous outcome if they made a wrong decision—or even, depending on the actions of Soviet Premier Nikita Khrushchev, if they made a correct one. This chapter provides an analysis of this momentous episode.

The discussion focuses on the rationality of the decision-making on both sides. As I have written elsewhere, I define "reason" and "rationality" as referring to both ends and means.[2]

Was Khrushchev being rational when he decided to install nuclear missiles in Cuba? What were his objectives, and were they reasonable? Was he rational about the means he devised and used to achieve those objectives?

Was JFK rational in his objective of removing the nuclear missiles from Cuba and preventing further shipments related to Khrushchev's scheme? Was he rational in the methods he employed to achieve that objective?

To what extent did Khrushchev and Kennedy use reason in resolving the crisis? Did their respective methods of decision-making facilitate or impede a rational and evidence-based solution?

The present study examines these questions in depth.

What is **political** leadership? Some scholars think it is analogous to **business** leadership; they apply corporate leadership models to evaluate presidents and prime ministers.[3] However, just as it is a category error and a false analogy to attempt to "run government like a business," so I oppose using corporate CEOs as models for government executives.

President Kennedy faced foreign policy challenges that no business executive ever encountered. His leadership during the Cuban Missile Crisis demonstrated his ability to rationally assess all the available options and choose the most prudent one under the circumstances. It had nothing to do with maximizing profits for corporate shareholders or other business owners.

One could make a similar statement about the political leadership of President Franklin D. Roosevelt and Prime Minister Winston Churchill during World War II. Although they occasionally made mistakes and even disagreed with each other, they brought reason to bear on many difficult issues of strategy and tactics.[4]

I was in high school during the 1962 Cuban Missile Crisis. At that time, most of us Americans believed it was quite possible that this confrontation would result in a nuclear war, leading to the deaths or radioactive poisoning of millions upon millions of people in the United States, the Soviet Union, and elsewhere. It was a sober time.

RELEVANT DEVELOPMENTS PRECEDING THE CUBAN MISSILE CRISIS

To understand the Cuban Missile Crisis, we must first consider the historical developments that led up to it. The appendix of this book provides a more detailed discussion and documentation of the events summarized in the following three subsections.

Communist Theory and Practice Before Castro

In the nineteenth century, Karl Marx and Friedrich Engels formulated the doctrine of Communism, based on the following premises. Human history is the history of class struggles. The dominant class struggle of that era was between the bourgeoisie (the capitalist owners of the means of production and employers of wage labor) and the proletariat (wage laborers). In reaction to the bourgeois exploitation of the proletariat, the proletariat would rise up and exterminate the bourgeoisie.

Marx and Lenin taught that the Communist revolution would proceed in two stages. The first stage would be the dictatorship of the proletariat, during which the bourgeois class would be eliminated and the capitalist system dismantled. The second stage would usher in Communism proper, a society in which class struggle would cease because the dictatorship of the proletariat would have eradicated the bourgeoisie and all its works and ways.

One version of the Communist phase was that the state (government) would "wither away" into a form of anarchism. The other version was that the state would persist and be operated by the proletariat rather than by the capitalists. In every Communist revolution since Marx and Engels, the state has never disappeared; the government has remained a dictatorship that violated individual rights.

Marx and Engels believed that Communist revolutions would occur in industrialized countries like Germany. But the first historical example of a Communist regime occurred in a nonindustrial country, Russia, where the Bolsheviks, under the leadership of Vladimir Lenin, came to power in 1917. Lenin made a critical amendment to the Marxist concept of the dictatorship of the proletariat. He maintained that the dictatorship was of the **vanguard** of the proletariat, namely, the Communist Party.

Lenin's government abolished the "bourgeois" ownership of land and redistributed it to the peasants who cultivated it. Proletarian workers displaced capitalist owners and assumed control of the factories. The vanguard of the proletariat executed and otherwise persecuted "class enemies." When Lenin died in 1924, Joseph Stalin took over as leader of the Soviet Union. Under Stalin, the Soviet Union was a totalitarian regime, featuring a cult of personality centered on himself.

Stalin died in 1953. A few years later, Nikita Khrushchev emerged as the dominant leader. Despite Khrushchev's somewhat more moderate approach, compared with Stalin, one distinguished scholar concluded, in December 1962, that "[Khrushchev's] regime remains totalitarian in its essence, still asserting its all-encompassing authority over the whole of Soviet society and tolerating no derogation of the monopoly powers of the Party leadership, but it can claim that it has responded to grievances which Stalin ignored."[5] Additionally, Khrushchev retained the Marxist-Leninist faith, which, to him, was sacrosanct. He held power until an internal Kremlin coup deposed him on October 14, 1964.

After World War II, totalitarian Communist regimes also emerged in China under Mao Zedong and in what became North Korea under Kim Il Sung.

For the Cold War between the United States and the Soviet Union, especially the developments regarding Berlin, see the section on the Cold War in the appendix.

The Rise of Castro and the Bay of Pigs Invasion

Fidel Castro's guerrilla forces successfully overthrew Cuban dictator Fulgencio Batista on January 1, 1959. At that time, Dwight D. Eisenhower was the president of the United States. Castro did not immediately identify himself as a Communist. However, he garnered the hostility of some US governmental officials by expropriating American companies and restricting foreign land ownership. Castro also began persecuting those who objected to the perceived Communist influence in his government.

The Central Intelligence Agency (CIA) of the United States had previously orchestrated successful coups in Iran and Guatemala. The CIA or its predecessor(s) had also been attempting to subvert foreign elections since the 1940s.

By January 1960, the Eisenhower administration was planning a coup to overthrow the Castro regime. Although the initial plan was to infiltrate Cuban exiles into Cuba to foment a rebellion, it evolved into a new strategy that included a coordinated sea and air assault on Cuba, along with general guerrilla activities. All this was to be accomplished under the facade of Cuban exile forces. The involvement of the US government in the plot was to be kept secret.

This was the plan that John F. Kennedy inherited upon becoming president of the United States on January 20, 1961. Additionally the Eisenhower administration had set up secret training bases for Cuban exile forces in Guatemala and the Canal Zone, while Cuban exile pilots received training in Nicaragua.

US military leadership and the CIA strongly supported the invasion plan. Kennedy was significantly

111

more skeptical. He repeatedly told the generals and the CIA that he did not want an invasion as such of Cuba. Rather, he preferred the earlier idea of secretly infiltrating exiles into Cuba to incite internal rebellion. Above all, he emphasized that no US forces were to be directly involved in any infiltration or invasion of Cuba.

Eventually, however, the president acquiesced in the plan of the CIA and the Joint Chiefs of Staff for an invasion of Cuba by exiles, assisted in the background by the US military.

The operation began on April 15, 1961, when Cuban exile pilots—operating US aircraft disguised as Castro's own warplanes—partially destroyed the Cuban government's air force. President Kennedy had approved this attack, but he canceled later air strikes after Castro publicly blamed the United States for the exiles' April 15 air attack. This kerfuffle included an embarrassing incident that afternoon at the United Nations, where US Ambassador Adlai Stevenson repeated the CIA's false cover story that the attack was perpetrated by defectors from Castro's own air force. Stevenson was unaware that this cover story, indirectly provided to him by the CIA, was a lie.

On April 17, the exile land invasion at the Cuban Bay of Pigs commenced. The invaders immediately encountered several problems. First, the CIA had been unaware of the coral reefs in the ocean near the beach, which forced the exiles to disembark from the landing craft much farther from shore than had been planned. Second, the landing, intended to be secret, was soon involved in a gunfight with one of Castro's local militias. Third, remaining planes in Castro's air force sank ships containing ammunition and other essential supplies, while additional supply ships headed out to sea. Fourth, Castro's regular army soon reached the Bay of Pigs and fought the invaders. At the end, the exiles had exhausted their ammunition, food, and medical supplies, leaving them with no effective option other than surrender. By April 19, the invasion was over.

Between the Bay of Pigs Invasion and the Missile Crisis (1961–1962)

Notwithstanding the collapse of the Bay of Pigs operation, the Kennedy administration persisted in its efforts to overthrow Castro during the period between the failed invasion and the onset of the Cuban Missile Crisis in the autumn of 1962. The president authorized Operation Mongoose, which involved sabotage, psychological warfare, and other covert activities in Cuba. The military prepared contingency plans for an overt US military invasion of Cuba, though Kennedy never ordered their implementation. The CIA continued its precedent from the Eisenhower administration of attempting to assassinate Castro by various fantastical methods. None of these schemes had achieved their objectives by October 1962, when the US first detected the existence of Soviet nuclear missiles in Cuba. This discovery fundamentally altered President Kennedy's analysis of the Cuban situation.

THE CUBAN MISSILE CRISIS

Khrushchev's Plan

The US-generated Bay of Pigs invasion had a profound effect on Soviet Premier Nikita Khrushchev and on Fidel Castro, who led the Cuban revolution and governed Cuba from January 1, 1959, until the early years of the twenty-first century. Both were convinced that the United States would keep trying, by another invasion or by assassination, to eliminate Castro.[6] As discussed above, this was, in fact, the US intention, even after the debacle of the Bay of Pigs invasion.

In his *Memoirs*, Khrushchev stated: "Although the counterrevolutionaries [the United States and the anti-Castro Cuban exiles] were defeated in the landing [at the Bay of Pigs], you would have had to be completely unrealistic to think everything had ended with that. That was only the beginning, even though it was an unsuccessful beginning. An unsuccessful effort arouses the desire to do it right a second time."[7]

"I was sure," Khrushchev continued, "that a new invasion was inevitable, that it was only a matter of time, and that in the very near future the Americans would make another attempt."[8]

Khrushchev described his thought process in arriving at the plan to install missiles in Cuba as follows:

We had to think of something. But what? It was a highly complicated matter trying to find something you could use as an effective counter to the United States. Naturally the following solution suggested itself: the United States had surrounded the Soviet Union with its military bases and placed its missiles all around our country. We knew that the United States had missile bases in Turkey and Italy, not to mention West Germany! We granted the possibility that they also existed in other countries. They had surrounded us with military bases; the planes at those bases were within effective range of our vital industrial and governmental centers, and those planes were armed with atomic bombs. Couldn't we counter with the very same thing? But of course that was not so simple! . . .

. . . And I thought to myself: "What if we were to come to an agreement with the government of Cuba and install missiles with atomic warheads there, but to do it in a concealed way, so that it would be kept a secret from the United States?" . . . I came to the conclusion that if we did everything secretly and the Americans found out about it only after the missiles were in place and ready to be launched, they would have to stop and think before making the risky decision to wipe out our missiles by military force.[9]

Khrushchev was well aware of what he was doing and the possible devastation that a nuclear strike from Cuba could cause to the United States.

Our missiles might be destroyed by the United States, but not all of them. It would be enough if one quarter or even one tenth of the missiles we installed were still in place and could be used to hit New York with one or two nuclear warheads. . . . [W]e knew from our nuclear-testing program that the destruction would be colossal. . . . It seemed to me that might restrain the United States from military action against Cuba. If things worked out that way, it wouldn't be bad. To some degree a "balance of fear"—a formula used in the West—might be reached.[10]

According to his *Memoirs*, Khrushchev explained his thinking to the Presidium (the top governing body of the Soviet Union) as follows:

"We have to do things in such a way as to preserve our country and not allow a world war to break out, but also not to let Cuba be crushed by U.S. troops. Our aim must be the preservation of the existing situation. But we must also contribute to the further development and strengthening of socialist construction in Cuba. Cuba must become a torch blazing in the night, a magnet of attraction for all the oppressed people of Latin America fighting against exploitation by the American monopolies. The warmth-giving light of socialism from Cuba will accelerate the process of struggle in countries fighting for independence."[11]

In this connection, it should be observed that Khrushchev and his comrades in the Presidium were well aware of the history of US corporate and governmental intervention in Cuba and other Latin American countries, including American support of corrupt dictators such as Fulgencio Batista who exerted authoritarian power in the interests of American multinational corporations, organized crime, and their own personal profit.[12]

Khrushchev further explained his intentions as follows: "What we were interested in was the essence of the matter: that Cuba should remain with its revolutionary gains, so that it could remain as the standard-bearer for the socialist countries on the American continent and carry on with its development under the banner of Marxism-Leninism."[13] "The reason we installed missiles with nuclear warheads, as I have said, was not to attack the United States but exclusively to defend Cuba. We wanted the United States not to attack Cuba, and that was all."[14]

Khrushchev's public account of the sole reason he decided to install nuclear missiles in Cuba should not be taken at face value. In their book *Khrushchev's Cold War*, Aleksandr Fursenko and Timothy Naftali explained:

> The release of additional Presidium materials in 2003 revealed for the first time how Khrushchev formally explained his idea [to the Presidium in May 1962]. **To second-tier officials, Khrushchev later emphasized the altruism of this scheme. He claimed to be purely motivated by the defense needs of Cuba. But in front of his colleagues, he said, "This will be an offensive policy." Although hinged on Castro's need to deter U.S. aggression, it was designed to do much more for the Soviet Union.** [Endnote omitted.] **Khrushchev in January ... had spoken confidently of the growth in Soviet power that by 1963 would force the United States to accommodate Moscow's perceived needs in Central Europe [Berlin] and elsewhere. The Cuba ploy would ensure that this necessary change in the balance of power occurred.**[15]

Although Anastas Mikoyan and some other Presidium members argued against Khrushchev's plan, they eventually acquiesced. According to Nikita's son Sergei, the practice of deferring to Khrushchev's wishes permeated the Soviet leadership, with the exception of Mikoyan, whose long history in the Soviet government allowed him to dissent without facing negative consequences. On this occasion, Mikoyan expressed the view that installing nuclear missiles in Cuba would be a dangerous step. However, he eventually signed on to the missile plan.[16]

Fidel Castro reluctantly agreed to the Khrushchev proposal. Planning and implementation of the plan now began in earnest. The Soviet government eventually shipped surface-to-surface nuclear missiles that could destroy major US cities, tactical (battlefield) nuclear weapons, surface-to-air missiles, rapid-firing antiaircraft guns, MiG-21 fighter jets, IL-28 bombers, tanks, artillery, and tens of thousands of Soviet troops to Cuba.[17]

Nikita Khrushchev told his son that only regular units of the Soviet Army, under command from Moscow, should have control of the nuclear missiles; he said he did not plan to let Cuba have control of these weapons.[18]

Did Khrushchev intend an overall shift in the balance of power between the Soviet Union and the United States with this action? Sergei Khrushchev wrote: "Of course, Father did think that deployment of the missiles had a certain strategic importance, but the principal aim of the operation was to defend the Cuban revolution. He was strongly of the opinion that the entire operation was expedient only because it might prevent a new landing on the island."[19] The Soviet military leaders, however, thought primarily in strategic terms, and there were, in fact, strategic reasons for the Soviet decision to install nuclear missiles in Cuba.[20]

Sergo Mikoyan (the son of Anastas Mikoyan) mostly agreed with the statements made by Nikita and Sergei Khrushchev that the main objective of sending missiles to Cuba was to prevent another invasion of that island: "The mission of the missiles in Cuba was designed to prevent its adversaries' attempts to impede with military force the worldwide victorious march of socialism." Although "another reason was the strategic intention to force the Americans to live under the same kind of threat from missiles close to the territory as the USSR had done from missiles deployed in Turkey, Italy, and Britain, . . . the issue of defending the Cuban Revolution could be easily traced in the secret communications between Khrushchev and [Anastas] Mikoyan when the latter visited Havanna to conduct negotiations with Fidel Castro."[21]

The official Soviet line was that the only purpose of sending nuclear missiles to Cuba was to defend the Castro regime. As noted above, however, Khrushchev acknowledged that he wanted to change the balance of power between the United States and the Soviet Union. This was also understood during the negotiations in early July 1962 between the Soviet and Cuban governments regarding the delivery of the weapons. As a result of their study of Soviet declassified primary-source documents, Aleksandr Fursenko and Timothy Naftali concluded:

> In making their request, the Cubans had differentiated between weapons necessary

119

for their defense and strategic weapons that Khrushchev wanted on the island for his purposes. Khrushchev accepted this distinction. In explaining the change in plans to his colleagues at the Presidium on July 6, following his first meeting with Raúl Castro, he said that the "defensive" weapons would go first and that the weapons that were part of his offensive plan, the strategic missiles, would follow.[22]

Above all, by the summer of 1962, Khrushchev figured that the installation of nuclear-armed surface-to-surface missiles in Cuba would provide him with significant leverage in his demands for withdrawal of Western troops from West Berlin. A declassified Soviet document shows that on July 1, 1962, Khrushchev outlined, at a Presidium meeting, his plan for cutting off Western access routes to West Berlin and removing Western military troops from the city. On July 5, 1962, Khrushchev sent a letter to President Kennedy stating his demands regarding Berlin.[23]

Evaluation of Khrushchev's Objectives and Means
According to Sergo Mikoyan, Khrushchev "never had any intention of starting World War III—both Moscow and the West knew that there would be no winners in such a war. Khrushchev belonged to the cohort of romantics (whose ranks seriously thinned in the 1930s due to Stalin's repressions); he believed in the victory of socialism in the global competition because it would more successfully address social issues and increase people's standard of living."[24] Thus,

Khrushchev was not a cynic but a romantic. That is why it was important for him to

120

rescue Cuba, and it was his main objective. But the story is different for military leaders such as Rodion Malinovsky and Sergey Biryuzov. It is very likely that strategic ideas prevailed in their minds. They interpreted strategic interests from a military standpoint.[25]

The Soviet government in 1962 was authoritarian or totalitarian in fact, if not on paper. Khrushchev, as premier and as first secretary of the Communist Party of the Soviet Union, held ultimate executive and even legislative authority.[26] Although he could have made an effort to rationally consider the opinions of other members of the Presidium and even the views of officials outside that supreme body, he failed to do so. In fact, he hand-picked the members of the Presidium, who, with the notable exception of Anastas Mikoyan, were "yes men" who normally acquiesced in what Khrushchev wanted to do.[27]

The decision to install nuclear missiles in Cuba was an example of how Khrushchev wielded power. He concluded on his own that nuclear missiles and other military equipment and troops should be sent to Cuba. Anastas Mikoyan and other Presidium members who initially opposed it bent to Khrushchev's will.[28]

Oleg Troyanovsky, Khrushchev's special assistant for international affairs, was not a member of the Presidium. Troyanovsky later recalled his reaction when he learned about Khrushchev's missile plan from another aide: "From the very beginning, the adventurism of the missile plan was obvious to me personally. I knew two things for sure: first of all, the Americans would not tolerate missiles in Cuba, and they would undertake some radical measures. Second, a military conflict was not envisioned in Khrushchev's plan, and it meant that at some critical moment he would be forced to retreat." In his book, Sergo Mikoyan commented on this incident as follows: "His colleagues agreed with him, but they advised him not to raise this issue in a conversation with Khrushchev, because the leader was unable to even listen to the opinions of people who disagreed with him—even of those people, who, due to their positions, had to express their viewpoints before any decision was adopted, for example, the foreign policy adviser."[29]

When, later in the crisis, the deputy minister of foreign affairs suggested a strategy to threaten the US with regard to West Berlin, Khrushchev, according to Sergo Mikoyan, "rudely cut the deputy minister: 'We do not need such advice!' It was not important whether [the deputy minister] was right, or wrong, but such kind of reactions of the first person of the country precluded many people from expressing their opinions. The majority of people from the Presidium of the Communist Party felt the same way."[30]

In deciding to proceed with the shipment of nuclear missiles and other military supplies to Cuba, Khrushchev relied on the advice of an adviser he had sent to Cuba to evaluate the ability to camouflage the missiles from US aerial surveillance. The adviser came back with news that they could be hidden under palm trees. This contradicted the views of several other Soviet officials who knew that the Cuban terrain would not successfully conceal the missiles. The palm trees grew foliage only at the top and were thinly interspersed on the ground. But Khrushchev did not want to hear any other comments about this matter. His unjustified reliance on the erroneous palm tree advice proved fatal. American aircraft discovered the missiles before they became operational, thereby triggering the Cuban Missile Crisis of October 1962.[31]

Apart from such details, was Khrushchev's missile plan rational? By 1962, international relations expert Hans J. Morgenthau had long argued that ideology was frequently a disguise for actual power politics. He observed that national political leaders often use ideology as a mere pretext for their exercise of power in an international context.[32]

However, it is clear that Communist ideology, as described earlier in this chapter and in the appendix, was a strong motivation for Khrushchev. His words and actions repeatedly demonstrated that he was a true believer in Marxist-Leninist dogma. For him and many others, Communism was, in effect, a religion. This devout belief motivated his hatred of capitalism and his glorification of centralized economic planning, no matter how unsuccessful the latter proved to be in practice.[33] This is what he meant when he famously said that "we will bury you": he was evidently not referring to military conquest but rather to his firm belief that Communism would prove itself much more successful than capitalism.[34] And this is why he was determined to protect the Castro regime against an American invasion. His following statement of faith bears repeating: "Cuba must become a torch blazing in the night, a magnet of attraction for all the oppressed people of Latin America fighting against exploitation by the American monopolies. The warmth-giving light of socialism from

Cuba will accelerate the process of struggle in countries fighting for independence."[35]

The ultimate problem with Khrushchev's objective in the Cuban Missile Crisis was his failure to acknowledge two fundamental facts: (1) every country that adopted the Marxist-Leninist creed, including the Soviet Union, was an authoritarian or totalitarian regime, and (2) a Marxist-Leninist "command economy" has always failed as a viable economic system.[36] Thus, it is fair to conclude that Khrushchev's ideological objectives in the Cuban Missile Crisis were not rational. He failed to use critical thinking to evaluate the rationality of his faith. Although some of his critiques of American capitalism were on point, the historical record paints a far grimmer picture of Communist regimes.

Furthermore, the means Khrushchev employed to achieve his objectives were not rational. As will be discussed in the following subsection, President Kennedy had stated earlier that the United States would not take forceful action regarding the shipment of defensive weapons to Cuba. Thus, although Kennedy was concerned about the buildup of conventional weapons in Cuba, he did not intend to trigger an international crisis over it. But JFK warned that the US would respond forcefully if Khrushchev sent offensive weapons, i.e., nuclear-armed surface-to-surface missiles, to Cuba. Khrushchev did not need nuclear missiles to achieve his objective of deterring a US invasion of Cuba; the massive conventional buildup already occurring would probably have prevented that. In placing offensive nuclear missiles in Cuba, Khrushchev generated an international crisis that risked a nuclear catastrophe. In fact, his decision to take such radical action indicated that his purpose was not only to defend Castro but also to change the international balance of power to the advantage of the Soviet Union and its Communist allies.

As discussed above, Khrushchev was motivated, at least in part, by a strategic decision to counter the US missiles in countries surrounding the Soviet Union. As will be seen later in this chapter, Kennedy secretly agreed to withdraw the obsolete American missiles in Turkey. He also made a public commitment that the United States would not invade Cuba if the Soviet Union withdrew the missiles in Cuba. It might thus be said that Khrushchev accomplished two of his objectives, whether or not those objectives were ultimately rational.

The following discussion also shows that Khrushchev hoped to achieve nuclear parity with the United States by installing medium-range and intermediate-range nuclear missiles in Cuba. The Soviet Union had only a few intercontinental ballistic missiles (ICBMs) that could reach the United States, and these were unreliable; installing missiles in Cuba would rectify that situation. In the event, however, Khrushchev was forced to withdraw all the nuclear missiles from Cuba. It was many years before the Soviet Union would have a sufficient stockpile of reliable ICBMs on its territory to obtain a nuclear balance of power with the United States.

Prelude to the Cuban Missile Crisis

The 1962 Soviet operation in Cuba involved two major stages. The first phase was to supplement conventional military defenses in Cuba by the addition of surface-to-air missiles (SAMs) and MiG-21 supersonic fighter jets. These were considered defensive weapons. The second phase was the concealed shipment of nuclear-capable ballistic missiles and Ilyushin-28 jet aircraft, both of which could reach major US cities. The Kennedy administration considered these to be offensive weapons.[37]

The shipments from the Soviet Union to Cuba began arriving in late July. About three weeks later, the CIA informed President Kennedy of these phase one developments, including the fact that there were thousands of Soviet "specialists" in Cuba and that military construction was ongoing. At this point, no one in the Kennedy administration knew about the Soviet plan for phase 2.[38]

White House Press Secretary Pierre Salinger read the following statement by President John F. Kennedy to news correspondents on September 4, 1962:

All Americans, as well as all of our friends in this Hemisphere, have been concerned over the recent moves of the Soviet Union to bolster the military power of the Castro regime in Cuba.

Information has reached this Government in the last four days from a variety of sources which establishes without doubt that the Soviets have provided the Cuban Government with a number of anti-aircraft defense missiles with a slant range of twenty-five miles which are similar to early models of our Nike. Along with these missiles, the Soviets are apparently providing the extensive radar and other electronic equipment which is required for their operation. We can also confirm the presence of several Soviet-made motor torpedo boats carrying ship-to-ship guided missiles having a range of fifteen miles. The number of Soviet military technicians now known to be in Cuba or en route— approximately 8,500—is consistent with assistance in setting up and learning to use this equipment. As I stated last week, we shall continue to make information available as fast as is obtained and properly verified.

There is no evidence of any organized combat force in Cuba from any Soviet bloc country; of military bases provided to Russia; of a violation of the 1984 treaty relating to Guantanamo; of the presence of offensive ground-to-ground missiles; or of other significant offensive capability either in Cuban hands or under Soviet direction and guidance. Were it to be otherwise, the gravest issues would arise.

The Cuban question must be considered as a part of the worldwide challenge posed by Communist threats to the peace. It must be dealt with as a part of that larger issue as well as in the context of the special relationships which have long characterized the inter-American System.

It continues to be the policy of the United States that the Castro regime will not be allowed to export its aggressive purposes by force or the threat of force. It will be prevented by whatever means may be necessary from taking action against any part of the Western Hemisphere. The United States, in conjunction with other Hemisphere countries, will make sure that while increased Cuban armaments will be a heavy burden to the unhappy people of Cuba themselves, they will be nothing more.[39]

Some Cuban refugees had been claiming for eighteen months (long before Khrushchev's plan to install surface-to-surface nuclear missiles in Cuba, as demonstrated above) that nuclear installations existed in Cuba, but no photographic or other evidence confirmed these rumors. Republican opponents of the Kennedy administration relied on such gossip to attack the administration for allegedly being soft on Communism. The Republicans were planning to make this a major talking point in the November midterm elections. In October, Republican Senator Kenneth Keating publicly stated that offensive missile bases were being established in Cuba, but he provided no evidence for this assertion. In any event, his statements to this effect were roughly contemporaneous with the Kennedy administration's discovery of the Soviet installation of missile sites in Cuba.[40]

The Kennedy Administration's Discovery, Deliberations, and Response

As a result of a directive from President Kennedy, a Secret Service officer installed a secret tape-recording system in the Oval Office and Cabinet Room of the White House on the weekend of July 28–29, 1962. The transcripts of many of these tapes are contained in *The Presidential Recordings: John F. Kennedy: The Great*

Crises (2001).[41] Much of the remainder of this chapter is based on these transcripts.

On Sunday, October 14, 1962, a U-2 reconnaissance plane of the US Strategic Air Command (SAC) photographed certain sites in Cuba. CIA analysis of the photographs on October 15 showed the existence of medium-range ballistic missile (MRBM) sites in Cuba. These MRBMs had a range of 1,100 nautical miles, which could reach Washington, DC, as well as Dallas, Cape Canaveral, St. Louis, and all SAC bases and cities in between.[42]

October 16 (Tuesday)

A CIA official informed McGeorge Bundy, the special assistant to the president for national security affairs, of the photographic evidence of MRBMs in Cuba during the evening of October 15. At that time, the president was out of town on a campaign trip. He returned to Washington early Tuesday morning. About 9:00 a.m. that morning, Bundy informed Kennedy of the CIA findings.[43]

At 11:50 a.m., the president convened a meeting of top officials, including, among others, CIA Acting Director Marshall Carter (CIA Director John McCone was out of town), CIA experts Arthur Lundahl and Sidney Graybeal, Vice President Lyndon Johnson, Secretary of State Dean Rusk, Under Secretary of State George Ball, Deputy Under Secretary of State U. Alexis Johnson, Secretary of Defense Robert McNamara, Deputy Secretary of Defense Roswell Gilpatric, Special Assistant to the President for National Security Affairs McGeorge Bundy, Attorney General Robert Kennedy, Chairman of the Joint Chiefs of Staff General Maxwell

Taylor, Secretary of the Treasury Douglas Dillon, and Special Counsel Theodore Sorensen.[44] This group, (which had varying attendees during their subsequent meetings), later became known as the Executive Committee of the National Security Council.[45]

Arthur Lundahl, who was the head of the CIA's National Photographic Interpretation Center, began the meeting with an explanation of what the aerial reconnaissance on Sunday had disclosed. He showed the president and the other officials the photographic evidence of MRBMs and associated equipment at different locations in Cuba.[46]

The United States did not yet have information regarding whether nuclear warheads were available for installation on the Soviet MRBMs.[47] Scholars Graham Allison and Philip Zelikow later wrote: "Unknown to the U.S., nuclear warheads for the MRBMs arrived on October 4, along with dozens of nuclear warheads for the Sopka coastal defense cruise missiles, 6 nuclear bombs for the IL-28 aircraft, and 12 nuclear warheads for short-range tactical nuclear rockets. Just before the blockade took effect [October 24, 1962], 24 more nuclear warheads for the IRBMs [intermediate-range ballistic missiles] arrived in Cuba. Indeed, a large number of dry-cargo ships, including those carrying the IRBM missiles themselves, were moving toward Cuba when the blockade was announced."[48]

The 11:50 a.m. meeting continued with discussions of Khrushchev's motives. Notably, the officials did not consider the possibility that the Soviet Union was installing nuclear missiles for defense of Cuba against a US invasion.

President Kennedy speculated that Khrushchev was not satisfied with the Soviet Union's ICBMs. It was known at that time that the US had significantly more ICBMs than the Soviet Union. General Taylor concurred, noting that Cuba gave the Soviets launching bases for short-range missiles that could supplement what he called their "rather defective" ICBM system.[49]

Secretary of State Rusk discussed the possibility that Khrushchev was trying to balance the previous US installation of Jupiter missiles in Turkey as well as attempting to leverage the situation in Berlin.[50] As discussed above, Rusk was correct about these Khrushchev motives.

With regard to possible responses, Secretary of Defense McNamara was skeptical about a US air attack, which, he said, would involve several hundred sorties. He opposed a limited air attack on the known missile sites without taking out the Cuban and Soviet capacity for reprisals[51]

Near the end of this meeting, President Kennedy summarized the options as follows:

1. Take out the missiles that had been located. The president said: "We're certainly going to do [option] number one. We're going to take out these missiles."
2. A general air strike. "That," said JFK, "we're not ready to say, but we should be in preparation for it."
3. A general invasion, for which the president said they should also be making preparations.[52]

The discussion ended with President Kennedy scheduling an additional meeting for 6:30 p.m. that day.

Following this first meeting on the Cuban Missile Crisis, President Kennedy attended a luncheon for a foreign dignitary. Adlai Stevenson, the US ambassador to the United Nations, was also present. After the luncheon, Kennedy invited Stevenson to the family quarters at the White House, where they discussed the U-2 photographs. Stevenson opposed an immediate air strike, saying the US should explore possibilities of a peaceful solution.[53] He elaborated upon his position in a letter to the president the following morning. Among other things, the letter stated: "Because an attack would very likely result in Soviet reprisals elsewhere— Turkey, Berlin, etc.—it is most important that we have as much of the world with us as possible. To start or risk starting a nuclear war is bound to be divisive at best and the judgments of history seldom coincide with the tempers of the moment." The letter added: "I know your dilemma is to strike before the Cuban sites are operational or to risk waiting until a proper groundwork of justification can be prepared. The national security must come first. But the means adopted have such incalculable consequences that I feel you should have made it clear that the existence of nuclear missile bases anywhere is negotiable before we start anything."[54]

At 6:30 p.m. on October 16, President Kennedy chaired a second meeting of governmental officials on the Cuban Missile Crisis.

CIA Acting Director Carter reported that they did not yet have a total readout of the photographs from the October 15 flights, but they had a much better readout of the October 14 film. He said the CIA concluded, "on the basis of information that we presently have, that these are solid propellant, inertial guidance missiles with 1,100 mile range . . . ." He added that "they could well be operational within 2 weeks, as we look at the pictures now. And once operational, they could fire on very little notice." Carter admitted that one of the missiles could be fully operational much sooner than two weeks. The CIA had no hard evidence at that time of nuclear warhead storage near the field launchers, though it was possible that an unusual facility, which had automatic antiaircraft weapon protection, could be storing nuclear warheads.[55]

President Kennedy, Secretary of State Rusk, and Special Assistant to the President for National Security Affairs Bundy then pressed Carter on the basis for the CIA's conclusions that these were MRBMs. Carter answered these questions in some detail.[56]

McNamara and Taylor pointed out that the Joint Chiefs of Staff and the relevant commanders were opposed to a selective air strike on only the three missile sites that had been discovered so far. General Taylor observed that they could never be sure of destroying all the missile sites in this manner, and such a limited attack would invite reprisal attacks. They recommended obtaining complete intelligence, including all the necessary photography. If such surveillance revealed a real threat to the United States, then "take it right out with one hard crack," including missile sites, airfields, fighter jets, bombers, and nuclear storage sites. This could not, however, be accomplished in one strike. They would have to come back, day after day, for perhaps five days to do a complete job. Meanwhile, they could decide whether to invade Cuba.[57]

McNamara observed that such an air attack would be extensive, including possibly 700 to 1,000 sorties per day for five days, according to the Joint Chiefs. A subsequent invasion would require perhaps up to 150,000 military personnel in the invasion force. Moreover, "[i]t seems to me almost certain that any of these forms of direct military action will lead to a Soviet military response of some type, some place in the world." All these factors would require "a very large-scale mobilization, certainly exceeding the limits of the authority we have from Congress, requiring a declaration therefore of a national emergency."[58]

McNamara suggested, as a possible alternative, a blockade against offensive weapons entering Cuba, and he outlined the advantages and disadvantages of such a course of action.[59] Thus, he was the first to introduce the option that the United States would ultimately adopt.

General Taylor noted that the US was quite vulnerable to a conventional bombing attack from Cuba in the Florida area, because the air defense had been oriented in other directions. Secretary of the Treasury Dillon then asked, "What if they carry a nuclear weapon?" President Kennedy responded that "you assume they wouldn't do that," and General Taylor added, "I think we could expect some conventional bombing." Bundy and Rusk concurred. The consensus was that neither the Soviet Union nor Cuba would use a nuclear weapon unless they were prepared to generate a nuclear war. The implicit assumption was that no nation would do that. However, as will later become clear,

Castro seemed to encourage Khrushchev to do exactly that, at least if the United States invaded Cuba.[60]

Bundy then posed the question, "What is the strategic impact on the position of the United States of MRBMs in Cuba? How gravely does this change the strategic balance?" McNamara responded, "I asked the Chiefs that this afternoon, in effect. And they said: 'Substantially.' My own personal view is: Not at all." Bundy concurred. President Kennedy pointed out that putting nuclear missiles in Cuba could result in the Soviets squeezing the United States in Berlin. He also queried whether it makes "any difference if you get blown up by an ICBM firing from the Soviet Union or one from 90 miles away. Geography doesn't mean that much . . . [ellipsis in the original]." The meeting attendees discussed these questions at some length, including psychological factors and the effect on Latin America.[61]

President Kennedy stated:
Last month I said we weren't going to [allow it]. Last month I should have said that we don't care. But when we said we're *not* going to, and then they go ahead and do it, and then we do nothing, then I would think that our risks increase.

I agree, what difference does it make? They've got enough to blow us up now anyway. I think it's just a question of . . . After all, this is a political struggle as much as military.[62]

President Kennedy was still thinking that a limited air strike might be preferable to a general air strike. He added, however, that they should proceed on the

135

assumption that it would be a general air strike and then reconsider whether a limited air strike was a better course of action. An invasion would be a third option.[63]

After further discussion, McNamara said, "I don't believe we have considered the consequences of any of these actions satisfactorily. And because we haven't considered the consequences, I'm not sure we're taking all the action we ought to take now to minimize those." He continued: "I don't know what kind of a world we live in after we've struck Cuba, and we've started it." [64]

General Taylor stated that "the Chiefs and the commanders feel so strongly about the dangers inherent in the limited strike that they would prefer taking *no* military action rather than to take that limited first strike. They feel that it's opening up the United States to attacks which they can't prevent if we don't take advantage of surprise."[65]

President Kennedy responded that the only argument for a limited strike was that the chances of it becoming a much broader struggle would be increased in a general attack. An attack on airports would trigger Cuban antiaircraft defenses. It would be "a much more major operation, therefore the dangers of the worldwide effects are substantial to the United States, are increased. That's the only argument for [the limited strike]."[66]

At this point, Special Counsel Theodore (Ted) Sorensen stated: "In that regard, Mr. President, there is a combination of the plans which might be considered, namely the limited strike and then the messages, or simultaneously the messages, to Khrushchev and Castro which would indicate to them that this was none other than simply the fulfilling of the statements we have made all along."[67] President Kennedy and Under Secretary of State Ball appeared to agree with this idea, with Kennedy suggesting that the Joint Chiefs favored a general strike because it would lead to an invasion. General Taylor responded that he was opposed to an invasion but rather wanted to eliminate as effectively as possible every weapon that could strike the United States.[68]

McNamara said, "This is why I think we have to think of the consequences here." He thought a general air strike would lead to an uprising among the people in Cuba. The United States would then feel obligated to respond by invasion. However, Deputy Undersecretary of State Alexis Johnson responded that, after discussing it that morning with "some of your people," it was concluded that a general attack against military targets, primarily, "would not result in any substantial unrest. People would just stay home and try to keep out of trouble." But McNamara again insisted that a general air strike would lead to an uprising.[69]

Following a question from Attorney General Robert Kennedy, McNamara said that a blockade would be necessary following a limited strike. The attorney general replied, "Then we're gonna have to sink Russian ships. Then we're gonna have to sink Russian submarines." RFK seemed to think the US was going to get into a war over this crisis whatever action the government took.[70]

President Kennedy turned again to the question of Khrushchev's motives. Under Secretary of State Ball observed that they had received word that Khrushchev was going to appear at the United Nations in November. Khrushchev might be assuming that the US would not discover the missiles before that time. In November, he might possibly offer to trade withdrawal of missiles in Cuba for a US concession in Berlin.[71]

Deputy Undersecretary of State Johnson pointed out that Khrushchev might be making up for his apparent deficiency in ICBMs by installing MRBMs, of which he had plenty, in Cuba. Bundy and Ball agreed that it was possible that this was an attempt to add to Soviet strategic capabilities.[72] (At this time, the attendees were unaware that Khrushchev was also installing IRBMs in Cuba.)

The remainder of this session addressed the issues already discussed in part, including the possibility of a blockade.[73]

October 17 (Wednesday)

Various governmental officials attended some or all of three separate meetings at the State Department on October 17. Because these meetings did not occur at the White House, they were not taped. President Kennedy and Vice President Johnson did not attend, though Kennedy was briefed regarding developments at the meetings. CIA Director John A. McCone, former Secretary of State Dean Acheson, Ambassador Charles E. Bohlen (newly appointed ambassador to France, previously special adviser to the president), and Ambassador-at-Large Llewellyn Thompson Jr. were also now present for at least portions of these meetings.

Although there is no transcript of the meetings, Director McCone prepared certain memoranda relating to them that shed light on his and others' views.

McCone's October 17, 1962 Memorandum for Discussion began by pointing out that "[t]he establishment of medium range strike capability in

Cuba by the Soviets was predicted by me in at least a dozen reports since the Soviet buildup was noted in early August." He stated that the purposes of the Soviet Union were to "[p]rovide Cuba with an offensive or retaliatory power for use if attacked," to "[e]nhance Soviet strike capability against the United States," and to increase Soviet influence in Latin America. More specifically the Soviet political objectives appeared to be "[t]he establishment of a 'trading position' to force removal of U.S. overseas bases and Berlin" and "[t]o satisfy their ambitions in Latin America by this show of determination and courage against the American Imperialist." Accordingly, McCone recommended, among other things, that the US give the Soviet Union and Cuba "24 hours to commence dismantling and removal of MRBMs, coastal defense missiles, surface to air missiles, IL 28s and all other aircraft which have a dual defensive-offensive capability, including MIG 21s" and "[i]f Khrushchev and Castro fail to act at once, we should make a massive surprise strike at air fields, MRBM sites and SAM sites concurrently."[74]

McCone also prepared a Memorandum for the File summarizing what he had observed at the October 17 meetings. Former Secretary of State Dean Acheson argued, in McCone's words, that "[w]e should proceed at once with the necessary military actions and should do no talking." Secretary Rusk seemed to favor a declaration of war against Cuba. Secretary McNamara made the point that the missiles in Cuba had no great military consequence. "Bohlen and Thompson questioned the real purpose of the Soviet's actions in Cuba and seemed to feel that their acts may be in preparation for a confrontation with President Kennedy at which time they would seek to settle the entire subject of overseas bases as well as the Berlin question." Although McCone thought this might be one of several objectives, he doubted that it was the primary purpose of such an elaborate and expensive installation as the Soviets were implementing in Cuba. According to his memorandum, McCone also "stated that the main objective of taking Cuba away from Castro had been lost and we have been overly consumed with the missile problem." The meeting included an extensive discussion of the advantages and disadvantages of a total or partial military blockade of Cuba.[75]

The Joint Chiefs of Staff also conducted a meeting on October 17 in which they outlined the following military options against Cuba:

    I.   Missile and nuclear storage sites only [requiring 52 sorties]

    II.   Same as above plus IL-28s, MiG-21s [requiring 52 sorties]

    III.   Same as above plus other aircraft, SAMs, cruise [missiles] and [missile] boats [requiring 104 sorties]

    IV.   All military targets but tanks [requiring 474 sorties]

    V.   All military targets, prelude to invasion[76]

Participants in later meetings on the Cuban Missile Crisis often referred to this military list of options.

October 18 (Thursday)

The previous discussions had been based on the premise that only MRBMs were being installed in Cuba. By the early morning of October 18, however, intelligence analysts had concluded that IRBM sites were also being constructed. The medium-range missiles could reach about 1,100 miles; intermediate-range missiles could hit targets up to 2,200 miles, which included all of the continental United States except the Pacific Northwest. Moreover, the nuclear warheads on intermediate-range missiles had about twice as much yield as those on medium-range missiles.[77]

This new knowledge was a wake-up call for many US officials. McNamara called McCone, saying that he now thought prompt and decisive action was necessary. Taylor told the Joint Chiefs that this information inclined him to favor an all-out invasion of Cuba.[78]

A White House meeting convened at 11:10 a.m. that morning.[79] The discussion began with a presentation by CIA expert Lundahl of the new photographic evidence of nuclear missile bases in Cuba.[80]

McNamara said that he and the Joint Chiefs "now consider nothing short of a full invasion as applicable military action. And this only on the assumption that we're operating against a force that does not possess operational nuclear weapons."[81] President Kennedy observed, "I would think you would have to go on the assumption that [the Soviets] are not going to permit nuclear weapons to be used against the United States from Cuba unless they're going to be using them from everyplace," to which McNamara responded, "I don't believe the Soviets would authorize their use against the U.S. but they might nonetheless be used."[82] McNamara's implicit premise seemed to be that either Castro or local Soviet commanders in Cuba might initiate a nuclear attack on the United States without approval from Moscow.

General Taylor noted that "the IRBMs really put a new factor in, as I look at it. Yesterday, when we looked at this we had only a few of the mobile type [MRBMs]. I was far from convinced that the big showdown would be required. Today we're getting new pictures, and the vision of an island that's going to be a forward base, can become a forward base, of major importance to the Soviets."[83] Under these circumstances, he thought that an air attack would be insufficient. "We can't take this threat out by actions from the air. So that we [the Joint Chiefs of Staff] have argued more and more that if indeed you're going to prevent that kind of thing, invasion is going to be required."[84]

In response to a question from Bundy, General Taylor stated: "Yes, you can't destroy a hole in the ground. We can't prevent this construction going ahead by any air actions. Conceivably diplomatic action might stop it, but only diplomatic action, or occupation as far as I can see, can prevent this kind of threat from building up."[85]

Ambassador Thompson pointed out that a first (air) strike would kill a lot of Russians. Thompson favored a blockade against military weapons, particularly offensive ones, along with a declaration of war. President Kennedy asked what we do with the weapons already there, to which Thompson responded, "Demand they're dismantled, and say that we're going to maintain constant surveillance, and if they are armed, we would then take them out. And then maybe do it." Thompson, who had been US ambassador to the Soviet Union from 1957 to 1962, noted that "[t]he Russians have curious faculty of wanting a legal basis despite all of the outrageous things they've done. They attach a lot of importance to this. The fact that you have a declaration of war. They would be running a military blockade legally established. I think it would greatly deter them."[86]

A long discussion followed about many related questions, including what would happen if the Soviets retaliated by taking action in Berlin and, if so, what the US response would be. McNamara asked, "what do we mean exactly? Does he take it with Soviet troops?" President Kennedy responded, "That's what it would seem to me." McNamara observed that US troops were in Berlin, and both he and General Taylor stated that they should fight the Soviet troops. The president noted, "And they get overrun," to which McNamara said, "Yes, they get overrun, exactly." Attorney General Kennedy queried, "Then, what do we do?" General Taylor responded, "Go to general war, if it's in the interest of ours." JFK asked, "You mean nuclear exchange?" General Taylor responded, "Guess you have to."[87]

Strangely, there was no immediate follow-up to these ominous remarks. But the discussion soon circled back to the question of imposing a blockade of Cuba to stop the influx of nuclear missiles. President Kennedy asked whether the US would have to issue a declaration of war in connection with a blockade. Although international law did not require a formal **declaration** of war, it had long considered a blockade to be an **act** of war. Some discussants thought a declaration of war in connection with a blockade was necessary and advisable. President Kennedy disagreed.[88] That evening, the State Department acting legal adviser, Leonard Meek, recommended that they should use the term "defensive quarantine" instead of "blockade."[89] The terminology "quarantine" rather than "blockade" was eventually adopted by administration officials. For the time being, however, they were still calling it a blockade.

The October 18 meeting discussed a possible agreement with the Soviet Union whereby the Soviets would withdraw the missiles from Cuba in exchange for a US withdrawal of its missiles in Turkey. This seemed to be more of a political rather than a military issue, since Polaris submarines capable of launching nuclear missiles were already making the Jupiter missiles in Turkey obsolete.[90]

The problem with the blockade strategy always was that it prevented new missiles and nuclear warheads from coming into Cuba but did not eliminate those already on the island. This problem was resolved by combining the announcement of the blockade or quarantine with an ultimatum to Khrushchev that the nuclear weapons already in Cuba must immediately be removed. If this were not done, the United States would proceed with air strikes and a possible invasion. After President Kennedy left the meeting, several attendees (Thompson, McNamara, Robert Kennedy, Taylor, Alexis Johnson, with others apparently approving) expressed agreement with this kind of plan.[91]

In the afternoon of October 18, President Kennedy met with former Secretary of State Dean Acheson, who again reiterated his preference for an immediate air strike against Cuba without previous notice.[92]

144

At 5:00 p.m. Kennedy met with Andrei Gromyko, the Soviet foreign minister. Secretary Rusk and Soviet Ambassador Dobrynin, among others, were also in attendance. Although Gromyko complained about the threat of US invasion of Cuba, he did not mention the Soviet buildup of nuclear missile sites on that island, and the president did not bring up the subject, waiting to see what, if anything, the Soviet foreign minister would say about it. Gromyko reiterated the earlier representation of the Soviet government that it would do nothing before the November midterm elections in the United States. However, he emphasized that the Berlin issue had to be resolved later in November. Absent agreement by the United States, the Soviet Union would unilaterally enter into a peace treaty with East Germany. As both Gromyko and Kennedy understood, this would result in East Germany demanding the withdrawal of Western forces from Berlin. Kennedy emphasized that the United States could never agree to such withdrawal.[93]

That evening, President Kennedy met with Rusk, Thompson, Bundy, Robert Lovett (secretary of defense in the Eisenhower administration), and Robert Kennedy in the Oval Office of the White House. Later, at 9:15 p.m., JFK met with McNamara, Gilpatrick, Taylor, Robert Kennedy, Ball, Alexis Johnson, Ed Martin, Bundy, and Sorensen. No tape recordings of these meetings appear to exist. However, the president later returned to the Oval Office, turned on the recording machine, and dictated a summary of the day's meetings that contained the following information.

President Kennedy said he had met with Dean Acheson that afternoon and that the former secretary of state "favored the first strike as being most likely to achieve our result and less likely to cause an extreme Soviet reaction. That strike would take place just against the missile sites."

Robert Lovett opposed any action, arguing, among other things, that it would endanger our alliances and that the Soviet reaction would endanger Berlin. Bundy had much the same view.

The last three paragraphs of the president's recorded statement were as follows:

> Everyone else felt that for us to fail to respond would throw into question our willingness to respond over Berlin, [and] would divide our allies and our country. [They felt] that we would be faced with a crunch over Berlin in two or three months and that by that time the Soviets would have a large missile arsenal in the Western Hemisphere which would weaken our whole position in this hemisphere and cause us, and face us with the same problems we're going to have in Berlin anyway.

> The consensus was that we should go ahead with the blockade beginning on Sunday night. Originally we should begin by blockading Soviets against the shipment of additional offensive capacity, [and] that we could tighten the blockade as the situation requires. I was most anxious that we not have to announce a state of war existing, because it would obviously be bad to have the word go out that we were having a war

146

rather than that it was a limited blockade for a limited purpose.

It was determined that I should go ahead with my speeches so that we don't take the cover off this, and come back Saturday night [October 20].[94]

Accordingly, by the end of the day on October 18, 1962, President Kennedy had decided to go with the blockade strategy. However, he had not yet experienced the blowback from the Joint Chiefs of Staff the following morning.

October 19 (Friday)

Kennedy met with the Joint Chiefs at 9:45 a.m. in the Cabinet Room In attendance were General Taylor (the chairman), Air Force Chief of Staff Curtis LeMay, Chief of Naval Operations George Anderson, Army Chief of Staff Earle Wheeler, Marine Corps Commandant David Shoup, and Secretary of Defense McNamara.

General LeMay opposed the blockade strategy. "This blockade and political action," he said, "I see leading into war. I don't see any other solution for it. It will lead right into war. This is almost as bad as the appeasement at Munich." If the blockade occurs, "their MiGs are going to fly. The IL-28s are going to fly against us. And we're just going to gradually drift into a war under conditions that are at great disadvantage to us, with missiles staring us in the face, that can knock out airfields in the southeastern portion [of the United States]. And if they use nuclear weapons, it's the population down there. We just drift into a war under conditions that I don't like. I just don't see any other

147

solution except direct military intervention *right now.*"[95]

Agreeing with General LeMay's analysis, Admiral Anderson stated: "I do not see that, as long as the Soviet Union is supporting Cuba, that there is any solution to the Cuban problem except a military solution."[96]

General Wheeler argued for a surprise air strike, a blockade, and an invasion of Cuba: "from a military point of view, I feel that the lowest risk course of action is the full gamut of military action by us."[97]

General Shoup indicated his support of an invasion in order to "take over the place and really put a new government that is non-Communist . . . ."[98]

The meeting also addressed additional issues, of which space does not permit a recapitulation here.

President Kennedy concluded: "I appreciate your views. As I said, I'm sure we all understand how rather unsatisfactory our alternatives are. The argument for the blockade was that what we want to do is to avoid, if we can, nuclear war by escalation or imbalance."[99]

After Kennedy, McNamara, and Taylor left he conference, the tape kept running with regard to the persons remaining in the room. With much profanity, Shoup exclaimed against doing anything piecemeal, indicating his support for an all-out invasion of Cuba.[100]

October 20 (Saturday)

Per the president's previous request, Robert Kennedy called JFK on Saturday morning, advising that he immediately return to Washington from a campaign trip. (As mentioned earlier, President Kennedy had continued with his public travel schedule in order to avoid media and public speculation.) At 2:30 p.m., President Kennedy and several others attended a

National Security Council meeting on the Cuban Missile Crisis. After listening at length to the several alternative views of his advisers, the president decided on a blockade, now called a quarantine, together with a demand on Khrushchev for the removal of the missiles. If Khrushchev did not comply, the US would launch an air strike.[101]

October 21 (Sunday)

The National Security Council met at 2:30 p.m. Admiral Anderson discussed with the president some of the details on how the blockade would work. President Kennedy brought up the subject of NATO missiles in Turkey. He said that the reason Turkey was promised Jupiter missiles in 1957 was that this was a response to Soviet MRBMs aimed at Europe. UN Ambassador Adlai Stevenson argued for a summit meeting with Khrushchev; Kennedy rejected that proposal.[102]

October 22 (Monday)

President Kennedy called former President Eisenhower at 10:40 a.m., explaining his strategy for dealing with the crisis. Eisenhower agreed with Kennedy's assessment that an air strike at that time would not be appropriate because they could not be sure that they had destroyed all the missiles. Eisenhower stated that "I personally think you're making the only move you can."[103]

Kennedy met with some of his advisers at 11:00 a.m. They discussed several matters related to the crisis.[104] This was followed at 11:47 a.m. with Kennedy's meeting with the Berlin Group on crisis planning.[105]

The president convened a meeting of the National Security Council at 3:00 p.m. All the Joint Chiefs of Staff as well as Secretary McNamara attended. Various details relating to the crisis were discussed. President Kennedy addressed the Joint Chiefs as follows:

> And I want to say this very clearly to the military, that I recognize we increase your problems in any military action we have to take in Cuba by the warning we're now giving.
>
> But I did want you to know that the reason we followed the course we have was because, while we would have been able to take out more planes and missiles without warning, as we *are* involved all around the world and not just in Cuba, I think the shock to the alliance might have been nearly fatal. Particularly as it would have excused very drastic action by Khrushchev.[106]

At 5:30 p.m., the president met with the congressional leadership to inform them of the discovery of nuclear missile sites in Cuba and his decision to impose a quarantine limited to blocking offensive weapons. CIA Director McCone and CIA expert Lundahl explained the status of intelligence gathering regarding the missile sites in Cuba. Senator Richard Russell, in particular, was not impressed with the quarantine/blockade strategy; he preferred a US invasion of Cuba. Russell was also opposed to "fooling with the Organization of American States," to which President Kennedy responded that "[t]he legality of the blockade depends—if it's a peacetime blockade—upon the endorsement, under the Rio Treaty of the OAS, which meets tomorrow morning." Senator Fullbright preferred an invasion to a blockade since a blockade would actually confront the Soviet Union. He commented, "I don't like the idea of a blockade at all. It seems to me that it complicates the whole thing." When Kennedy asked, "What are you in favor of, Bill?," the senator responded, "I'm in favor, on the basis of this information, of an invasion, and an all-out one, and as quickly as possible."[107]

At 7:00 p.m., President Kennedy delivered his famous television address regarding the crisis to the American people. The following are important excerpts from that speech:

> This Government, as promised, has maintained the closest surveillance of the Soviet Military buildup on the island of Cuba. Within the past week, unmistakable evidence has established the fact that a series of offensive missile sites is now in preparation on that imprisoned island. The purpose of these bases can be none other than to provide a nuclear strike capability against the Western Hemisphere.
>
> Upon receiving the first preliminary hard information of this nature last Tuesday morning at 9 a.m., I directed that our surveillance be stepped up. And having now confirmed and completed our evaluation of the evidence and our decision on a course of action, this Government feels obliged to report this new crisis to you in fullest detail.

The characteristics of these new missile sites indicate two distinct types of installations. Several of them include medium range ballistic missiles capable of carrying a nuclear warhead for a distance of more than 1,000 nautical miles. Each of these missiles, in short, is capable of striking Washington, D.C., the Panama Canal, Cape Canaveral, Mexico City, or any other city in the southeastern part of the United States, in Central America, or in the Caribbean area.

Additional sites not yet completed appear to be designed for intermediate range ballistic missiles—capable of traveling more than twice as far—and thus capable of striking most of the major cities in the Western Hemisphere, ranging as far north as Hudson Bay, Canada, and as far south as Lima, Peru. In addition, jet bombers, capable of carrying nuclear weapons, are now being uncrated and assembled in Cuba, while the necessary air bases are being prepared.

This urgent transformation of Cuba into an important strategic base—by the presence of these large, long range, and clearly offensive weapons of sudden mass destruction—constitutes an explicit threat to the peace and security of all the Americas, in flagrant and deliberate defiance of the Rio Pact of 1947, the traditions of this Nation and hemisphere, the joint resolution of the 87th Congress, the Charter of the United

Nations, and my own public warnings to the Soviets on September 4 and 13. . . .

Acting, therefore, in the defense of our own security and of the entire Western Hemisphere, and under the authority entrusted to me by the Constitution as endorsed by the resolution of the Congress, I have directed that the following initial steps be taken immediately:

First: To halt this offensive buildup, a strict quarantine on all offensive military equipment under shipment to Cuba is being initiated. All ships of any kind bound for Cuba from whatever nation or port will, if found to contain cargoes of offensive weapons, be turned back. This quarantine will be extended, if needed, to other types of cargo and carriers. We are not at this time, however, denying the necessities of life as the Soviets attempted to do in their Berlin blockade of 1948.

Second: I have directed the continued and increased close surveillance of Cuba and its military buildup. The foreign ministers of the OAS, in their communique of October 6, rejected secrecy in such matters in this hemisphere. Should these offensive military preparations continue, thus increasing the threat to the hemisphere, further action will be justified. I have directed the Armed Forces to prepare for any eventualities; and I trust that in the interest of both the Cuban people and the Soviet technicians at the sites, the hazards to all concerned in continuing this threat will be recognized.

Third: It shall be the policy of this Nation to regard any nuclear missile launched from Cuba against any nation in the Western Hemisphere as an attack by the Soviet Union on the United States, requiring a full retaliatory response upon the Soviet Union.

Fourth: As a necessary military precaution, I have reinforced our base at Guantanamo, evacuated today the dependents of our personnel there, and ordered additional military units to be on a standby alert basis.

Fifth: We are calling tonight for an immediate meeting of the Organ of Consultation under the Organization of American States, to consider this threat to hemispheric security and to invoke articles 6 and 8 of the Rio Treaty in support of all necessary action. The United Nations Charter allows for regional security arrangements--and the nations of this hemisphere decided long ago against the military presence of outside powers. Our other allies around the world have also been alerted.

Sixth: Under the Charter of the United Nations, we are asking tonight that an emergency meeting of the Security Council be convoked without delay to take action against this latest Soviet threat to world peace. Our resolution will call for the prompt dismantling and withdrawal of all offensive weapons in Cuba, under the supervision of U.N. observers, before the quarantine can be lifted.

Seventh and finally: I call upon Chairman Khrushchev to halt and eliminate this clandestine, reckless and provocative threat to world peace and to stable relations between our two nations. I call upon him further to abandon this course of world domination, and to join in an historic effort to end the perilous arms race and to transform the history of man. . . .

The path we have chosen for the present is full of hazards, as all paths are—but it is the one most consistent with our character and courage as a nation and our commitments around the world. The cost of freedom is always high—and Americans have always paid it. And one path we shall never choose, and that is the path of surrender or submission.

Our goal is not the victory of might, but the vindication of right—not peace at the expense of freedom, but both peace and freedom, here in this hemisphere, and, we hope, around the world. God willing, that goal will be achieved.[108]

A copy of this statement was delivered to Soviet Ambassador Dobrynin, and Kennedy also sent a letter to Khrushchev with additional details about the position of the United States on these issues.[109]

Additionally, on October 22, 1962, President Kennedy executed National Security Action Memorandum 196, which formally established the Executive Committee (ExComm) of the National Security Council: "I hereby establish, for the purpose of effective conduct of the operations of the Executive Branch in the current crisis, an Executive Committee of the National Security Council. This committee will meet, until further notice, daily at 10:00 a.m. in the Cabinet Room. I shall act as Chairman of this committee, and its additional regular members will be as follows: the Vice President [Lyndon Johnson], the Secretary of State [Dean Rusk], the Secretary of Defense [Robert McNamara], the Secretary of the Treasury [Douglas Dillon], the Attorney General [Robert Kennedy], the Director of Central Intelligence [John McCone], the Under Secretary of State [George Ball], the Deputy Secretary of Defense [Roswell Gilpatrick], the Chairman of the Joint Chiefs of Staff [Maxwell Taylor], the Ambassador-at-Large [Llewellyn Thompson], the Special Counsel [Ted Sorensen], and the Special Assistant to the President for National Security Affairs [McGeorge Bundy]."[110]

October 23 (Tuesday)
After obtaining OAS approval of the quarantine procedure, President Kennedy signed Proclamation 3504, authorizing a naval quarantine of Cuba.[111] The cover of the present book contains a photograph of the president signing the Proclamation.

Khrushchev sent a letter to Kennedy on this date, objecting to the quarantine and claiming that all the weapons given to Cuba were "intended solely for defensive purposes in order to secure the Republic of

Cuba against the attack of an aggressor."[112] The president responded with a short message, concluding as follows: "I hope that you will issue immediately the necessary instructions to your ships to observe the terms of the quarantine, the basis of which was established by the vote of the Organization of American States this afternoon, and which will go into effect at 1400 hours Greenwich time October twenty-four."[113]

President Kennedy also attended ExComm and other meetings and conversations discussing strategy details throughout the day.[114]

Confrontation and Agreement

October 24 (Wednesday)

The president again attended meetings and conferences discussing strategy details relating to the crisis.[115] At an ExComm meeting on this day, General Taylor reported that three of the Soviet ships headed for Cuba "are definitely turning back." Other ships appeared to be continuing on to Cuba.[116]

Meanwhile, however, Khrushchev sent an angry letter to Kennedy, stating in part:

> You, Mr. President, are not declaring a quarantine, but rather are setting forth an ultimatum and threatening that if we do not give in to your demands you will use force. Consider what you are saying! And you want to persuade me to agree to this! What would it mean to agree to these demands? It would mean guiding oneself in one's relations with other countries not by reason, but by submitting to arbitrariness. You are no

157

longer appealing to reason, but wish to intimidate us. . . .

The Soviet Government considers that the violation of the freedom to use international waters and international air space is an act of aggression which pushes mankind toward the abyss of a world nuclear-missile war. Therefore, the Soviet Government cannot instruct the captains of Soviet vessels bound for Cuba to observe the orders of American naval forces blockading that Island. Our instructions to Soviet mariners are to observe strictly the universally accepted norms of navigation in international waters and not to retreat one step from them. And if the American side violates these rules, it must realize what responsibility will rest upon it in that case. Naturally we will not simply be bystanders with regard to piratical acts by American ships on the high seas. We will then be forced on our part to take the measures we consider necessary and adequate in order to protect our rights. We have everything necessary to do so.[117]

October 25 (Thursday)

In response to Khrushchev's October 24 letter, Kennedy again reiterated the sequence of historical events, concluding as follows: "I repeat my regret that these events should cause a deterioration in our relations. I hope that your Government will take the necessary action to permit a restoration of the earlier situation."[118]

At today's ExComm meetings, Deputy Under Secretary of State Alexis Johnson reported that fourteen ships had turned back in response to the quarantine, while CIA Director McCone stated that fifteen ships were still on their way to Cuba. The question arose whether tankers not containing deck cargo should be allowed to pass through the quarantine line without being searched. The ExComm members generally thought it unlikely that a tanker could contain missiles in the absence of visible storage facilities on deck. Secretary McNamara reported that a number of tankers were passed through without deck cargo. However, ExComm was considering additional bans on POL (petroleum, oil, and lubricants), aviation gas, and missile fuel, in the event the Soviets failed to remove the offensive nuclear weapons from Cuba. Air surveillance continued to show ongoing work on the Cuban sites, and the ExComm members were discussing the possible use of force against those sites as well as the interception of a tanker called the *Grozny* that had a deck load.[119]

On this day, there was a famous confrontation between US Ambassador Adlai Stevenson and the Soviet Ambassador Valerin Zorin in the United Nations Security Council. Objecting to Zorin's obfuscation of the issue, Stevenson asked: "All right, sir, let me ask you one simple question: Do you, Ambassador Zorin, deny that the U.S.S.R. has placed and is placing medium- and intermediate-range missiles and sites in Cuba? Yes or no—don't wait for the translation—yes or no?" Zorin refused to answer, saying that Stevenson would have his answer in due course. Stevenson then replied: "You can answer yes or no. You have denied

159

they exist. I want to know if I understood you correctly. I am prepared to wait for my answer until hell freezes over, if that's your decision. And I am also prepared to present the evidence in this room." He then proceeded to show the Security Council the photographic evidence of the Soviet missiles in Cuba.[120]

October 26 (Friday)

Castro sent a letter to Khrushchev, warning of an imminent US attack on Cuba and discussing a military response:

> Given the analysis of the situation and the reports which have reached us, [I] consider an attack to be almost imminent—within the next 24 to 72 hours. There are two possible variants: the first and most probable one is an air attack against certain objectives with the limited aim of destroying them; the second, and though less probable, still possible, is a full invasion. This would require a large force and is the most repugnant form of aggression, which might restrain them. . . .
>
> **If the second variant takes place and the imperialists invade Cuba with the aim of occupying it, the dangers of their aggressive policy are so great that after such an invasion the Soviet Union must never allow circumstances in which the imperialists could carry out a nuclear first strike against it.**
>
> **I tell you this because I believe that the imperialists' aggressiveness makes them extremely dangerous, and that if they**

manage to carry out an invasion of Cuba—a brutal act in violation of universal and moral law—then that would be the moment to eliminate this danger forever, in an act of the most legitimate self-defense. However harsh and terrible the solution, there would be no other.[121]

Castro's intelligence was mostly correct. The United States was, indeed, preparing for an air attack and invasion against Cuba in the event the Soviet-installed nuclear weapons were not removed. The Joint Chiefs of Staff had even advocated an immediate air strike and invasion against Cuba regardless of whether the Kremlin promised to remove the weapons. But President Kennedy considered the air strike and invasion options as necessary and advisable only if the nuclear weapons in Cuba were not removed. Castro was now talking about a Soviet nuclear attack on the United States in the event the US invaded Cuba. Of course, that was not necessarily a novel view, since the whole point of the Soviet nuclear buildup in Cuba, according to Khrushchev, was to permit nuclear retaliation against a US invasion.

However, Khrushchev apparently misread or misremembered Castro's letter to mean that the Soviet Union should immediately launch a nuclear attack against the United States. In his *Memoirs*, which he dictated during the years after he was forced out of office and living in a country dacha without access to relevant documents, Khrushchev wrote that Castro "reasoned that since an invasion was inevitable, it was necessary to forestall it. He proposed that to prevent destruction of our missile installations, we should immediately strike first, dealing a [preemptive] thermonuclear blow to the United States. [¶] When this message was read aloud to us, we sat there in silence, looking at one another for a long time." Castro's letter evidently terrified Khrushchev and made him more amenable to a quick resolution of the crisis.[122]

This may explain why Khrushchev now wrote a lengthy letter to Kennedy, the important language of which was the following:

> **If assurances were given by the President and the Government of the United States that the USA itself would not participate in an attack on Cuba and would restrain others from actions of this sort, if you would recall your fleet, this would immediately change everything.** I am not speaking for Fidel Castro, but I think that he and the Government of Cuba, evidently, would declare demobilization and would appeal to the people to get down to peaceful labor. **Then, too, the question of armaments would disappear, since, if there is no threat, then armaments are a burden for every people. Then too, the question of the destruction, not only of the armaments which you call offensive, but of all other armaments as well, would look different. . . .**
>
> Let us therefore show statesmanlike wisdom. **I propose: We, for our part, will declare that our ships, bound for Cuba, will not carry any kind of armaments.**

You would declare that the United States will not invade Cuba with its forces and will not support any sort of forces which might intend to carry out an invasion of Cuba. Then the necessity for the presence of our military specialists in Cuba would disappear.[123]

At 7:00 p.m., Washington time, the US embassy in Moscow began transmitting the English translation of this long letter to the US government. In the meantime, however, the Kennedy administration had been getting hints by way of U Thant, the acting UN secretary-general, and other sources that the Soviet Union might agree to remove the missiles in Cuba for a US pledge not to invade Cuba. Secretary Rusk informed the president of this development about 4:30 p.m.. In fact, President Kennedy had already indicated his willingness to resolve the crisis on that basis in an ExComm meeting earlier that day. When, after 7:40 p.m., President Kennedy and several of his advisers reviewed Khrushchev's letter, they became more optimistic that a resolution was in sight.[124]

October 27 (Saturday)

That optimism was, however, short-lived. An October 27 letter from Khrushchev was inconsistent with his letter of October 26. The operative language in the second letter was as follows:

I therefore make this proposal: We are willing to remove from Cuba the means which you regard as offensive. We are willing to carry this out and to make this pledge in the United Nations. Your

representatives will make a declaration to the effect that the United States, for its part, considering the uneasiness and anxiety of the Soviet State, will remove its analogous means from Turkey. Let us reach agreement as to the period of time needed by you and by us to bring this about. And, after that, persons entrusted by the United Nations Security Council could inspect on the spot the fulfillment of the pledges made. Of course, the permission of the Governments of Cuba and Turkey is necessary for the entry into those countries of these representatives and for the inspection of the fulfillment of the pledge made by each side . . . .

We, in making this pledge, in order to give satisfaction and hope of the peoples of Cuba and Turkey and to strengthen their confidences in their security, will make a statement within the framework of the Security Council to the effect that **the Soviet Government gives a solemn promise to respect the inviolability of the borders and sovereignty of Turkey, not to interfere in its internal affairs, not to invade Turkey, not to make available our territory as a bridgehead for such an invasion, and that it would also restrain those who contemplate committing aggression against Turkey, either from the territory of the Soviet Union or from**

the territory of Turkey's other neighboring states.

The United States Government will make a similar statement within the framework of the Security Council regarding Cuba. It will declare that the United States will respect the inviolability of Cuba's borders and its sovereignty, will pledge not to interfere in its internal affairs, not to invade Cuba itself or make its territory available as a bridgehead for such an invasion, and will also restrain those who might contemplate committing aggression against Cuba, either from the territory of the United States or from the territory of Cuba's other neighboring states.[125]

This proposal, unlike the October 26 private message to Kennedy, was public: it was broadcast on Radio Moscow.

The problem was the new demand to exchange the removal of the NATO missiles in Turkey for the removal of Soviet missiles in Cuba. President Kennedy considered those Jupiter missiles as obsolete and easily replaced by US Polaris submarines in the Mediterranean containing nuclear missiles. But Turkey had adamantly opposed removing the missiles the previous year. The situation with Turkey was quite difficult from a diplomatic perspective. Much of the ExComm meetings of October 27 addressed this problem. Kennedy ardently wanted to remove the missiles in Turkey, but the Turks had stubbornly refused, and Kennedy could not push the issue without jeopardizing the NATO alliance. Technically, the missiles belonged to Turkey, and they were manned by Turks, but the warheads were under US control. The missiles were committed to NATO, and the United States was merely the custodian of the warheads for the account of the Turks, in recognition that the US was obligated to release them under NATO nuclear release procedures. Meanwhile, work on the missile sites in Cuba continued at a rapid pace.[126]

The White House press office, at the direction of the president, released the following statement to the world media:

> Several inconsistent and conflicting proposals have been made by the U.S.S.R. within the last 24 hours, including the one just made public by Moscow. The proposal broadcast this morning involves the security of nations outside the Western Hemisphere. But it is the Western Hemisphere countries and they alone that are subject to the threat that has produced the current crisis—the action of the Soviet Government in secretly introducing offensive weapons into Cuba. Work on these offensive weapons is still proceeding at a rapid pace. The first imperative must be to deal with this immediate threat, under which no sensible negotiations can proceed.
>
> It is therefore the position of the United States that as an urgent preliminary to consideration of any proposals work on the Cuban bases must stop; offensive weapons must be rendered inoperable; and further

shipment of offensive weapons to Cuba must cease—all under effective international verification.

As to proposals concerning the security of nations outside this hemisphere, the United States and its allies have long taken the lead in seeking properly inspected arms limitations, on both sides. These efforts can continue as soon as the present Soviet-created threat is ended.[127]

The Joint Chiefs of Staff (not including General Taylor), consistent with their previous position, recommended a massive air strike against Cuba, followed by an invasion. The air strikes were to commence within the next two days.[128]

Other dangerous incidents occurred on this day. A U-2 reconnaissance plane, obtaining air samples from Soviet nuclear tests, accidentally veered into Soviet airspace, resulting in a confrontation with Soviet MiG fighters. The US pilot managed to get back outside Soviet airspace without further incident.[129]

However, a U-2 flying on a reconnaissance mission over Cuba was shot down by a SAM site; the pilot died.[130]

Additionally, US planes conducting low-level reconnaissance over Cuba were being attacked by ground fire.[131] President Kennedy informed the other ExComm members that "Castro just announced that any plane that intruded over the airspace over Cuba would be fired upon."[132]

The situation was very tense. Construction on the missile sites was continuing, and air surveillance over Cuba was becoming very dangerous. The swap of missiles in Turkey for missiles in Cuba seemed impossible as well as inadvisable. Some ExComm members were becoming inclined toward a military solution.[133]

President Kennedy, however, was collaborating with Ted Sorenson and Robert Kennedy on a letter to Khrushchev. This letter was sent to the US embassy in Moscow at 8:05 p.m. with instructions to deliver it to the highest available Soviet official. The text of the letter was released to the press at the same time. President Kennedy dispatched Robert Kennedy to meet immediately with Soviet Ambassador Dobrynin and give him a copy of the letter. The letter read, in significant part, as follows:

> I have read your letter of October 26 with great care and welcomed the statement of your desire to seek a prompt solution to the problem. The first thing that needs to be done, however, is for work to cease on offensive missile bases in Cuba and for all weapons systems in Cuba capable of offensive use to be rendered inoperable, under effective United Nations arrangements.
>
> Assuming this is done promptly, I have given my representatives in New York instructions that will permit them to work out this week and—in cooperation with the Acting Secretary General and your representative—an arrangement for a permanent solution to the Cuban problem along the lines suggested in your letter of October 26. As I read your letter, the key

elements of your proposals—which seem generally acceptable as I understand them—are as follows:

1. You would agree to remove these weapons systems from Cuba under appropriate United Nations observation and supervision; and undertake, with suitable safeguards, to halt the further introduction of such weapons systems into Cuba.

2. We, on our part, would agree—upon the establishment of adequate arrangements through the United Nations to ensure the carrying out and continuation of these commitments—(a) to remove promptly the quarantine measures now in effect and (b) to give assurances against an invasion of Cuba and I am confident that other nations of the Western Hemisphere would be prepared to do likewise.

If you will give your representative similar instructions, there is no reason why we should not be able to complete these arrangements and announce them to the world within a couple of days. The effect of such a settlement on easing world tensions would enable us to work toward a more general arrangement regarding "other armaments", as proposed in your second letter which you made public. I would like to say again that the United States is very much interested in reducing tensions and halting the arms race; and if your letter signifies that you are prepared to discuss a detente affecting NATO and the Warsaw Pact, we are quite prepared to consider with our allies any useful proposals.

But the first ingredient, let me emphasize, is the cessation of work on missile sites in Cuba and measures to render such weapons inoperable, under effective international guarantees. The continuation of this threat, or a prolonging of this discussion concerning Cuba by linking these problems to the broader questions of European and world security, would surely lead to an intensification of the Cuban crisis and a grave risk to the peace of the world. For this reason I hope we can quickly agree along the lines outlined in this letter and in your letter of October 26.[134]

In his meeting that evening with Ambassador Dobryin, Robert Kennedy directly addressed the subject that had not been explicitly discussed in President Kennedy's public letter. If Khrushchev accepted the terms of the letter, after a lapse of time of four or five months, the US would see to it that the Jupiter missiles would be removed from Turkey. But this part of the understanding had to be kept totally secret.[135] These missiles were, in fact, withdrawn from Turkey in 1963.

Robert Kennedy emphasized in his conversation with Dobrinyn that the US had to have a commitment from Khrushchev by the next day to withdraw the missiles under UN supervision, or otherwise there would be drastic consequences.[136]

October 28 (Sunday)

On Sunday morning, Khrushchev responded to Kennedy's letter in a message that was also broadcast over Radio Moscow. Khrushchev agreed to Kennedy's terms, though with a great deal of verbiage.[137]

The US military chiefs, apart from General Taylor, were not happy campers. Notwithstanding the Khrushchev-Kennedy agreement, they argued, in a letter to the president, for an air strike, beginning the next day, to be followed by an invasion of Cuba, absent "irrefutable evidence" that dismantling of the missile sites had actually begun.[138]

Aftermath

Several aspects of the agreement between Kennedy and Khrushchev proved difficult to implement due to the intransigence and noncooperation of Fidel Castro, who, among other things, refused UN on-site inspection and wanted to keep nuclear-capable bombers and tactical nuclear weapons. However, the US president and the Soviet premier found a workaround regarding the inspection issue, and the Soviets forced Castro to give up all the nuclear weapons they had given him. The nightmare of the Cuban Missile Crisis finally came to an end. The experience of being at the brink of nuclear war chastened both leaders, especially Khrushchev. In succeeding months, they worked toward a kind of détente between the Soviet Union and the United States, including the signing of a partial nuclear test ban treaty. It might have gone much further in that direction had JFK not been assassinated on November 22, 1963, and Khrushchev not deposed in October 1964.[139] In the last analysis, the hardliners won.

Final Evaluations of the Political Leadership of President Kennedy and Premier Khrushchev in the Cuban Missile Crisis

This chapter has had to be long in order to capture the breadth and depth of the political leadership of John F. Kennedy and Nikita Khrushchev during the Cuban Missile Crisis.

Khrushchev used brinkmanship as a tactical weapon during his years in office up to the Cuban Missile Crisis. As discussed above, his ideological objectives were irrational, failing to acknowledge that his Communist dreams were based on anti-human authoritarianism or totalitarianism. His means were extremely dangerous, bringing the world to the edge of nuclear war. But Khrushchev, though not well educated, had a kind of common sense that permitted him to work with Kennedy to resolve a crisis that could well have led to nuclear war. And, to some extent, he was a changed man after his experience in the Cuban Missile Crisis.

Kennedy had his own faults, though most of them were personal. For example, following in his father's footsteps, there is evidence that he had a number of extramarital affairs. But my study of political leadership has resulted in the conclusion that JFK was one of the most rational political figures in human history. Unlike some later presidents, he did not decide difficult questions by his "gut" but rather by reason and evidence. And he consulted advisers of many different persuasions in order to be sure he understood all the available options.

On April 4, 1964, historian Arthur M. Schlesinger Jr., a former special assistant to President Kennedy, conducted an oral history interview with Robert S. McNamara, the secretary of defense in the Kennedy administration and, until February 29, 1968, the administration of President Lyndon B. Johnson. Among other things, the following exchange took place:

> McNAMARA: On the 22nd of January, 1963, the President, during a meeting with his advisors, emphasized the lesson we had learned from Cuba. In his opinion it was this: we provided the Soviet Union with time for consideration of their response, and thereby we avoided a spasm response. This was the major argument in favor of the blockade instead of the air strike. This should be our objective for future confrontations with the Soviets.
>
> SCHLESINGER: What was the demeanor of the President during this period?
>
> McNAMARA: Calm and cool—and highly rational and unemotional during the period.[140]

At the time of the Bay of Pigs invasion in April 1961, John F. Kennedy had just recently assumed the presidency. He had not yet figured out whom he could trust for reliable information and advice. As a result, he went against his better instincts in finally approving the invasion plan, which had already been in the planning stages during the last year of the Eisenhower administration.

By the time of the October 1962 Cuban missile crisis, President Kennedy had learned how to navigate the surrounding bureaucracy. He resisted the urging of

Chapter 5. Political Leadership in the Cuban Missile Crisis

several military and civilian advisers who believed that only a bombing and invasion of Cuba would be effective. He instead adopted a quarantine plan and entered into a negotiation with Premier Khrushchev that led to the removal of the missiles without triggering World War III.

Ted Sorensen was Kennedy's friend, speechwriter, and counselor. He was a member of ExComm, and he drafted some of the most memorable lines of JFK's speeches. In the spring of 1963—some months after the Cuban Missile Crisis and a few months before JFK's assassination—Sorensen give two lectures at Columbia University. These were turned into a book, with a June 1963 foreword by President Kennedy. The book, titled *Decision-Making in the White House: The Olive Branch or the Arrows*, discusses how Kennedy arrived at presidential decisions, consulting with many experts and other advisers, and rationally evaluating their various perspectives and recommendations. Sorensen observed, "To make informed decisions, the President must be at home with a staggering range of information—about history, economics, politics and personalities in fifty states and now in a hundred or more countries. . . . For the essence of decision is choice; and, to choose, it is first necessary to know."[141]

Or, as President John F. Kennedy said (adapting words from a poem by Domingo Ortego) in a presidential backgrounder on October 16, 1962, which was the day he first learned of Soviet missiles in Cuba:

Bullfight critics row on row
Fill the enormous Plaza de toros
But only one is there who knows
And he is the one who fights the bull.[142]

EPILOGUE

REASON AND EMOTION IN POLITICAL PHILOSOPHY AND PRACTICE

As elaborated in my book *Reason and Human Ethics*, reason, understood as correct reasoning about both ends and means, should supervise—not eliminate—emotion in human life. Reason is especially important in political philosophy and politics, because many human lives other than that of one individual are at stake. Irrationality regarding ends or means can be catastrophic, as the political history of humankind has demonstrated time and time again.

What, then, is the place of emotion in political matters? The word "empathy" means different things to different people, and I use the term here to refer to a rational and occasionally emotional concern about the welfare of others. Empathy in this sense surely plays an important role in formulating governmental policy at all levels—from international politics to national, regional, and local government treatment of people who have not been fortunate. We see, to cite just a few examples, a total lack of empathy in the Nazi actions against Jews, the populist mistreatment of migrants, and the persecution of religious minorities throughout history.

In the final analysis, however, even empathy should be governed by reason. Empathy assists reason in formulating the proper objectives of government, but the means to achieve those ends should be rationally and ethically devised to ensure they do not result in the opposite of what was intended. As the proverb says, the road to hell is paved with good intentions. Moreover, empathy should not be limited to those in one's own in-group.

Once reason, accompanied by empathy, ascertains correct political ends and means, it often needs to be fortified by yet another emotion—courage or, as Plato called it, spiritedness. One must have the courage of one's convictions and not bow to irrationality and prejudice from any quarter. Individuals should use reason to identify the times and places in which courage should be manifested in public speech or political action. That will depend on particular circumstances, many of which cannot be predicted in advance of their occurrence.

Politics, as we know it, often involves irrational anger and other emotional excesses. Such extreme behavior has no place in a reasonable and decent society. As Hamlet said to Horatio, "Give me that man / That is not passion's slave and I will wear him / In my heart's core, ay, in my heart of heart, / As I do thee."[1]

THE GOOD SOCIETY

It has long been a dream of some human beings that a good society might be possible. In such a sociopolitical order, everyone would have sufficient economic resources to live comfortably, and no one would be corrupted by excessive wealth. All people would be guided by reason to treat themselves and other humans with dignity. Crime, wars, and interpersonal hostility would no longer exist.

History does not give cause for optimism that such a political society will ever be achieved. Indeed, all historical experience suggests otherwise. Ethics and politics appear to be forever separated.

We should keep the good society in mind as we think about political philosophy and politics. But it is counterproductive to attempt to realize the good society through authoritarianism, military imperialism, or anarchism. Such approaches lead to the opposite of a good society.

Political philosophy and political action require the utmost sobriety. We should use reason to formulate ethical ends and devise workable means that do not entail unintended, negative consequences.

For the current and foreseeable centuries, we should focus not on realizing the currently impossible task of a perfectly good society (or a perfectly good world order) but rather on improving the society and world we now have. Perhaps in some distant century the perfectly good society and world will be visible and within reach. But that time is not now. However much it may break our hearts, we must deal with human ethics and politics as we find it. Our immediate goal should be improvement, not utopian perfection.[2]

THE ULTIMATE RECONCILIATION OF ETHICAL AND POLITICAL PHILOSOPHY

This book began with the quandary of the incompatibility between ethics and politics. Do the principles of individual ethics apply to politics? If so, does this not require the logical conclusion that government should not be allowed to do anything that an individual cannot ethically do? An individual may not ethically initiate force against another human being absent very unusual circumstances amounting to a rational need for immediate, preemptive action in the context of the defense of oneself or others. But government claims a right, in the formulation of Max Weber and many others, to the legitimate use of force, including, for example, the initiation of force by way of taxation or government economic regulation.

Chapter 3 of this book elaborates some of the kinds of force that are, in my view, appropriate for government. Chapter 1 refutes the contrary view of anarchism. The human condition does not allow anarchism as a viable option in advanced societies.

It is a category error to conflate ethics and politics in the anarchist manner. Government, as outlined in the preceding chapters of this book, is necessary, though humans should work to promote the best possible kind of government under existing circumstances. And political leaders and individual people and their organizations should strive to be as rational and ethical as possible.

The fact that some ultimate principles of ethics and politics cannot currently be reconciled does not mean that they will never be reconciled. But such reconciliation requires the kind of precedent ethical and rational reformation that is outlined in my book *Reason and Human Ethics*. Then, and only then, will ethical and political philosophy converge, with a consequent happiness for humankind that it has not to date experienced.

SUMMARY OF THIS PHILOSOPHICAL TRILOGY

This concludes my philosophical trilogy on free will (*Free Will and Human Ethics*), ethics (*Reason and Human Ethics*), and political philosophy (*Reason and Human Government*). The following is a brief summary of the principal themes of these books.

Human beings have some free will to lead rational and ethical lives. That free will is not perfect, but people who are not seriously brain damaged have some power to overcome negative attitudes and prejudices in favor of thoughts and actions that are consistent with reason and ethics. As a result of negative habituation, some people find this task harder than others, and severely negative environmental factors may make such reformation extremely difficult, though, hopefully, not impossible.

Human ethics involves the proper understanding of rational ends and the use of ethical, rational means to achieve those ends. This applies to the four kinds of ethics: individual, social, citizen (including media), and political ethics.

Human life in complex societies requires government. Anarchism is not possible in complex societies for the reasons articulated in chapter 1 of the present book. Government should recognize and protect correctly defined individual rights (chapter 2). Government also has some proper affirmative powers (chapter 3). The best workable form of government is a democratic republic that—based ultimately on a democratic franchise—recognizes and protects individual human rights and has a separation of powers between executive, legislative, and judicial functions as well as checks and balances within and between these branches (chapter 4). Political leaders should be rational and base their political decisions on appropriate ends and means. Chapter 5 provides a model of such political deliberation.

We benefit ourselves and others by thinking and acting ethically and rationally. Individual human beings have different abilities and interests. In a complex economy with division of labor, individuals can, when possible, contribute to society through participation in the economy, the proper raising of the next generation of humans, charitable endeavors, obeying just laws, and paying their taxes.

For millennia, some form of what we call capitalism has been the default economic mechanism. Totalitarian, command economies have never worked. At the present time, however, human societies are facing the possibility of massive unemployment due to automation and artificial intelligence. It may be that more and more people are left behind in this brave new economic world. It is perhaps too soon to predict whether such a calamity will actually occur. If it does happen, governments will have to figure out a way to preserve the human species in the face of unprecedented economic circumstances. Some modification of laissez-faire capitalism may be necessary. The subject of political economy will become all-important. At my advanced age, I will not be around if and when the worst of this phenomenon occurs. It is a question for younger generations to solve.

APPENDIX

THE HISTORICAL BACKGROUND OF THE 1962 CUBAN MISSILE CRISIS

The Cuban Missile Crisis was perhaps the most significant event of the Cold War between the United States and the Union of Soviet Socialist Republics (USSR), also known as the Soviet Union. Each side of the Cold War had its allies; other nations were nonaligned. Most people alive today were born after the 1962 Cuban Missile Crisis, and many were born after the Cold War ended in 1991 with the disintegration of the USSR. That large empire was replaced by the smaller Russian Federation, which unsuccessfully attempted a conversion to democracy during the 1990s. Since the first decade of the twenty-first century, Russia has become an increasingly authoritarian country ruled by Vladimir Putin. The Soviet Union was a totalitarian Communist empire. Putin's government is a nostalgic fascist regime evoking the centuries of rule by Russian tzars before the 1917 Russian Revolution. It also has features of kleptocracy.[1]

The present appendix is written for those readers interested in understanding the relevant philosophical and historical developments leading up to the Cuban Missile Crisis, including but not limited to the 1961 US–instigated invasion of the Cuban Bay of Pigs.

The Marxist Roots of Soviet Communism

The founding fathers of modern Communism were Karl Marx (1818–83) and Friedrich Engels (1820–95). Their most famous joint work was titled *The Manifesto of the*

Communist Party (often called *The Communist Manifesto*), [2] though each wrote other related books and tracts.

The following are some of the salient points in the *Manifesto*:

- "The history of all hitherto existing society is the history of class struggles" (*Manifesto*, 1:29).
- "Society as a whole is more and more splitting up into two great hostile camps, into two great classes directly facing each other—Bourgeoisie and Proletariat" (1:29).
- "By bourgeoisie is meant the class of modern capitalists, owners of the means of social production and employers of wage labour. By proletariat, the class of modern wage labourers who, having no means of production of their own, are reduced to selling their labour power in order to live" (Friedrich Engels, Note in the 1888 English edition of the *Manifesto*, 1:165).
- "The bourgeoisie, wherever it has got the upper hand, has put an end to all feudal, patriarchal, idyllic relations. . . . It has resolved personal worth into exchange value, and in place of the numberless indefeasible chartered freedoms, has set up that single, unconscionable freedom—Free Trade. In one word, for exploitation, veiled by religious and political illusions, it has substituted naked, shameless, direct, brutal exploitation" (*Manifesto*, 1:31).

- "The weapons with which the bourgeoisie felled feudalism to the ground are now turned against the bourgeoisie itself. [¶] But not only has the bourgeoisie forged the weapons that bring death to itself; it has also called into existence the men who are to wield those weapons—the modern working class—the proletarians" (1:34–35).

- "When, in the course of development, class distinctions have disappeared, and all production has been concentrated in the hands of a vast association of the whole nation, the public power will lose its political character. Political power, properly so called, is merely the organised power of one class for oppressing another. If the proletariat during its contest with the bourgeoisie is compelled, by the force of circumstances, to organise itself as a class, if, by means of a revolution, it makes itself the ruling class, and, as such, sweeps away by force the old conditions of production, then it will, along with these conditions, have swept away the conditions for the existence of class antagonisms and of classes generally, and will thereby have abolished its own supremacy as a class" (2:49).

- "The Communists disdain to conceal their views and aims. They openly declare that their ends can be attained only by the forcible overthrow of all existing social conditions. Let the ruling classes tremble at a Communistic revolution. The proletarians have nothing to lose but their chains. They have a world to win" (4:61).

In the *Critique of the Gotha Program*, Marx explicitly used the phrase "dictatorship of the proletariat" to describe the transitional phase between capitalism and communism: "Between capitalist and communist society there lies the period of the revolutionary transformation of the one into the other. Corresponding to this is also a political transition period in which the state can be nothing but **the revolutionary dictatorship of the proletariat**."[3]

Throughout his writings, Marx deprecated what he called "bourgeois rights." As Joseph Cropsey explained:

> Civil society is the stratum of common life that is given its essential character by the self-assertiveness of men, one against the other, in the name of their inalienable, irreducible rights. The sanctity of those rights, thought by writers like Locke to be the ground for guaranteeing the freedom and thus the humanity of men, is rejected by Marx because he views the assertion of those rights as the source of, surely the expression of man's dehumanization. The war of Marxism against the ruling principles of Western constitutionalism must never be mistaken for a mere skirmish.[4]

Marx and Engels regarded the dictatorship of the proletariat as the transition between capitalism and communism. What, then, did they mean by the final phase of communism? Here, they were vague and obfuscatory. Engels talked about the withering away of the state. This suggested a kind of anarchism. A close look at the writings of Marx and Engels suggests, however, that they did not foresee an anarchist society but rather one in which the state itself supervised the "classless society." As Richard Adamiak concluded after an exhaustive analysis of Marxian semantics:

> The future communist society envisioned by Marx and Engels was antithetical to Anarchism; the state was foreseen as being its one indispensable institution. By exploiting the unique semantics of their ideology to maximum political advantage, Marx and Engels adroitly constructed a specious anarchistic facade to ward off the successive threats from their more radical rivals, the Anarchists. The theory of "the withering away of the state," and its earlier variations, were no more than misleading myths. Marxism, from 1848 to 1894, was a statist ideology.[5]

We now consider how this Marxist ideology played out in the history of the Soviet government up to the 1961 Bay of Pigs invasion and the 1962 Cuban Missile Crisis.

The 1917 Bolshevik Revolution and Its Aftermath

The Russian Revolution against the historic tsarist regime occurred in 1917. Vladimir Lenin (1870–1924) led the second phase, called the Bolshevik Revolution, which took over the Russian government in late 1917 and 1918. In his contemporaneous pamphlet titled *The State and Revolution: The Marxist Theory of the State and the Tasks of the Proletariat in the Revolution*, Lenin expressed his agreement with Marx regarding the dictatorship of the proletariat, which was to be the "socialist" intermediary phase between "capitalism" and "communism." In this "socialist" phase, according to Lenin, "[t]he means of production are no longer the private property of individuals. The means of production belong to the whole of society." He defined "the means of production" as "the factories, machines, land, etc." The revolutionary proletariat will "crush, smash to atoms, wipe off the face of the earth the bourgeois, even the republican-bourgeois, state machine, the standing army, the police and the bureaucracy and to substitute for them a more democratic state machine, but a state machine nevertheless, in the shape of armed workers who proceed to form a militia involving the entire population."[6]

After taking power, Lenin ruled Russia and the emerging Soviet Union until 1924. He put a unique twist on the Marxist doctrine of the dictatorship of the proletariat. Lenin said that the dictatorship would be of the "vanguard" of the proletariat, i.e., the Communist Party:

> [T]he **dictatorship of the proletariat**, i.e., the organization of the **vanguard** of the oppressed as the ruling class for the purpose of suppressing the oppressors, cannot result merely in an expansion of democracy. Simultaneously with an immense expansion of democracy, which for the first time becomes democracy for the poor, democracy for the people, and not democracy for the money-bags, **the dictatorship of the proletariat imposes a series of restrictions**

**on the freedom of the oppressors, the
exploiters, the capitalists. We must
suppress them in order to free humanity
from wage slavery, their resistance must
be crushed by force . . . .[7]**

The new Bolshevik government immediately
announced that all land belonged to the peasants who
worked it, thereby displacing the "bourgeois"
landowners and landlords. Meanwhile, the proletarian
workers took control of the factories through their
soviets (councils). These were the first major steps of
the dictatorship of the proletariat or the dictatorship of
the vanguard of the proletariat. Many more
governmental actions were taken against the
bourgeoisie and other "class enemies" (including
executions of political dissidents) during succeeding
years and decades.

As Michael McFaul, a former US ambassador to
Russia and noted Russian scholar, has explained,

After seizing power in October 1917
(November, by the Gregorian calendar),
Lenin and his comrades tried to construct an
entirely new political and economic system
in Russia in which the Communist Party
owned all property, set all prices, and
managed all commerce allegedly on behalf
of the peasants, workers, and soldiers. At the
time, Lenin aspired to export this new
communist model to the entire world,
threatening not just democracies but
capitalist economies.[8]

Generally speaking, the Leninist regime was, at the
very least, authoritarian, and the successor Stalinist

regime (1924–1953) was totalitarian.[9] The promised "withering away of the state" never happened.

After Stalin died in 1953, Nikita Khrushchev (1894–1971) eventually emerged as the undisputed leader of the Soviet Union, occupying the post of first secretary of the Central Committee of the Communist Party of the Soviet Union in 1953 and the governmental post of chairman of the Council of Ministers (premier) in 1958. He held both positions until he was ousted by Leonid Brezhnev and other ministers on October 14, 1964.

In a February 25-26, 1956 speech before the Twentieth Congress of the Communist Party of the Soviet Union, Khrushchev severely criticized Stalin's tyrannical rule, focusing especially on the latter's paranoid torture and executions of party cadres. Although this is often called the "Secret Speech," it did not remain secret for long.[10]

Khrushchev was a somewhat more moderate leader than Stalin, but his government remained totalitarian in important ways.[11] The "bourgeois rights" of Western democracies were unknown in the Soviet Union at any time of its existence, except for some relaxation of governmental control during the leadership of Mikhail Gorbachev (1985–91). Nor have they existed, except perhaps for a fleeting moment during the 1990s, in the post-Soviet era. Since the early years of the present century, Vladimir Putin has avidly pursued his fever dream of returning Russia to the presumed glories of its pre-Communist authoritarian past.

The Cold War

The post-World War II phase of the Cold War between the Soviet Union and its allies and the United States and its allies began after the end of the war in 1945 and concluded with the dissolution of the Soviet Union in 1991. For summaries of its major developments, see standard encyclopedia articles and the many books and articles about same.

One aspect of the Cold War that was particularly relevant to the developments in Cuba during 1961 and 1962 was the situation in Berlin. [12]

At the end of World War II, the victorious Allies (the United States, the United Kingdom, France, and the Soviet Union) divided the conquered nation of Germany into four separate sectors, each separately controlled by one of the four Allied powers. Berlin, which was in the Soviet sector, was also divided into four similar sectors, controlled, respectively, by the same governments. Germany remained divided into what became East Germany (controlled by a Soviet client government) and West Germany (controlled, initially, by the United States, the United Kingdom, and France).

The division of Berlin became a repeated flash point of the Cold War. The Soviet Union wanted to deny Western air and land access to West Berlin (controlled by the Western Allies) by signing a peace treaty with East Germany that would allow its Communist government to prevent such access. Western abandonment of West Berlin was a major desideratum of Khrushchev's government, and he used many pressure tactics to try to achieve that result. All of them were unsuccessful.

The Soviet and East German leaders were especially concerned about the fact that an estimated 3.5 million East Germans—dissatisfied with the dictatorial control of the East German government over their

190

persons and property—had escaped to West Berlin, in which civil liberties were protected. Finally, in August 1961, East Germany, supported by the Soviet Union, built a wall around Berlin. This alleviated the problem of the defection of East Germans to West Berlin and somewhat alleviated the Berlin issue in international politics. However, Khrushchev kept exerting pressure on the West over Berlin and was considering increasing that pressure after the Soviet missiles were installed in Cuba.

THE 1961 BAY OF PIGS INVASION

The Cuban Revolution

After years of warfare against Cuban dictator Fulgenico Batista, Fidel Castro and his guerrilla forces succeeded in taking over the Cuban government on January 1, 1959. At first, it was not clear whether Castro shared the Communist sympathies of some of his chief supporters, especially that of Ernesto "Che" Guevara; even Khrushchev was confused.[13]

In April 1959, Fidel and his entourage undertook a what amounted to a "charm offensive" in an eleven-day visit to the United States. Although the US was, during the 1950s, obsessed with a perceived threat from Communist countries such as the Soviet Union and the People's Republic of China, many Americans now came to believe Castro's repeated statements during this trip that he was not a Communist.

Nevertheless, the United States gradually realized that the new Cuban leader was not going to be friendly to US interests and ideology. As elsewhere in Latin America, huge landowners (including US companies) dominated agriculture. In May 1959, Castro's government promulgated land reforms that limited foreign ownership of land and restricted most land ownership to 1,000 acres. Castro also expropriated US companies (which largely controlled Cuba's economy), thereby resulting in a major negative impact to American corporate interests. Many Americans saw these developments as manifestations of socialism at a time when socialism was equated with Communism.

And it did not take Castro long to exhibit a more brutal side to his revolution. In October 1959, Hugo Matos, who had fought with Castro and was then military governor of a province in central Cuba, sent a letter to Castro resigning his position and criticizing the influence of Communists in the new regime. In response, Castro had Matos arrested for treason, for which he served twenty years in prison.[14]

The Eisenhower Administration

Castro came to power during the US presidential administration of Dwight D. Eisenhower (1953-61). In 1959 and 1960, the US Department of State began to consider Castro's regime a threat to American interests in Latin America and an advantage to international Communism. But as late as November 5, 1959, the deputy director of the US Central Intelligence Agency (CIA) told Congress that Fidel Castro was not himself a Communist. On November 6, an internal CIA document stated: "For the moment, CIA operations should be carried out on the assumption that the revolutionary government is basically non-Communist, with legitimate reform goals that deserve US respect and support."[15]

By 1960, however, the CIA had begun planning to overthrow the Castro regime. It had already successfully engineered coups in Iran (1953) and Guatemala (1954) and had been subverting elections in foreign countries since the 1940s. Such practices, which continued during later decades, had become essential to its operations. Covert action had replaced spying as the CIA's most important function: it was an actor, not merely an observer, in international politics.[16]

Preparations for what became the Bay of Pigs invasion began in earnest on January 13, 1960, when the Special Group (also called the 5412 Committee) of the National Security Council authorized CIA Director Allen Dulles to continue planning for such a covert operation. On March 16, the Special Group produced a "Secret-Eyes Only" document titled "A Program of Covert Action Against the Castro Regime," portions of which were later declassified. This plan contemplated, among other things,

> the development of an adequate paramilitary force outside of Cuba, together with mechanisms for the necessary logistic support of covert military operations on the Island. Initially a cadre of leaders will be recruited after careful screening and trained as paramilitary instructors. In a second phase a number of paramilitary cadres will be trained at secure locations outside of the U.S. so as to be available for immediate deployment into Cuba to organize, train and lead resistance forces recruited there both before and after the establishment of one or more active centers of resistance. [17]

An undated, unsigned note attached to the source text of this program reads: "This document is our basic policy paper. It was approved by the President at a meeting in the White House on 17 March 1960." At this meeting, CIA Director Dulles met with President Eisenhower, Vice President Richard Nixon, Secretary of State Christian Herter, Assistant Secretary of State Roy Rubottom, Secretary of the Treasury Robert B. Anderson, Special Assistant for National Security Affairs Gordon Gray, and others to discuss the program of covert action against the Castro regime. The official record of this meeting is a "Top Secret" (later mostly declassified) memorandum of the conference. Among other things, this document stated:

> Mr. Allen Dulles said that preparations of a para-military force will begin outside of Cuba, the first stage being to get a cadre of leaders together for training. The formation of this force might take something like eight months.

> The President said that he knows of no better plan for dealing with this situation. The great problem is leakage and breach of security. Everyone must be prepared to swear that he has not heard of it. . . .

> The President told Mr. Dulles he thought he should go ahead with the plan and the operations. He and the other agencies involved should take account of all likely Cuban reactions and prepare the actions that we would take in response to these. . . .

> Mr. Gray asked whether OAS [Organization of American States] support will only be forthcoming if the Cubans actually attack Americans on the island. Mr.

Rubottom thought that the OAS might be brought to act prior to such an attack on the basis of Castro being tied up with international communism. **The President asked whether we have to base it on the word "communism" or whether we couldn't base it on dictatorship, confiscation, threats to life, etc.** Mr. Nixon said he thought the [March 28, 1954 OAS] Caracas Resolution was based on the term "international communism."[18]

The quadrennial US presidential election was scheduled for November 1960. The Democratic Party nominated Senator John F. Kennedy for president. The Republican Party nominated Vice President Richard Nixon. During the campaign, Kennedy repeatedly criticized the Eisenhower administration for permitting Castro to take over Cuba. At one point, the Kennedy campaign stated: "We must attempt to strengthen the non-Batista democratic anti-Castro forces in exile, and in Cuba itself, who offer eventual hope of overthrowing Castro. Thus far these fighters for freedom have had virtually no support from our Government."[19]

When Nixon learned of this statement by the Kennedy campaign, he concluded that CIA Director Dulles had told Kennedy about the Eisenhower plan for what became the Bay of Pigs invasion on one of the occasions that Dulles briefed him about current foreign policy. However, Dulles denied that he communicated such details to Kennedy. Nixon, of course, could not reveal the ongoing governmental plans for covert action against the Castro regime in public. Instead, he issued

what, under the circumstances, was a somewhat bizarre
statement:

> I think that Senator Kennedy's policies and
> recommendations for the handling of the
> Castro regime are probably the most
> dangerously irresponsible recommendations
> that he's made during the course of this
> campaign. . . . I do know this: that if we were
> to follow that recommendation, that we
> would lose all of our friends in Latin
> America, we would probably be condemned
> in the United Nations, and we would not
> accomplish our objective. I know something
> else. It would be an open invitation for Mr.
> Khrushchev to come in, to come into Latin
> America and to engage us in what would be
> a civil war, and possibly even worse than
> that.[20]

John Kennedy won the November 1960 presidential
election and shortly thereafter decided to keep Allen
Dulles as CIA director. Meanwhile, the Eisenhower
administration had modified its plan for covert action
against the Castro regime. The original intention was to
infiltrate people into Cuba in order to foment a
rebellion. This plan was now viewed as being unlikely
to succeed. The new plan involved a combined sea-air
assault on Cuba coordinated with general guerrilla
activity, followed, if necessary, by an air assault on the
Havana area with the guerrilla forces moving on the
ground into the Havanna area. Additionally, there was a
contingency plan for overt US military intervention,
including planning for coordinated use of CIA assets.
Allen Dulles and CIA Director of Plans Richard Bissell

informed President-elect Kennedy of the current concept on November 18, 1961.[21]

The Kennedy Administration

John F. Kennedy was inaugurated as president of the United States on January 20, 1961; his administration ended on November 22, 1963, when he was assassinated.

The situation in Cuba occupied much of the Kennedy administration's attention during these months. President Kennedy made it clear that he did not oppose land and other reforms in Cuba or other Latin American countries. He did, however, oppose authoritarian or totalitarian Communism as well as Castro's attempts to export his Communist revolution in Cuba to other Latin American countries.

For example, in a January 28, 1961 meeting involving the president, "it was agreed that the United States must make entirely clear that its position with respect to the Cuban Government is currently governed by its firm opposition to Communist penetration of the American Republics, and not by any hostility to democratic social revolution and economic reform."[22] In his January 30, 1961 State of the Union address, President Kennedy stated:

> In Latin America, Communist agents seeking to exploit that region's peaceful revolution of hope have established a base on Cuba, only 90 miles from our shores. Our objection with Cuba is not over the people's drive for a better life. Our objection is to their domination by foreign and domestic tyrannies. Cuban social and economic reform should be encouraged. Questions of

economic and trade policy can always be negotiated. But Communist domination in this Hemisphere can never be negotiated.

We are pledged to work with our sister republics to free the Americas of all such foreign domination and all tyranny, working toward the goal of a free hemisphere of free governments, extending from Cape Horn to the Arctic Circle.[23]

In the background of these developments was the long-established Monroe Doctrine, announced by US President James Monroe in his December 2, 1823 State of the Union message to Congress. The historical context of this pronouncement was that, following the defeat of Napoleon, several monarchies in Europe had allied to stamp out revolutions in Europe and were possibly intending to suppress revolutions in Latin America against European colonial powers. These nations might also wish to colonize new areas of the Western Hemisphere. Regarding such potential threats, Monroe announced

a principle in which the rights and interests of the United States are involved, that **the American continents, by the free and independent condition which they have assumed and maintain, are henceforth not to be considered as subjects for future colonization by any European powers**. . . .

. . . In the wars of the European powers in matters relating to themselves we have never taken any part, nor does it comport with our policy so to do.

It is only when our rights are invaded or seriously menaced that we resent injuries or make preparation for our defense. With the movements in this hemisphere we are of necessity more immediately connected, and by causes which must be obvious to all enlightened and impartial observers.

The political system of the allied powers is essentially different in this respect from that of America. This difference proceeds from that which exists in their respective Governments; and to the defense of our own . . . .

We ... declare that we should consider any attempt on their part to extend their system to any portion of this hemisphere as dangerous to our peace and safety. With the existing colonies or dependencies of any European power we have not interfered and shall not interfere, but with the Governments who have declared their independence and maintained it, and whose independence we have, on great consideration and on just principles, acknowledged, we could not view any interposition for the purpose of oppressing them, or controlling in any other manner their destiny, by any European power in any other light than as the manifestation of an unfriendly disposition toward the United States.[24]

In 1823, when President Monroe first articulated these principles, the United States had no military capacity to enforce them. By the 1960s, of course, the situation on the ground was much different.

As the Soviet government increased its economic and military ties to the Castro government (which had adopted the Soviet "dictatorship of the vanguard of the proletariat" form of government and was attempting to export it to other Latin American countries), the United States considered such developments to be inconsistent with the Monroe Doctrine.

The foregoing highlights the **objectives** of the Kennedy administration regarding Cuba and the export of Marxist-Leninist authoritarianism to other counties in Latin America. The question of **means** was much more difficult and engendered considerable discussion and debate within the administration.

In a February 15, 1961 memorandum to Secretary of State Dean Rusk, Assistant Secretary of State for Inter-American Affairs Thomas Mann concluded, for a number of reasons, that it would not be in the national interest to proceed with a proposed plan for the landing of a brigade of approximately 800 men from bases in Guatemala and Nicaragua, supported by an air strike from the same bases either simultaneously with the landing or twenty-four hours preceding it.[25]

On February 17, Richard Bissell, who had continued in the Kennedy administration with his position as CIA Director of Plans, reported the following developments regarding the Castro government:

> The regime is proceeding methodically to solidify its control over all the major institutions of the society and to employ

them on the Communist pattern as instruments of repression. The Government now directly controls all radio, television, and the press. It has placed politically dependable leadership in labor unions, student groups, and professional organizations. It has nationalized most productive and financial enterprises and is using a program of so-called land reform to exercise effective control over the peasantry. It has destroyed all political parties except the Communist party. Politically reliable and increasingly effective internal security and military forces are being built up . . . .

At the present time the regular Cuban military establishment, especially the Navy and Air Force, are of extremely low effectiveness. Within the next few months, however, it is expected that Cuba will begin to take delivery of jet aircraft and will begin to have available trained Cuban pilots of known political reliability. During the same period the effectiveness of ground forces will be increasing and their knowledge of newly acquired Soviet weapons will improve. Therefore, after some date probably no more than six months away it will become militarily infeasible to overthrow the Castro regime except through the commitment to combat of a sizeable organized military force. The option of action by the Cuban opposition will no longer be open.[26]

In this paper, Bissell quoted the following CIA National Intelligence Estimate: "For the Communist powers, Cuba represents an opportunity of incalculable value. More importantly, the advent of Castro has provided the Communists with a friendly base for propaganda and agitation throughout the rest of Latin America and with a highly exploitable example of revolutionary achievement and successful defiance of the United States."

Under the heading "Possible Courses of Action," Bissell noted: "For reasons which require no elaboration the overt use of U.S. military forces to mount an invasion of Cuba has been excluded as a practical alternative." He did not state whether he agreed with that conclusion.

After examining various alternatives, Bissell arrived at the following recommendation: "The Cuban paramilitary force, if used, has a good chance of overthrowing Castro or at the very least causing a damaging civil war without requiring the U.S. to commit itself to overt action against Cuba."

On February 18, McGeorge Bundy, the special assistant to the president for national security affairs, informed President Kennedy of the divergent views of the State Department and the CIA, forwarding to him the contending memoranda of Mann and Bissell.[27] Secretary of State Rusk, Bissell, and others met with the president later that day. Although no definite decision was reached, Kennedy indicated that he would be in favor of a more moderate approach to the problem such as mass infiltration. He also asked if there was anything he could do to develop a political position to support action such as a speech on traditional liberalism in the western hemisphere.[28]

In preparation for a March 11 meeting with President Kennedy, Bissell prepared a memorandum that concluded: "The Cuban paramilitary force if effectively used has a good chance of overthrowing Castro, or of causing a damaging civil war, without the necessity for the United States to commit itself to overt action against Cuba. . . . Among the alternative courses of action here reviewed, an assault in force preceded by a diversionary landing offers the best chance of achieving the desired result."[29]

The March 11 meeting with the president included Vice President Lyndon Johnson, Secretary of Defense McNamara, Secretary of State Rusk, CIA Director Dulles, CIA Director of Plans Bissell (apparently), McGeorge Bundy, and others. In a subsequent memorandum, Bundy summarized Kennedy's position at the meeting as follows: "The President expects to authorize U.S. support for an appropriate number of patriotic Cubans to return to their homeland. He believes that the best possible plan, from the point of view of combined military, political and psychological considerations, has not yet been presented, and new proposals are to be concerted promptly."[30]

In a March 15 paper titled "Revised Cuban Operation," Bissell noted: "The plan for a Cuban operation and the variants thereof presented on 11 March were considered to be politically objectionable on the ground that the contemplated operation would not have the appearance of an infiltration of guerrillas in support of an internal revolution but rather that of a small-scale World War II type of amphibious assault."

Among other things, he proposed: "The initial landing should be as unspectacular as possible and should have neither immediately prior nor concurrent tactical air support. It should conform as closely as possible to the typical pattern of the landings of small groups intended to establish themselves or to join others in terrain suited for guerrilla operations. In the absence of air support and in order to fit the pattern, it should probably be at night." It is clear from his extended analysis that Bissell did not approve of any such modification of his earlier plan.[31]

The Joint Chiefs of Staff also opposed a modification of the earlier plan. Although its March 15 memorandum considered various alternatives, it concluded: "None of the alternative concepts are considered as feasible and likely to accomplish the objective as the basic para-military plan."[32]

President Kennedy met with Vice President Johnson, McNamara, Rusk, Mann, Dulles, Bissell, McGeorge Bundy, Under Secretary of Defense William Bundy, and others at 4:30 p.m. on March 15. The following notes were taken by Major General David W. Gray of the Joint Chiefs of Staff:

> At this meeting the [CIA's] Zapata plan was presented to the President and a full-length discussion of it followed. The President expressed the belief that uprisings all along the island would be better than to concentrate and strike. The President asked how soon it was intended to break out from this area and Mr. Bissell stated that not before about D+10. The President was also concerned about ability to extricate the

forces. The President did not like the idea of the dawn landing and felt that in order to make this appear as an inside guerrilla-type operation, the ships should be clear of the area by dawn. He directed that this planning be reviewed and another meeting be held the following morning.[33]

By this point in time, the operation was scheduled for the Bay of Pigs. It was initially called the Zapata plan, named after a swamp adjacent to this bay.[34]

At 4:15 p.m. on March 16, the same officials convened again at the White House. General Gray's notes of this meeting stated:

At meeting with the President, CIA presented revised concepts for the landing at Zapata wherein there would be air drops at first light with the landing at night and all of the ships away from the objective area by dawn. The President decided to go ahead with the Zapata planning; to see what we could do about increasing support to the guerrillas inside the country; to interrogate one member of the force to determine what he knows; and he reserved the right to call off the plan even up to 24 hours prior to the landing.[35]

According to an Editorial Note in the official records, Chief of Naval Operations Admiral Arleigh Albert Burke, who apparently also attended the March 16 meeting,

provided the [Joint Chiefs of Staff] with additional details about the discussion of the revised Zapata plan. According to Burke,

the President wanted to know what the consequences would be if the operation failed. He asked Burke how he viewed the operation's chance of success. Burke indicated that he had given the President a probability figure of about 50 percent. President Kennedy also inquired what would happen if it developed after the invasion that the Cuban exile force were pinned down and being slaughtered on the beach. If they were to be re-embarked, the President wanted to know where they could be taken. According to Burke's account of the meeting: "It was decided they would not be re-embarked because there was no place to go. Once they were landed they were there." **In the course of the discussion, it was emphasized that the plan was dependent on a general uprising in Cuba, and that the entire operation would fail without such an uprising.**[36]

President Kennedy conducted a further meeting on these issues on March 29. In attendance were, among others, McGeorge Bundy, McNamara, Dulles, Bissell, Mann, and Schlesinger. Details of the Zapata plan were discussed. The Editorial Note in the governmental records notes:

Secretary of Defense McNamara later recalled that the President issued instructions at this meeting that prior to the invasion the brigade leaders were to be informed that U.S. strike forces would not be allowed to participate in or support the invasion in any way. McNamara wrote that Kennedy asked that the brigade leaders be queried as to whether they believed the operation would be successful with this restriction and whether they wished on that basis to proceed. McNamara recalled that the President was subsequently informed that the brigade leaders indicated that, despite the prohibition on the use of U.S. strike forces, they wished to proceed with the invasion. McNamara noted that his recollection of these details was confirmed in discussions with McGeorge Bundy and Bissell.[37]

From 6:00 p.m. to 8:18 p.m. on April 4, President Kennedy met with members of the Joint Chiefs of Staff and others involved in the Zapata operation. General Gray's notes, prepared on May 8, state the following:

This meeting was held in the State Department and Senator Fulbright was also present. Senator Fulbright spoke out against the plan. The President again indicated his preference for an operation which would infiltrate the force in units of 200-250 and then develop them through a build up. Colonel Hawkins from CIA expressed the belief that landing small groups would merely serve to alert Castro and they would be eliminated one by one. He indicated that a group of 200 was below the critical number able to defend themselves. Mr. Rusk expressed opposition to the plan but Mr. [Adolph A.] Berle [Jr.] and Mr. Mann expressed general approval. Mr. McNamara also expressed approval of the general concept. The President indicated that he still wished to make the operation appear as an internal uprising and wished to consider the matter further the next morning.[38]

The official Editorial Note for this meeting adds: "After the conference with the President on April 4, **Secretary McNamara requested that the Joint Chiefs of Staff reconsider the rules of engagement for the Bumpy Road [Zapata] operation to ensure that the United States would not become overtly engaged with Castro's armed forces.**"[39]

Adolph A. Berle Jr. was a consultant to Secretary of State Rusk. In a later oral history interview, he was evidently referring to the April 4, 1961 meeting when reading from a memorandum he had written on or about May 3, 1961:

"At a subsequent White House meeting the plan was discussed. **By this time President Kennedy had made it clear that he would not back it with American forces. I had difficulty with this, but the president made known his decision and we had no further discussion on the point. The Joint Chiefs of Staff and the CIA thought the plan of getting ashore was a sound one. Thereafter, the success of the expedition depended entirely on its support within Cuba.** As it presented itself then, the operation was substantially a commando operation, getting into Cuba with a relatively small group of trained men—in other words, doing exactly what Fidel Castro had done.

The Joint Chiefs and the CIA were sure they could get ashore without opposition, and that adhesions would come automatically. I did not dissent, though two elements were absent: willingness of the United States to assume responsibility, and willingness to assume a cold war front levied against the United States would imply that America would lose force [face?] if need be."[40]

In an April 5 memorandum to President Kennedy, Special Assistant Arthur Schlesinger expressed opposition to the Zapata plan in a detailed analysis of the pros and cons.[41]

Per General Gray's notes, in an April 6 meeting with Rusk, McNamara, Dulles, Berle, Mann, Rusk, and others, "the President indicated a desire to use the force but he wanted to do everything possible to make it appear to be a Cuban operation partly from within Cuba but supported from without Cuba, the objective being to make it more plausible for US denial of association with the operation although recognizing that we would be accused." Other details of the Zapata plan were also discussed.[42]

At an April 12 White House meeting with Rusk, McNamara, Attorney General Robert Kennedy, General Lyman Lemnitzer (chairman of the Joint Chiefs of Staff), Bissell, and others, the CIA outlined the latest changes for the Zapata operation. President Kennedy did not give final approval to the CIA plan at this meeting. However he had gradually came around to supporting the operation with the condition that no US military forces would be directly involved.[43] On April 13, the CIA informed the leadership of the invasion brigade that "[t]he President has stated that under no conditions will U.S. intervene with any U.S. forces."[44]

After further developments, the military operation commenced on April 15 with air strikes by eight US airplanes disguised as planes in Castro's air force and manned by Cuban exile pilots. These attacks were only partially successful in achieving their mission of destroying Castro's actual air force. Meanwhile, air strikes scheduled for the afternoon of April 15 and for April 16 were canceled.[45]

On April 15, Castro immediately accused the United States of being behind the air assault. His foreign secretary requested and obtained an emergency meeting of the United Nations Political Committee for that afternoon. Adlai Stevenson, the US ambassador to the United Nations, had been given only the official cover story that these were Castro's pilots who had turned against him. The CIA, via intermediaries, communicated this fabrication to Stevenson despite the fact that, according to Schlesinger, President Kennedy had "told the group in the Cabinet Room that he wished Stevenson to be fully informed, and that nothing said at the UN should be less than the truth, even if it could not be the full truth. 'The integrity and credibility of Adlai Stevenson,' he had remarked to me on April 7, 'constitute one of our great national assets. I don't want anything to be done which might jeopardize that.' " Contrary to these explicit instructions, Stevenson had instead been told the mendacious cover story, and he unknowingly repeated that lie in the UN Political Committee that afternoon.[46]

The international political embarrassment of the United States over the CIA's absurd cover story seriously threatened US foreign policy around the world. Consequently, President Kennedy canceled a further airstrike, unless it could be sourced to a landing strip on a beachhead established by Cuban exile fighters at the Bay of Pigs. This, indeed, is what Kennedy thought he had authorized:

> It was now late Sunday [April 16] afternoon. When Rusk said that the projected strike was one which could only appear to come from Nicaragua, Kennedy said, "I'm not signed on to this"; the strike he knew about was the one coming ostensibly from the beachhead. After a long conversation, the President directed that the strike be canceled. When he put down the phone, he sat on in silence for a moment, shook his head and began to pace the room in evident concern, worried perhaps less about this decision than about the confusion in the planning; what would go wrong next?[47]

In response to the April 15 air attacks, Castro had thousands of suspected dissenters arrested. Dozens of alleged spies or traitors were executed during the following days. These actions helped prevent any coup or mass uprising against Castro on the island.[48] This development should not have been a surprise. Schlesinger noted: "It was . . . recognized that the pre-invasion strikes would probably cause Castro to move against the underground; but, since CIA did not put much stock in the underground anyway, its elimination was considered less important than the elimination of Castro's air power."[49]

President Kennedy had reserved the right to cancel the imminent land invasion of the Bay of Pigs up to twenty-four hours before the event. On Sunday, April 16, Richard Bissell waited anxiously, alone at his desk at the CIA. Finally, the call from the president arrived. "Go ahead," he ordered.[50]

The Bay of Pigs land invasion turned out to be a disaster. Somehow, the CIA and others had failed to adequately explain to Kennedy that the Cuban air force planes that had survived the April 15 attack could seriously threaten the viability of the April 17 land invasion. On the other hand, it is arguable that JFK, who had been a commissioned naval officer in World War II and had famously experienced actual combat in that war, should have known better. Notwithstanding the immense historical literature on the Bay of Pigs episode, the precise details of what the president knew about these matters at the relevant time is still not entirely clear. Schlesinger, who has been derided by some as the official Kennedy court historian, wrote that "[t]he Cuban air force, according to the CIA estimate, was 'entirely disorganized,' its planes 'for the most part obsolete and inoperative,' its combat efficiency 'almost nonexistent.' "[51] If this statement reflects what the CIA actually communicated to the president at that time, it might help explain why Kennedy made the decision to cancel a further pre-invasion air strike.

However this may be, in the evening of April 16, CIA Deputy Director Cabell and CIA Director of Plans Bissell, deeply disturbed by the decision [to cancel the April 17 pre-invasion air strike], arrived at [Secretary of State] Rusk's office . . . and tried to reopen the case. They argued that both the flotilla and the landing would be endangered if there were no dawn strike. Rusk replied that the ships could unload in darkness before Castro's planes located them and that after the landing the B-26s could defend the beaches from airstrips on shore. The vigorous discussion gave Rusk the impression that CIA regarded the Nicaraguan strike as important but not vital. He suggested to Cabell and Bissell that, if they wanted to carry their case further, they could appeal to the President, but they declined to do so.[52]

No matter what the CIA and other officials did or did not tell Kennedy, the quantity and quality of Castro's land and air forces were sufficient to cause substantial damage to the invading forces on and after April 17. The first impediment was the existence of coral reefs—previously undetected by US intelligence—that forced the exile forces to disembark from their landing crafts much farther out from the beach than had been planned. Then, they met hostile fire from a Cuban militia. "At nine-thirty in the morning, a [Castro plane] sank the ship carrying the ammunition reserve for the next ten days and most of the communications equipment: an inexplicable concentration of treasure in a single hull. Other ships suffered damage, and the rest of the flotilla put out to sea." Necessary supplies—food, medical, and ammunition—for the Cuban exile forces were lost, and the invaders eventually ran out of ammunition. Castro's substantial infantry forces moved into the area and fought the exiles. By April 19, the jig was up. The invasion had failed, and most of the anti-Castro invaders surrendered.[53]

That same day, CIA Director Allen Dulles met with Richard Nixon and told the former vice president about President Kennedy's decision to cancel the air strikes. "I should have told him that we must not fail. And I came very close to doing so, but I didn't," Dulles said. "It was the greatest mistake of my life."[54]

Although I do not agree with all of the interpretations and conclusions of Jim Rasenberger's well-researched book *The Brilliant Disaster: JFK, Castro, and America's Doomed Invasion of Cuba's Bay of Pigs*, I think some of his assessments are on point. For example, he accurately describes the overall quandary of the Bay of Pigs problem as follows:

> The operation was, in fact, undertaken by well-intentioned people attempting to achieve the best solution to what they perceived to be a serious problem. Castro's ouster, most Americans believed at the time, was a requirement of national security. Given the risks of overt action, a covert operation was judged to be a safer method. Eisenhower set the "Program" in motion based on this assumption, and once that snowball began to roll and grow, it was nearly unstoppable. Coming into office in the winter of 1961, Kennedy found himself

instantly in a bind. On the one hand, he could not easily halt the operation; on the other hand, he grasped the potential for serious repercussions if he went ahead; and on the third hand—you needed more than two to grapple with this mess—nobody had any better ideas for getting rid of Castro.[55]

Rasenberger explains the more concrete issues as follows:

But what would have happened had the beachhead been sustained? Could the invasion ever have achieved its ultimate goal of overthrowing Fidel Castro? Probably not.

As the CIA understood from the very beginning, there were only two ways an operation that pitted fourteen hundred men against a national army made sense over the long term. The first was for the brigade to somehow spark an internal reaction against Castro by serving as "a rallying point for the thousands who are estimated to be ready for overt resistance," as described in an early briefing paper for Secretary Rusk. The second was for an American military presence to sooner or later make itself known in Cuba. "If matters do not eventuate as predicted above," the CIA informed Rusk, "the lodgment established by our force can be used as the site for establishment of a provisional government which can be recognized by the United States, and hopefully by other American States."[56]

Ultimately, however, success in this enterprise may have entangled the United States in a quagmire similar to that which it later encountered in Vietnam:

> The United States would have become an occupying force in Cuba. The administration would have been faced not only with the prospect of fighting "house to house in Havana," as Richard Goodwin predicted, but also contending with resentment from countries throughout Latin America. And the Soviet Union—what would Khrushchev have done? The consequences can only be imagined, but they were potentially catastrophic. "An invasion force that succeeded in overthrowing Castro without a demonstrative show of popular support," wrote the historian Theodore Draper in 1962, "could have ruled Cuba only in a state of perpetual civil war or as a thinly disguised American occupation."[57]

Accordingly, it is my view that the entire Bay of Pigs project should never have been pursued by the presidential administrations of Dwight D. Eisenhower and John F. Kennedy. The risks and possible downsides were too great.

OPERATION MONGOOSE AND PLOTS TO ASSASSINATE CASTRO

President John F. Kennedy and his brother, Attorney General Robert F. Kennedy ("RFK"), blamed the CIA for not properly advising JFK regarding the Bay of Pigs operation. Consequently, Allen Dulles was replaced by John McCone as CIA director on November 29, 1961, and Richard Bissell was replaced by Richard Helms as CIA director of plans on February 17, 1962.[58]

Notwithstanding the Bay of Pigs fiasco, JFK and RFK still hoped to overthrow the Castro regime. In November 1961, the president authorized Operation Mongoose, a project to engage in sabotage, economic coercion, psychological warfare, and other covert activities in Cuba. Contingency plans were drawn for US military action. At one point, however, Mongoose was limited to intelligence gathering and sabotage operations. As it had done in the Eisenhower administration, the CIA formulated and attempted to execute plots to assassinate Castro, but all such plots were unsuccessful.[59]

In October of 1962, everything changed when the US government learned that the Soviet Union was installing nuclear-tipped missiles in Cuba. See chapter 5 ("Case Study: Political Leadership in the 1962 Cuban Missile Crisis") of this book.

NOTES

Preface

[1] *The Analects of Confucius*, trans. and ed. Simon Leys (New York: W. W. Norton, 1997), 2.17.

[2] Alan E. Johnson, *Free Will and Human Life* (Pittsburgh, PA: Philosophia, 2021).

[3] Alan E. Johnson, *Reason and Human Ethics* (Pittsburgh, PA: Philosophia, 2022).

[4] Alan E. Johnson, *The First American Founder: Roger Williams and Freedom of Conscience* (Philosophia, 2015); Johnson, *The Electoral College: Failures of Original Intent and Proposed Constitutional and Statutory Changes for Direct Popular Vote*, 2nd ed. (Philosophia, 2021).

[5] https://chicago.academia.edu/AlanJohnson.

[6] https://www.goodreads.com/group/show/137714-political-philosophy-and-ethics.

Introduction

[1] Cf. Leo Strauss, *What Is Political Philosophy? and Other Studies* (Free Press, 1959), 11–12: "Of philosophy thus understood, political philosophy is a branch. Political philosophy will then be the attempt to replace opinion about the nature of political things by knowledge of the nature of political things."

[2] Alan E. Johnson, *Reason and Human Ethics* (Philosophia, 2022).

Chapter 1. Is Government Necessary?

[1] Max Weber, "Politics as a Vocation," in Weber, *The Vocation Lectures*, ed. David Owen and Tracy B. Strong, trans. Rodney Livingstone (Hackett, 2004) (italics in the original), Kindle.

2 *Merriam-Webster Dictionary*, "anarchism," accessed December 29, 2025, https://www.merriam-webster.com/dictionary/anarchism.

3 Matthew Sanger, "Anarchic Theory and the Study of Hunter-Gatherers," *The SAA Archaeological Record* 17, no. 1 (2017): 39–44, https://theanarchistlibrary.org/library/matthew-sanger-anarchic-theory-and-the-study-of-hunter-gatherers.

4 Murray N. Rothbard, *For a New Liberty: A Libertarian Manifesto*, 2nd ed. (Ludwig von Mises Institute, 2006), Kindle.

5 Murray N. Rothbard, *Power and Market: Government and the Economy*, 4th edition (Ludwig von Mises Institute, 2006), Kindle (first edition published in 1970 by the Institute for Humane Studies).

6 Murray N. Rothbard, *The Ethics of Liberty* (New York University Press, 2002), Kindle (first edition published 1982).

7 Rothbard, *For a New Liberty*, 27, 28.

8 J. Michael Oliver, *The New Libertarianism: Anarcho-Capitalism* (published by the author, 2013).

9 Murray N. Rothbard (Aubrey Herbert, pseud.), "Are Libertarians 'Anarchists'?," 1950s, https://archive.lewrockwell.com/rothbard/rothbard167.html.

10 Rothbard, *The Ethics of Liberty*, "Preface."

11 Rothbard, *The Ethics of Liberty*,172–73.

12 Rothbard, *For a New Liberty*, 241–42.

13 Rothbard, *For a New Liberty*, 242–43 (italics in the original, bold emphasis added).

14 See chapter 11 ("II. The Public Sector: Streets and Roads") of *For a New Liberty*.

15 Rothbard, *For a New Liberty*, 255.

16 Georgetown Law, Institute for Constitutional Advocacy and Protection, "Fact Sheet: Private Security Services," accessed July 20, 2025, https://www.law.georgetown.edu/icap/wp-

content/uploads/sites/32/2024/05/Private-Security-Forces-Fact-Sheet_FINAL.pdf.

[17] Holley South, "Is It Legal for a Security Guard to Detain You?," FindLaw, last updated June 2, 2022, https://www.findlaw.com/legalblogs/criminal-defense/is-it-legal-for-a-security-guard-to-detain-you/.

[18] Rothbard, *For a New Liberty*, 282–91.

[19] Rothbard, *The Ethics of Liberty*, 89.

[20] The scenario in this and the following paragraph is based on Rothbard's discussion in Chapter 12 of *For a New Liberty*.

[21] "A Declaration of Some Proceedings of Lt. Col. John Lilburne," 1648, in *The Leveller Tracts*, ed. William Haller and Godfrey Davies (Peter Smith, 1944), 120 (spelling as in the original).

[22] Rothbard, *For a New Liberty*, 296 (italics in the original).

[23] Rothbard, *For a New Liberty*, 297–98.

[24] Rothbard, *For a New Liberty*, 298-300.

[25] Wikipedia, "German military administration in occupied France during World War II," last modified, December 1, 2025, 12:05 (UTC), https://en.wikipedia.org/w/index.php?title=German_military_administration_in_occupied_France_during_World_War_II&action=history.

[26] Rothbard, *For a New Liberty*, 248.

Chapter 2. Governmental Recognition and Protection of Individual Rights

[1] Robert Kagan, *Rebellion: How Antiliberalism Is Tearing America Apart—Again* (Knopf Doubleday, 2024), 13, Kindle; cf. Leo Strauss, *Natural Right and History* (University of Chicago Press, 1953), 1–2.

[2] *Merriam-Webster's Unabridged Dictionary*, s.v. "judicial review," accessed December 30, 2025, https://unabridged.merriam-webster.com/unabridged/judicial%20review.

[3] United Nations Universal Declaration of Human Rights, proclaimed by the United Nations General Assembly, December 10, 1948, https://www.un.org/en/about-us/universal-declaration-of-human-rights. For the history of the UDHR, see the official UN history at https://www.un.org/en/about-us/udhr/history-of-the-declaration, the *Encyclopedia Brittanica* article at https://www.britannica.com/topic/Universal-Declaration-of-Human-Rights (accessed December 30, 2025), and the Wikipedia article at https://en.wikipedia.org/wiki/Universal_Declaration_of_Human_Rights (accessed December 30, 2025).

[4] Declaration of Independence of the United States of America, proclaimed by the Second Continental Congress, July 4, 1776, https://founders.archives.gov/documents/Jefferson/01-01-02-0176-0006.

[5] United States Constitution, https://constitutioncenter.org/the-constitution/full-text.

[6] For explanations of the status of individual rights in many different countries, see the various discussions of same in John McCormick, Rod Hague, and Martin Harrop, *Comparative Government and Politics*, 13th ed. (Bloomsbury Academic, 2025). For individual rights recognized by the European Union, see Ulrich Haltern, *The Constitution of the European Union: A Contextual Analysis* (Hart, 2025), esp. chap. 7.

[7] Alan E. Johnson, "John Locke, Thomas Jefferson, Abraham Lincoln, and the Declaration of Independence," Academia.edu, August 9, 2024, https://www.academia.edu/122721285/John_Locke_Thomas_Jefferson_Abraham_Lincoln_and_the_Declaration_of_Independence; Alan E. Johnson, "Deism, Unitarianism, and the US Founders," Academia.edu, August 29, 2015, https://www.academia.edu/15269565/Deism_Unitarianism_and_the_US_Founders.

[8] See, for example the following: AvvoStories, "8 People Who Were Executed and Later Found Innocent," May 5, 2010, https://stories.avvo.com/crime/murder/8-people-who-were-executed-and-later-found-innocent.html; Death Penalty Information Center, "Executed But Possibly Innocent," accessed December 30, 2025, https://deathpenaltyinfo.org/policy-issues/policy/innocence/executed-but-possibly-innocent.

[9] Melanie A. Howard, "What the Bible actually says about abortion may surprise you," *Religious News*, July 25, 2022, https://religionnews.com/2022/07/25/what-the-bible-actually-says-about-abortion-may-surprise-you/.

[10] *Roe v. Wade*, 410 U.S. 113 (1973), which can be located at https://www.loc.gov/resource/usrep.usrep410113/?pdfPage=1.

[11] *Dobbs v. Jackson Women's Health Organization*, 597 U.S. 215 (2022), which can be located at https://www.supremecourt.gov/opinions/21pdf/597us1r58_gebh.pdf.

[12] John E. Nowak and Donald D. Rotunda, *Constitutional Law*, 8th ed. (West, 2010), § 13.4(a), p. 648, Kindle.

[13] Douglas A. Blackmon, *Slavery by Another Name: The Re-Enslavement of Black Americans from the Civil War to World War II* (Anchor Books, 2008), Kindle.

[14] See Alan E. Johnson, "Due Process, Procedural," in *Encyclopedia of the U.S. Supreme Court*, ed. Thomas T. Lewis and Richard L. Wilson (Salem Press, 2001), 1:290–92.

[15] Apart from due process, the US Supreme Court frequently analyzes criminal procedure in terms of the Fourth, Fifth, and Sixth Amendments (applied to state and local governments by way of the Fourteenth Amendment). These detailed constitutional protections, as well as the subject of "substantive due process," are beyond the scope of the present book, as are the related provisions of Articles 9–12 of the UDHR.

[16] *Board of Regents v. Roth*, 408 U.S. 566, 572 (1972) (bold emphasis added).

[17] Thomas Jefferson to John Trumbull, February 15, 1789, *Founders Online,* National Archives, https://founders.archives.gov/documents/Jefferson/01-14-02-0321.

[18] Thomas Jefferson to John Minor, August 30, 1814, including Thomas Jefferson to Bernard Moore, [ca. 1773?]," *Founders Online,* National Archives, https://founders.archives.gov/documents/Jefferson/03-07-02-0455 (bold emphasis added).

[19] John Locke, *An Essay Concerning Human Understanding,* ed. Peter H. Nidditch (Oxford University Press, 1975), bk. 2, chap. 21, §§ 51–52 (quotations at § 51, p. 266, bold emphasis added); cf. Johnson, *Reason and Human Ethics*, chaps. 2–3.

[20] See Alan E. Johnson, "Property Rights," in *Encyclopedia of the U.S. Supreme Court*, ed. Thomas T. Lewis and Richard L. Wilson (Salem Press, 2001), 2:751–55, for a summary of the constitutional history of property rights.

[21] For historical details, see Alan E. Johnson, *The First American Founder: Roger Williams and Freedom of Conscience* (Philosophia, 2015).

[22] Brown University, Watson Institute for International & Public Affairs, "Torture," https://watson.brown.edu/costsofwar/costs/social/rights/torture.

[23] *United States v. Windsor*, 570 U.S. 744, 769 (2013); *Weinberger v. Wiesenfeld*, 420 U.S. 636, 638 n.2 (1975) ("This Court's approach to Fifth Amendment equal protection claims has always been precisely the same as to equal protection claims under the Fourteenth Amendment"); *Bolling v. Sharpe*, 570 U. S. 744, 769–70 (1954).

[24] For a general account of judicial review, see Richard L. Wilson, "Judicial Review," in *Encyclopedia of the U.S. Supreme Court*, ed. Thomas T. Lewis and Richard L. Wilson (Salem Press, 2001), 2:521–26.

[25] See McCormick et al., *Comparative Government and Politics*, 13th ed., 167–75, Kindle.

[26] To my knowledge, the version of *The Federalist* that is most faithful to the original (as edited by the original authors) is the Gideon edition, which is currently available in print as follows: Alexander Hamilton, John Jay, and James Madison, *The Federalist*, Gideon edition, edited by George W. Carey and James McClellan (Liberty Fund, 2001). This publication is freely available online for viewing and download at https://oll.libertyfund.org/titles/jay-the-federalist-gideon-ed.

[27] The opponents of the ratification of the Constitution were called the Anti-Federalists. Their tracts, which address the federal judiciary provisions of the proposed Constitution as well as many other issues, are contained in *The Complete Anti-Federalist*, edited with commentary and notes by Herbert J. Storing (University of Chicago Press, 1981). A convenient abridgement of this work is *The Anti-Federalist: Writings by the Opponents of the Constitution*, edited by Herbert J. Storing and selected by Murray Dry from *The Complete Anti-Federalist* (University of Chicago Press, 1985). See also Herbert J. Storing, *What the Anti-Federalists Were For: The Political Thought of the Opponents of the Constitution* (University of Chicago Press, 1981) and numerous other books and essays about the Anti-Federalists.

[28] U.S. Const. art. 2, § 4.

[29] *Marbury v. Madison*, 5 U.S. (1 Cranch) 137 (1803), https://www.loc.gov/resource/usrep.usrep005137/.

[30] U.S. Const. art. 3, § 9, cl. 2.

[31] *Marbury*, 5 U.S. at 136–38.

[32] *Id.* at 173–81.

[33] *Id.* at 176–80 (italics in the original).

[34] *Id.* at 179–80 (italics in the original).

[35] Ciara Torres-Spelliscy, "The History of Corporate Personhood," Brennan Center for Justice, April 8, 2014, https://www.brennancenter.org/our-work/analysis-opinion/history-corporate-personhood.

Notes

Chapter 3. Legitimate Affirmative Powers of Government

[1] For general legal histories, see, among other books, John Maxcy Zane, *The Story of Law*, 2nd ed. (Liberty Fund, 1998, originally published in 1927 by Ives Washburn); Oliver Wendell Holmes, *The Common Law*, ed. Mark DeWolfe Howe (Back Bay Books, 1936, originally published in 1881 by Little, Brown); Arthur R. Hogue, *Origins of the Common Law* (Liberty Fund, 1986); and Lawrence M. Friedman, *A History of American Law*, 4th ed. (Oxford University Press, 2019).

[2] John Locke, *The Second Treatise of Government*, in Locke, *Two Treatises of Government*, ed. Peter Laslett (Cambridge University Press, 1988), §§ 87, 123, 143 (italics and capitalization as in the original), Kindle.

[3] Locke, *Second Treatise of Government*, §§ 124–26 (italics, capitalization, and spelling as in the original, bold emphasis added).

[4] Locke, *Second Treatise of Government*, §§ 4, 6–8, 26, 31–33, 36–38, 45–50, 77–243.

[5] Zane, *The Story of Law*, 2nd ed., 218 (Kindle edition, 236) (bold emphasis added).

[6] Legal Dictionary, "Tort Law," accessed January 3, 2026, https://legaldictionary.net/tort-law/.

[7] See, for example, Joseph E. Stiglitz, *The Road to Freedom: Economics and the Good Society* (W. W. Norton, 2024), esp. chap. 3, Kindle; Richard H. Thaler, *Misbehaving: The Making of Behavioral Economics* (W. W. Norton, 2015), Kindle; Robert J. Shiller, *Irrational Exuberance*, rev. and exp. 3rd ed. (Princeton University Press, 2015), Kindle; Justin Fox, *The Myth of the Rational Market: A History of Risk, Reward, and Delusion on Wall Street* (HarperCollins, 2009); Robert B. Reich, *The Common Good* (Alfred A. Knopf, 2018), esp. 81–82, Kindle; and Bethany McLean and Joe Nocera, *All the Devils Are Here: The Hidden History of the Financial Crisis* (Portfolio, 2010), Kindle. For an excellent discussion of the various alternative approaches to political economy, see Lucas McGranahan, "Delicate Dance: Two Faculty Projects

Examine the Awkward Partnership Between Democracy and Capitalism," *University of Chicago Magazine* 117, no. 1 (Fall 2024): 27–31, https://mag.uchicago.edu/law-policy-society/delicate-dance.

[8] Alan E. Johnson, *The First American Founder: Roger Williams and Freedom of Conscience* (Philosophia, 2015).

[9] Alan E. Johnson, *Reason and Human Ethics* (Philosophia, 2022).

[10] Alan E. Johnson, *Free Will and Human Life* (Philosophia, 2021).

[11] See, generally, Reich, "Civic Education for All," chap. 10 in *The Common Good*.

[12] See, on this and other educational issues, Diane Ravitch, *An Education: How I Changed My Mind about Schools and Almost Everything Else* (Columbia University Press, 2025).

[13] See the video of this February 28, 2025 conference at https://www.bing.com/videos/riverview/relatedvideo?&q=zelensky+trump+meeting+video&qpvt=zelensky+trump+meeting+video&mid=635A95F4CB23A3D85330635A95F4CB23A3D85330&&FORM=VRDGAR. A partial transcript is at https://en.wikisource.org/wiki/Transcript_of_the_2025_Trump%E2%80%93Zelenskyy_meeting.

[14] https://www.thisdayinquotes.com/2022/04/we-have-met-the-enemy-and-he-is-us/.

[15] Annie Lowry, "How the Richest People in America Avoid Paying Taxes," *The Atlantic*, August 25, 2025, https://www.theatlantic.com/economy/archive/2025/08/billionaire-tax-study/683987/?gift=jvRXZia7Ag6tGK6Imt0JSx7BaigEIQHVDEbcbO1mVx0; Akcan S. Balkir et al., "How Much Tax Do US Billionaires Pay? Evidence from Administrative Data," National Bureau of Economic Research, Working Paper 34170, August 2025, https://www.nber.org/papers/w34170, https://gabriel-zucman.eu/files/BSYZ2025NBER.pdf; Chuck Marr, Samantha Jacoby and Kathleen Bryant, "Substantial Income of Wealthy Households Escapes Annual Taxation Or

Enjoys Special Tax Breaks: Reform Is Needed," Center on Budget and Policy Priorities, November 13, 2019, https://www.cbpp.org/research/substantial-income-of-wealthy-households-escapes-annual-taxation-or-enjoys-special-tax; Kelley R. Taylor, "IRS Updates Capital Gains Tax Thresholds: What to Know," Kiplinger, November 7, 2024, https://www.kiplinger.com/taxes/new-irs-long-term-capital-gains-tax-thresholds; Anna-Louise Jackson and Ashley Barnett (ed. Miranda Marquit), "What Are Capital Gains Taxes?," Buy Side from WSJ, February 18, 2025, https://www.wsj.com/buyside/personal-finance/taxes/capital-gains-tax.

[16] Ayn Rand, *The Virtue of Selfishness: A New Concept of Egoism* (Signet Books, 1964).

[17] Rand, 112 (Kindle page 149) (italics in the original).

[18] Rand, chaps. 14 and 15.

Chapter 4. Forms of Government

[1] James Madison in the Virginia Ratifying Convention, June 20, 1788, *Documentary History of the Ratification of the Constitution,* digital edition, ed. John P. Kaminski and Gaspare J. Saladino (University of Virginia Press, 2009), 10:1417, http://rotunda.upress.virginia.edu/founders/RNCN-02-10-02-0002-0009.

[2] See Alan E. Johnson, *Reason and Human Ethics* (Philosophia, 2022), esp. chap. 5 ("Citizen and Media Ethics").

[3] Johnson, *Reason and Human Ethics*, esp. chaps. 1 and 2.

[4] For a discussion of feudalism, see *Britannica*, "Feudalism," last updated December 5, 2025, https://www.britannica.com/topic/feudalism.

[5] *Merriam-Webster Unabridged Dictionary*, s.v. "mercantilism," accessed January 4, 2026, https://unabridged.merriam-webster.com/unabridged/mercantilism.

[6] Ralph Lerner, "Prologue: Commerce and Character: The Anglo-American as New-Model Man" (1979) (quoting

Montesquieu, *De L'Esprit des Lois*, III, 7, IV, 2, XIII, 1), in *Commerce and Character: The Political Economy of the Enlightenment and the American Founding*, ed. Steven Frankel and John Ray (University Press of Kansas, 2025), 13–14, Kindle.

[7] See, among other discussions, Alan E. Johnson, *The First American Founder: Roger Williams and Freedom of Conscience* (Philosophia, 2015), chap. 10; Matthew D. Taylor, *The Violent Take It by Force: The Christian Movement That Is Threatening Our Democracy* (Broadleaf Books, 2024), Kindle; and Katherine Stewart, *Money, Lies, and God: Inside the Movement to Destroy American Democracy*, (Bloomsbury, 2025), Kindle.

[8] Declaration of Independence of the United States of America, July 4, 2024, https://www.archives.gov/founding-docs/declaration-transcript#:~:text=We%2C%20therefore%2C%20the%20Rep resentatives%20of%20the%20united%20States,Things%20w hich%20Independent%20States%20may%20of%20right%20d o.

[9] Julian P. Boyd, *The Declaration of Independence: The Evolution of the Text*, rev. ed., ed. Gerard W. Gewalt (Library of Congress, 1999), 60 (Document IV), 67 (Document V) (emphasis added). Note: Jefferson had initially written "sacred & undeniable" instead of "self-evident," and it is not clear whether Jefferson or another committee member changed that language to "self-evident," but the change was made early on in the process. Boyd, 26-27. For further information, see Alan E. Johnson, "John Locke, Thomas Jefferson, Abraham Lincoln, and the Declaration Of Independence," Academia.edu, August 11, 2024, https://www.academia.edu/122721285/John_Locke_Thomas_ Jefferson_Abraham_Lincoln_and_the_Declaration_of_Indepe ndence.

[10] James Madison, *Federalist* no. 10, https://founders.archives.gov/documents/Madison/01-09-02-0001.

[11] The text of the United States Constitution and amendments thereto can be accessed at https://constitutioncenter.org/the-constitution/full-text.

[12] US Constitution, Preamble (emphasis added).

[13] See *McCulloch v. Maryland*, 17 U.S. 316, 402-5, 412 (1819) ("A government is created by the people, having legislative, executive, and judicial powers").

[14] James Madison, *Federalist* no. 39, https://founders.archives.gov/documents/Madison/01-10-02-0234.

[15] See Alan E. Johnson, *The Electoral College: Failures of Original Intent and Proposed Constitutional and Statutory Changes for Direct Popular Vote*, 2nd ed. (Philosophia, 2021), chap. 1 ("The Intentions of the Framers of the Electoral College") and the appendix ("A Detailed Narrative of the Debates in the 1787 Constitutional Convention on the Selection of the President").

[16] Mary Annette Pember, "Death by Civilization," *The Atlantic*, March 8, 2019, https://www.theatlantic.com/education/archive/2019/03/traumatic-legacy-indian-boarding-schools/584293/?gift=jvRXZia7Ag6tGK6Imt0JS2rcpc2iGtom79oBTnCkGaw&utm_source=copy-link&utm_medium=social&utm_campaign=share.

[17] *McCulloch v. Maryland*, 17 U.S. at 407, 415, 421 (1819). See, generally, Erwin Chemerinksy, *Worse Than Nothing: The Dangerous Fallacy of Originalism* (Yale University Press, 2022), Kindle; David A. Strauss, *The Living Constitution* (Oxford University Press, 2010), Kindle; Richard L. Hasen, *The Justice of Contradictions: Antonin Scalia and the Politics of Disruption* (Yale University Press, 2018), Kindle; and Jack N. Rakove, *Original Meanings: Politics and Ideas in the Making of the Constitution* (Vintage Books, 1997), Kindle.

[18] See John E. Nowak and Donald D. Rotunda, *Constitutional Law*, 8th ed. (West, 2010), §§ 5.6(a)– 5.6(b)(iii), pp. 231–35, Kindle (discussing cases).

[19] For details, see John McCormick et al., *Comparative Government and Politics*, 13th ed. (Bloomsbury Academic, 2025), 200, 288–89, Kindle.

[20] For details regarding the United Kingdom, see McCormick, *Comparative Government and Politics*, 234–35. Additional information about the UK and other parliamentary democracies is scattered throughout McCormick's book. See also Peter Leyland, *The Constitution of the United Kingdom: A Contextual Analysis*, 4th ed. (Hart, 2021), Kindle.

[21] See, for example, Ulrich Haltern, *The Constitution of the European Union: A Contextual Analysis* (Hart, 2025).

[22] Plato, *Apology of Socrates*; Plato, *Crito*; Plato, *Phaedo*; Xenophon, *Apology of Socrates to the Jury*.

[23] Leo Strauss, *The Argument and the Action of Plato's "Laws"* (University of Chicago Press, 1975), 1.

[24] Plato, *Republic* 450c–d, 471c–473c, 591c–592b; Leo Strauss, *The City and Man* (Rand McNally, 1964), 63 ("we are thus prepared for the possibility that the restoration attempted in the *Republic* will not take place on the political plane"), 138 ("As Cicero has observed, the *Republic* does not bring to light the best possible regime, but rather the nature of the city [citing Cicero, *De republica* II 53]—the nature of political things"); Leo Strauss, "Plato," in *History of Political Philosophy*, 3rd ed., ed. Leo Strauss and Joseph Cropsey (University of Chicago Press, 1987), 34 ("there are also a few indications in the *Republic* to the effect that the longed-for reformation is not likely to succeed on the political plane or that the only possible reformation is that of the individual man").

[25] Strauss, *City and Man*, 138 ("the *Republic* . . . abstracts from the body and *eros*; by abstracting from the body and *eros*, the *Republic* in fact abstracts from the soul; the *Republic* abstracts from nature" [italics in the original]); cf. *Republic* 450c. See also Aristotle's critique of the *Republic* in Book 2 of his treatise titled *Politics*.

[26] Jaqueisse, *The Philosopher Kingdom* (Jabroni, 2024), Kindle.

Notes

[27] Alan E. Johnson, "Review of Jaqueisse's *The Philosopher Kingdom*," Academia.edu, June 12, 2024, https://www.academia.edu/120896197/Review_of_Jaqueisses_The_Philosopher_Kingdom_.

[28] Jason Brennan, *Against Democracy, with a New Preface* (Princeton University Press, 2017), 14, Kindle.

[29] Alan E. Johnson, "From Philosopher Kings to Libertarian Elitists: A Critical Appraisal of Jason Brennan, *Against Democracy*," Academia.edu, October 23, 2023, https://www.academia.edu/106405232/From_Philosopher_Kings_to_Libertarian_Elitists_A_Critical_Appraisal_of_Jason_Brennan_Against_Democracy_With_A_New_2017_Preface_by_the_Author_Princeton_Princeton_University_Press_2017_edited_June_7_2024_.

[30] See, for example, Ricardo Neves e Castro, *Global Disorder: The World Adrift* (pub. by author, 2024), 312–15, Kindle.

[31] McCormick, *Comparative Government and Politics*, 126.

[32] On authoritarianism generally, see chapter 5 ("Authoritarian Rule") of *Comparative Government and Politics* as well as scattered discussions of authoritarianism throughout that book. See also *Constitutions in Authoritarian Regimes*, ed. Tom Ginsburg and Alberto Simpser (Cambridge University Press, 2014), Kindle; Timothy Snyder, *On Tyranny: Twenty Lessons from the Twentieth Century* (Tim Duggan Books, 2017), Kindle; Snyder, *The Road to Unfreedom: Russia, Europe, America* (Crown, 2018), Kindle; Ruth Ben-Ghiat, *Strongmen: Mussolini to the Present* (Norton, 2020), Kindle; Anne Applebaum, *Twilight of Democracy: The Seductive Lure of Authoritarianism* (Vintage, 2020), Kindle; Applebaum, *Autocracy, Inc: The Dictators Who Want to Rule the World* (Doubleday, 2024), Kindle; Pippa Norris, and Robert Inglehart, *Cultural Backlash: Trump, Brexit, and Authoritarian Populism* (Cambridge University Press, 2019), Kindle; and Erica Frantz, *Authoritarianism: What Everyone Needs to Know* (Oxford University Press, 2018), Kindle. For a discussion of the authoritarianism of Vladimir Putin and the

emerging authoritarianism of Donald J. Trump (first presidential term), see chapters 5 and 6 passim of Johnson, *Reason and Human Ethics*. With regard to Putin, see also Nina Khrushcheva, "Russia's Descent Into Tyranny: How Four Years of War Have Remade Society," *Foreign Affairs*, December 30, 2025, https://www.foreignaffairs.com/russia/russias-descent-tyranny. Trump's second term, as of this writing (December 2025), is clearly an attempt to actualize an authoritarian regime, as can be authenticated by many journalistic and other sources too numerous to cite here. For an excellent account of Trump's authoritarian measures in his second term, as of December 11, 2025, see Stephen Levitsky et al., "The Price of American Authoritarianism: What Can Reverse Democratic Decline?," *Foreign Affairs*, December 11, 2025, https://www.foreignaffairs.com/united-states/american-authoritarianism-levitsky-way-ziblatt. See also parts II and III of Joonhong Park, *Another Civil War: Why Our Instincts Choose Trumpism over Democracy?* (pub. by author, 2025).

[33] McCormick, *Comparative Government and Politics*, 113.

[34] See, generally, David D. Roberts, *Totalitarianism* (Polity, 2020), Kindle. See also Johnson, *Reason and Human Ethics*, 140–44 (discussion of Stalin and Hitler). In the present book, see the sections "The Marxist Roots of Soviet Communism" and "The Bolshevik Revolution and Its Aftermath" in the appendix ("The Historical Background of the 1962 Cuban Missile Crisis") and the subsection "Communist Theory and Practice" in Chapter 5 ("Case Study: Political Leadership in the 1962 Cuban Missile Crisis").

[35] George Orwell, *1984* (Mariner Books, 1949). Many editions of this book have been published over the decades.

[36] Among other references, see Alan E. Johnson, "Theocracy in Sixteenth-Century Geneva and Seventeenth-Century Massachusetts Bay," app. B in *The First American Founder*; Matthew D. Taylor, *The Violent Take It by Force*; and *Britannica*, "Theocracy," last updated Nov. 21, 2025, https://www.britannica.com/topic/theocracy.

[37] Margaret Atwood, *The Handmaid's Tale* (Ecco, 1986). The six seasons of the television series based on this novel are currently available on Hulu and Amazon Prime Video.

[38] See Johnson, *The Electoral College.*

[39] See Wikipedia, "Ranked-choice voting in the United States," last modified, January 1, 2026, 12:45 (UTC), https://en.wikipedia.org/wiki/Ranked-choice_voting_in_the_United_States.

[40] See Wikipedia, "Independent agencies of the United States federal government," last modified Oct. 2, 2025, 06:17 (UTC), https://en.wikipedia.org/wiki/Independent_agencies_of_the_United_States_federal_government.

[41] Cf. *Britannica*, "Sovereignty," last updated Dec. 8, 2024, https://www.britannica.com/topic/sovereignty.

[42] Confucius, *The Great Learning*, ¶¶ 6 and 7, in *The Chinese Classics*, trans. and ed. James Legge, vol. 1, *The Life and Teachings of Confucius*, 2nd ed. (London: N. Trüber, 1869), 267 (italics in the Legge translation), https://babel.hathitrust.org/cgi/pt?id=uva.x000304472&view=1up&seq=7&skin=2021 (also available in a 2016 Owlfoot Kindle edition with Trüber print edition pagination in brackets, https://www.amazon.com/gp/product/B01MCUC6UD/ref=ppx_yo_dt_b_d_asin_title_o02?ie=UTF8&psc=1).

Chapter 5. Case Study: Political Leadership in the 1962 Cuban Missile Crisis

[1] Graham Allison, "The Cuban Missile Crisis at 50: Lessons for U.S. Foreign Policy Today," *Foreign Affairs*, July 1, 2012, https://www.foreignaffairs.com/articles/cuba/2012-07-01/cuban-missile-crisis-50.

[2] Alan E. Johnson, *Reason and Human Ethics* (Philosophia, 2022), esp. chap. 2 ("Human Reason").

[3] See, for example, John McCormick, Rod Hague, and Martin Harrop, *Comparative Government and Politics*, 5th ed. (Bloomsbury Academic, 2025), 187, Kindle.

[4] Churchill's subsequent account of the war exhibited, with frequent references to and quotations from primary-source documents, his careful reasoning about both ends and means when he was a cabinet member and later prime minister immediately before and during the conflict. Winston S. Churchill, *The Second World War*, 6 vols. (Mariner Books, 1986) (originally published 1948–53 by Houghton Mifflin). Churchill, like FDR and JFK, was not perfect and sometimes erred, but all three of these political leaders demonstrated remarkable powers of rational analysis in the most important international crises that confronted them.

[5] Merle Fainsod, *How Russia Is Ruled*, rev. ed. (Harvard University Press, 1964), 128.

[6] Sergei Khrushchev, *Nikita Khrushchev and the Creation of a Superpower*, trans. Shirley Benson (Pennsylvania State University Press, 2000), 794, Kindle.

[7] *Memoirs of Nikita Khrushchev*, ed. Sergei Khrushchev, trans. George Shriver and Stephen Shenfield, vol. 3, *Statesman, 1953–1964* (Pennsylvania State University Press, 2007), 320.

[8] *Memoirs of Nikita Khrushchev*, 3:324.

[9] *Memoirs of Nikita Khrushchev*, 3:325.

[10] *Memoirs of Nikita Khrushchev*, 3:325–26.

[11] *Memoirs of Nikita Khrushchev*, 3:327 (quotation marks in the original).

[12] *Memoirs of Nikita Khrushchev*, 3:322–23, 347. See generally Wikipedia, "United States involvement in regime change in Latin America," last modified December 18, 2025, 22:09 (UTC), https://en.wikipedia.org/wiki/United_States_involvement_in_regime_change_in_Latin_America.

[13] *Memoirs of Nikita Khrushchev*, 3:331. As explained in "The 1917 Bolshevik Revolution and Its Aftermath" section of the appendix, Marxist-Leninist thought calls the transition between capitalism and Communism the "socialist" phase, which is characterized by the "dictatorship of the vanguard of

the proletariat." The term "socialism" is thus a very technical term in Marxism-Leninism. It is to be distinguished from democratic socialism or social democracy, which are opposed to a one-party dictatorship and which support individual rights, though not unlimited private property rights. See the *Britannica* articles on "democratic socialism" (https://www.britannica.com/topic/democratic-socialism) and "social democracy" (https://www.britannica.com/topic/social-democracy) for further information.

[14] *Memoirs of Nikita Khrushchev*, 3:335.

[15] Aleksandr Fursenko and Timothy Naftali, *Khrushchev's Cold War: The Inside Story of an American Adversary* (W. W. Norton, 2006), 435 (emphasis added).

[16] Fursenko and Naftali, *Khrushchev's Cold War*, 435–36; *Memoirs of Nikita Khrushchev*, 3:328; Sergei Khrushchev, *Nikita Khrushchev and the Creation of a Superpower*, 801–5; Sergo Mikoyan, *The Soviet Cuban Missile Crisis: Castro, Mikoyan, Kennedy, Khrushchev, and the Missiles of November*, ed. Svetlana Savranskaya, trans. National Security Archive (Stanford University Press, 2014), 96–98, 102. Other members of the Presidium finally deposed Khrushchev in October 1964. "Khrushchev had lost favor because of his increasingly authoritarian management of the Kremlin." *Khrushchev's Cold War*, 531; see, generally, chap. 21 of *Khrushchev's Cold War* for a more detailed account of Khrushchev's downfall.

[17] *Memoirs of Nikita Khrushchev*, 3:329–31, 358n27; Sergei Khrushchev, *Nikita Khrushchev and the Creation of a Superpower*, 823–24; Allison, "The Cuban Missile Crisis at 50"; Sergo Mikoyan, *The Soviet Cuban Missile Crisis*, 101–2, 223–27, 266–67, 479–80, 482, 484–485, 487.

[18] Sergei Khrushchev, *Nikita Khrushchev and the Creation of a Superpower*, 805.

[19] Sergei Khrushchev, *Nikita Khrushchev and the Creation of a Superpower*, 805.

[20] Sergo Mikoyan, *The Soviet Cuban Missile Crisis*, 98–100; cf. Graham Allison and Philip Zelikow, *Essence of Decision:*

Explaining the Cuban Missile Crisis, 2nd ed. (Longman, 1999), 91–109, 260–1.

[21] Sergo Mikoyan, *The Soviet Cuban Missile Crisis*, 95, 96.

[22] Fursenko and Naftali, *Khrushchev's Cold War*, 444.

[23] Fursenko and Naftali, *Khrushchev's Cold War*, 441–47. For the historical background of the Berlin dispute, see the section "The Cold War" in the appendix ("The Historical Background of the 1962 Cuban Missile Crisis") of the present book.

[24] Sergo Mikoyan, *The Soviet Cuban Missile Crisis*, 95.

[25] Sergo Mikoyan, *The Soviet Cuban Missile Crisis*, 100.

[26] Fainsod, *How Russia Is Ruled*, 125–28, 168–75, 200, 204, 207, 210–11, 213–221, 307, 323–28, 335–38, 450–51, 580–81; John A. Armstrong, *Ideology, Politics, and Government in the Soviet Union: An Introduction*, 4th ed. (University Press of America, 1986), 159–71; William Taubman, *Khrushchev: The Man and His Era* (W. W. Norton, 2003), 324, 364–67, 370–71, 381, 513–16, 524–25.

[27] Sergo Mikoyan, *The Soviet Cuban Missile Crisis*, 166–68.

[28] Sergo Mikoyan, *The Soviet Cuban Missile Crisis*, 96–98, 102.

[29] Sergo Mikoyan, *The Soviet Cuban Missile Crisis*, 102–3.

[30] Sergo Mikoyan, *The Soviet Cuban Missile Crisis*, 572n22.

[31] Sergo Mikoyan, *The Soviet Cuban Missile Crisis*, 100, 102.

[32] Hans J. Morgenthau, *Politics Among Nations: The Struggle for Power and Peace*, 3rd ed. (Alfred A. Knopf, 1961), chap. 7 ("The Ideological Element in International Policies").

[33] See Sergei Khrushchev, *Nikita Khrushchev and the Creation of a Superpower*, 1129–30.

[34] Sergei Khrushchev, *Nikita Khrushchev and the Creation of a Superpower*, 218.

[35] *Memoirs of Nikita Khrushchev*, 3:327 (quotation marks in the original).

[36] "The Soviet command economy began a slow death spiral in the late 1950s that would be delayed only by the dramatic

increase in the price of oil in the 1970s." Fursenko and
Naftali, *Khrushchev's Cold War*, 543.

[37] Arthur M. Schlesinger, *A Thousand Days: John F. Kennedy
in the White House* (Mariner Books, 1993), 797 (originally
published in 1965 by Houghton Mifflin).

[38] Schlesinger, *A Thousand Days*, 798–99.

[39] "Statement of President John F. Kennedy," September 4,
1962, *Department of State Bulletin*, 47, No. 1213 (September
24, 1962): 450, https://www.tep-
online.info/laku/usa/cuba/jfkstate.htm (emphasis added).

[40] Schlesinger, *A Thousand Days*, 800–1; Ted Sorensen,
Kennedy: The Classic Biography (Harper Perennial, 2009),
669–72, Kindle (originally published in 1965 by Harper).

[41] Philip Zelikow and Ernest May, eds., *The Presidential
Recordings: John F. Kennedy; The Great Crises*, 3 vols
(W.W. Norton, 2001). For details of the history of President
Kennedy's recording system see the preface to volume 1 by
Philip Zelikow and Ernest May, *Presidential Recordings:
Kennedy*, 1:xvii–xxiv.

[42] *Presidential Recordings: Kennedy*, 2:395–99; Allison and
Zelikow, *Essence of Decision*, 204; Sorensen, *Kennedy*, 675.

[43] *Presidential Recordings: Kennedy*, 2:395–96; cf. Laurence
Chang and Peter Kornbluh, eds., *The Cuban Missile Crisis,
1962: A National Security Archive Documents Reader* (The
New Press, 1998), 370–71.

[44] The discussion in the text of the 11:50 a.m. meeting on
October 16, 1962, is based on the transcript of same at
Presidential Recordings: Kennedy, 2:397–427. In some
instances, subsequent endnotes identify the specific page(s) of
this lengthy transcript.

[45] Robert Kennedy later explained why President Kennedy did
not attend all of the meetings on the Cuban Missile Crisis:
"To keep the discussions from being inhibited and because
[President Kennedy] did not want to arouse attention, he
decided not to attend all the meetings of our committee. This
was wise. Personalities change when the President is present,

and frequently even strong men make recommendations on the basis of what they believe the President wishes to hear. He instructed our group to come forward with recommendations for one course or possibly several alternative courses of action." Robert F. Kennedy, *Thirteen Days: A Memoir of the Cuban Missile Crisis* (W. W. Norton, 2011), 26–27, Kindle (originally published in 1969 by W. W. Norton).

[46] *Presidential Recordings: Kennedy*, 2:397–404.

[47] *Presidential Recordings: Kennedy*, 2:399, 400–1, 411–12.

[48] Allison and Zelikow, *Essence of Decision*, 203 (endnote omitted).

[49] *Presidential Recordings: Kennedy*, 2:409.

[50] *Presidential Recordings: Kennedy*, 2:410–11.

[51] *Presidential Recordings: Kennedy*, 2:410.

[52] *Presidential Recordings: Kennedy*, 2:422.

[53] *Presidential Recordings: Kennedy*, 2:428.

[54] Chang and Kornbluh, *The Cuban Missile Crisis*, 129–30 (underscoring in the original), facsimile; reproduced in *Foreign Relations of the United States* [FRUS], 1961–1963, vol. 11, *Cuban Missile Crisis and Aftermath*, doc. 25 (italics replacing underscoring), https://history.state.gov/historicaldocuments/frus1961-63v11/d25.

[55] *Presidential Recordings: Kennedy*, 2:429–31.

[56] *Presidential Recordings: Kennedy*, 2:431–33.

[57] *Presidential Recordings: Kennedy*, 2:435–36.

[58] *Presidential Recordings: Kennedy*, 2:437–38.

[59] *Presidential Recordings: Kennedy*, 2:437.

[60] *Presidential Recordings: Kennedy*, 2:439–40.

[61] *Presidential Recordings: Kennedy*, 2:440–42.

[62] *Presidential Recordings: Kennedy*, 2:442–43 (brackets, italics, and ellipsis in the original).

[63] *Presidential Recordings: Kennedy*, 2:444–45.

[64] *Presidential Recordings: Kennedy*, 2:448.

[65] *Presidential Recordings: Kennedy, 2:448* (italics in the original).

[66] *Presidential Recordings: Kennedy*, 2:448 (brackets in the original).

[67] *Presidential Recordings: Kennedy*, 2:448–49.

[68] *Presidential Recordings: Kennedy*, 2:449.

[69] *Presidential Recordings: Kennedy*, 2:449.

[70] *Presidential Recordings: Kennedy*, 2:450.

[71] *Presidential Recordings: Kennedy*, 2:450–51.

[72] *Presidential Recordings: Kennedy*, 2:451.

[73] *Presidential Recordings: Kennedy*, 2:451–68.

[74] McCone, Memorandum for Discussion, FRUS, 1961–1963, vol.11, doc. 26, https://history.state.gov/historicaldocuments/frus1961-63v11/d26.

[75] McCone, Memorandum to the File, FRUS, 1961–1963, vol.11, doc. 23, https://history.state.gov/historicaldocuments/frus1961-63v11/d23.

[76] *Presidential Recordings: Kennedy*, 2:513.

[77] *Presidential Recordings: Kennedy*, 2:516.

[78] *Presidential Recordings: Kennedy*, 2:516.

[79] See *Presidential Recordings: Kennedy*, 2:510, 516–72.

[80] *Presidential Recordings: Kennedy*, 2:516–21.

[81] *Presidential Recordings: Kennedy*, 2:526.

[82] *Presidential Recordings: Kennedy*, 2:528 (bracketed text added).

[83] *Presidential Recordings: Kennedy*, 2:529 (brackets in the original).

[84] *Presidential Recordings: Kennedy*, 2:529 (bracketed text added).

[85] *Presidential Recordings: Kennedy*, 2:529.

[86] *Presidential Recordings: Kennedy*, 2:532.

[87] *Presidential Recordings: Kennedy*, 2:540–41.

[88] *Presidential Recordings: Kennedy*, 2:541–42.

[89] *Presidential Recordings: Kennedy*, 2:575.

[90] See, for example, *Presidential Recordings: Kennedy*, 2:249 (remarks of Ambassador Thompson).

[91] *Presidential Recordings: Kennedy*, 2:54 –50, 565–69.

[92] *Presidential Recordings: Kennedy*, 2:572.

[93] Memorandum of Conversation, October 18, 1962, FRUS, 1961–1963, vol. 11, doc. 29, https://history.state.gov/historicaldocuments/frus1961-63v11/d29; Memorandum of Conversation, October 18, 1962, FRUS, 1961–1963, vol.15, doc. 138, https://history.state.gov/historicaldocuments/frus1961-63v15/d135.

[94] The foregoing information and quotations are from President Kennedy's summary (brackets in the original).

[95] *Presidential Recordings: Kennedy*, 2:583–84 (brackets and italics in the original).

[96] *Presidential Recordings: Kennedy*, 2:584.

[97] *Presidential Recordings: Kennedy*, 2:586.

[98] *Presidential Recordings: Kennedy*, 2:587.

[99] *Presidential Recordings: Kennedy*, 2:593.

[100] *Presidential Recordings: Kennedy*, 2:597–98.

[101] *Presidential Recordings: Kennedy*, 2:600–614.

[102] *Presidential Recordings: Kennedy*, 3:5–7.

[103] *Presidential Recordings: Kennedy*, 3:11–15.

[104] *Presidential Recordings: Kennedy*, 3:16–32.

[105] *Presidential Recordings: Kennedy*, 3:33–39.

[106] *Presidential Recordings: Kennedy*, 3:42–58 (quotation at p. 43).

[107] *Presidential Recordings: Kennedy*, 3:58–90.

[108] Transcript of President John F. Kennedy's November 22, 1962 address, John F. Kennedy Library, https://www.jfklibrary.org/node/11861. A video of the speech can be accessed at https://www.youtube.com/watch?v=EgdUgzAWcrw.

[109] Letter From President Kennedy to Chairman Khrushchev, October 22, 1962, FRUS, 1961–1963, vol. 11, doc. 44, https://history.state.gov/historicaldocuments/frus1961-63v11/d44.

[110] National Security Action Memorandum 196, October 22, 1962, FRUS, 1961–1963, vol. 11, doc. 42, https://history.state.gov/historicaldocuments/frus1961-63v11/d42.

[111] President John F. Kennedy, Proclamation 3504 regarding the interdiction of the delivery of offensive weapons to Cuba, October 23, 1962, JFK Library, https://microsites.jfklibrary.org/cmc/oct23/doc4.html. The second "Whereas" clause of this Proclamation referred to the "Joint Resolution passed by the Congress of the United States and approved on October 3, 1962, [in which it] was declared that the United States is determined to prevent by whatever means may be necessary, including the use of arms, the Marxist-Leninist regime in Cuba from extending, by force or the threat of force, its aggressive or subversive activities to any part of this hemisphere, and to prevent in Cuba the creation or use of an externally supported military capability endangering the security of the United States. . . ." Thus, the Proclamation explicitly relied upon congressional authorization.

[112] Chairman Khrushchev's Letter to President Kennedy, October 23, 1962, JFK Library, https://microsites.jfklibrary.org/cmc/oct23/doc6.html.

[113] Telegram From the Department of State to the Embassy in the Soviet Union, October 23, 1962, FRUS, 1961–1963, vol. 11, doc. 52, https://history.state.gov/historicaldocuments/frus1961-63v11/d52.

[114] *Presidential Recordings: Kennedy*, 3:102–83.

[115] *Presidential Recordings: Kennedy*, 3:183–232.

[116] *Presidential Recordings: Kennedy*, 3:200.

[117] Letter From Chairman Khrushchev to President Kennedy, October 24, 1962, JFK Library, https://microsites.jfklibrary.org/cmc/oct24/doc2.html.

[118] Letter From President Kennedy to Chairman Khrushchev, October 25, 1962, JFK Library, https://microsites.jfklibrary.org/cmc/oct25/doc1.html.

[119] *Presidential Recordings: Kennedy*, 3:233–84 passim.

[120] James M. Lindsay, "TWE Remembers: Adlai Stevenson Dresses Down the Soviet Ambassador to the UN (Cuban Missile Crisis, Day Ten)," Council on Foreign Relations, October 25, 2012, https://www.cfr.org/blog/twe-remembers-adlai-stevenson-dresses-down-soviet-ambassador-un-cuban-missile-crisis-day-ten. This article includes a link to a video of this exchange. See also *Presidential Recordings: Kennedy*, 3:270.

[121] Letter from Castro to Khrushchev, October 26, 1962, PBS, https://www.pbs.org/wgbh/americanexperience/features/jfk-attack/ (emphasis added).

[122] *Memoirs of Nikita Khrushchev*, 3:340–41 (bracketed word "preemptive" in the published edition of this work).

[123] Department of State Telegram Transmitting Letter From Chairman Khrushchev to President Kennedy, October 26, 1962, JFK Library, https://microsites.jfklibrary.org/cmc/oct26/doc4.html (emphasis added).

[124] *Presidential Recordings: Kennedy*, 3:305, 331–33, 335, 344–55.

[125] Letter From Chairman Khrushchev to President Kennedy, October 27, 1962, JFK Library, https://microsites.jfklibrary.org/cmc/oct27/doc4.html (emphasis added).

[126] *Presidential Recordings: Kennedy*, 3:358–87.

[127] *Presidential Recordings: Kennedy*, 3:385–86.

[128] *Presidential Recordings: Kennedy*, 3:388, 437.

[129] *Presidential Recordings: Kennedy*, 3:288.

[130] *Presidential Recordings: Kennedy*, 3:445–56.

[131] *Presidential Recordings: Kennedy*, 3:389.

[132] *Presidential Recordings: Kennedy*, 3:452.

[133] See, generally, the transcript of the ExComm meeting from 4:00 p.m. to 7:45 p.m. on October 27, 1962, at *Presidential Recordings: Kennedy*, 3:387–482.

[134] Telegram From the Department of State to the Embassy in the Soviet Union, October 27, 1962, 8:05 p.m., FRUS, 1961–1963, vol.11, doc. 95, https://history.state.gov/historicaldocuments/frus1961-63v11/d95.

[135] *Presidential Recordings: Kennedy*, 3:484–88.

[136] *Presidential Recordings: Kennedy*, 3:488.

[137] Letter From Chairman Khrushchev to President Kennedy, October 28, 1962, JFK Library, https://microsites.jfklibrary.org/cmc/oct28/doc1.html.

[138] *Presidential Recordings: Kennedy*, 3:517.

[139] For details, see, for example, Sergo Mikoyan, *The Soviet Cuban Missile Crisis*, chaps. 5–9, and Fursenko and Naftali, *Khrushchev's Cold War*, chap. 20.

[140] Robert S. McNamara, recorded interview by Arthur M. Schlesinger, Jr., April 4, 1964, transcript p. 20, John F. Kennedy Library Oral History Program, https://static.jfklibrary.org/7g7x88l15361l52170omarl73dv014xa.pdf?odc=20231115180846-0500.

[141] Theodore C. Sorensen, *Decision-Making in the White House: The Olive Branch or the Arrows* (Columbia University Press, 2005), 38–39 (originally published in 1963).

142

https://www.democraticunderground.com/discuss/duboard.php?az=show_mesg&forum=364&topic_id=991380&mesg_id=992153; cf. https://www.jfklibrary.org/asset-viewer/archives/jfkwhsfps-165-004#?image_identifier=JFKWHSFPS-165-004-p0001.

Epilogue

[1] William Shakespeare, *Hamlet*, 3.2.76–79 (Folger Shakespeare), https://folger-main-site-assets.s3.amazonaws.com/uploads/2022/11/hamlet_PDF_Folg erShakespeare.pdf.

[2] I originally wrote and published this paragraph in the text on March 16, 2025. On September 2, 2025, William Galston published a book that contained a similar thought: "This is not the world of our dreams; it is the world in which we live. While public-spirited citizens and leaders must never abandon hope for the improvement of the human condition, their first duty is to see things as they are and act accordingly. We do not live in a world dominated by rational self-interest, let alone altruism or love. Political action can achieve its goals only when it is undertaken in full awareness of the threat the darker side of human nature will always pose." William A. Galston, *Anger, Fear, Domination: Dark Passions and the Power of Political Speech* (Yale University Press, 2025), 135, Kindle. I recommend Galston's book for further study and reflection.

Appendix: The Historical Background of the 1962 Cuban Missile Crisis

[1] Anne Applebaum, *Autocracy, Inc.: The Dictators Who Want to Run the World* (Doubleday, 2024), Kindle; Applebaum, *Twilight of Democracy: The Seductive Lure of Authoritarianism* (Doubleday, 2020), Kindle; Timothy Snyder, "We Should Say It. Russia Is Fascist," *New York Times*, May 19, 2022, https://www.nytimes.com/2022/05/19/opinion/russia-fascism-ukraine-putin.html; Snyder, *The Road to Unfreedom: Russia, Europe, America* (Tim Duggan Books, 2018), Kindle; Ruth Ben-Ghiat, *Strongmen: Mussolini to the Present* (W. W. Norton, 2020), Kindle; Masha Gessen, *The Future Is History: How Totalitarianism Reclaimed Russia* (Riverhead Books, 2017), Kindle; Gessen, *Words Will Break Cement: The Passion of Pussy Riot* (Riverhead Books, 2014), Kindle; Gessen, *The Man without a Face: The Unlikely Rise of*

Notes

Vladimir Putin (Riverhead Books, 2012), Kindle; Gessen, *Surviving Autocracy* (Riverhead Books, 2000), Kindle.

[2] *The Manifesto of the Communist Party*, originally published in 1848 in German, was translated into several different languages. The text used here is the official English translation (approved by Frederich Engels in 1888) by Samuel Moore. This translation has been reproduced in many editions, including in *The Marx Reader: Manifesto of the Communist Party; Wage Labour & Capital; and Value, Price & Profit* (Mockingbird, 2020). Quotations herein are from the Samuel Moore translation in this publication. Citations are to chapter numbers as well as to page numbers of the Kindle edition of *The Marx Reader*. For example 1:5 means chapter 1 of the *Manifesto* at page 5 of *The Marx Reader* (Kindle edition).

[3] Karl Marx, *Critique of the Gotha Program*, trans. anon. (Grapevine, 2023), 29 (emphasis added), Kindle. This writing was based on an 1875 letter of Marx to the Social Democratic Workers' Party of Germany, published after his death by Engels.

[4] Joseph Cropsey, "Karl Marx," in *History of Political Philosophy*, 3rd ed., ed. Leo Strauss and Joseph Cropsey (University of Chicago Press, 1987), 807.

[5] Richard Adamiak, "The 'Withering Away' of the State: A Reconsideration," *Journal of Politics* 32, no. 1 (February 1970): 17, https://doi.org/10.2307/2128862, https://www.jstor.org/stable/2128862.

[6] Vladimir Lenin, *The State and Revolution: The Marxist Theory of the State and the Tasks of the Proletariat in the Revolution*, 2nd ed. (December 2018), chap. 5 passim, in *Communism: Selections from Marx, Engels, Kropotkin, Lenin, Stalin, Trotsky* (Andrii Ponomarenko, 2023), Kindle.

[7] Lenin, *The State and Revolution*, chap. 5 (emphasis added).

[8] Michael McFaul, *Autocrats vs. Democrats: China, Russia, America, and the New Global Disorder* (Mariner Books, 2025), 25, Kindle.

[9] For additional information, see, among other references, *Britannica*, "Vladimir Lenin," last updated December 7, 2025, https://www.britannica.com/biography/Vladimir-Lenin; Robert Service, *Lenin: A Biography* (Belknap Press of Harvard University Press, 2000); Richard Pipes, ed., *The Unknown Lenin: From the Secret Archive* (Yale University Press, 1995); Danny Bird, "How the 'Red Terror' Exposed the True Turmoil of Soviet Russia 100 Years Ago," *Time*, September 5, 2018, https://time.com/5386789/red-terror-soviet-history/; Robert Service, *Stalin: A Biography* (Belknap Press of Harvard University Press, 2005); Stephen Kotkin, *Stalin: Paradoxes of Power, 1878–1929* (Penguin Books, 2015), Kindle; Kotkin, *Stalin: Waiting for Hitler, 1929–1941* (Penguin Books, 2018), Kindle; and Nikita Khrushchev, *Memoirs of Nikita Khrushchev*, 3 vols., ed. Sergei Khrushchev, trans. George Shriver and Stephen Shenfield (Pennsylvania State University Press, 2004, 2006), 1:1–704 passim, 2:3–170.

[10] For an English translation of this speech, see https://www.marxists.org/archive/khrushchev/1956/02/24.htm .

[11] See Merle Fainsod, *How Russia Is Ruled*, rev. ed. (Harvard University Press, 1963), esp. 128.

[12] For the following paragraphs in the text about Berlin, see Aleksander Fursenko and Timothy Naftali, *Khrushchev's Cold War: The Inside Story of an American Adversary* (W. W. Norton, 2006), 22–24, 381–84, 355–65, 399–408, 421–23.

[13] The factual statements in the present section of this book about the rise of Castro and his actions up to and including the 1961 Bay of Pigs invasion are generally supported by the well-researched historical account in Jim Rasenberger, *The Brilliant Disaster: JFK, Castro, and America's Doomed Invasion of Cuba's Bay of Pigs* (Scribner, 2011), Kindle. As for Khrushchev's initial uncertainty about Fidel Castro's view of Communism, see *The Memoirs of Nikita Khrushchev*, 3:315–17.

[14] Rasenberger, *The Brilliant Disaster*, 69–70.

Notes

[15] Rasenberger, *The Brilliant Disaster*, 83–84.

[16] Rasenberger, *The Brilliant Disaster*, 85–88; Tim Weiner, *Legacy of Ashes: The History of the CIA* (Doubleday, 2007), chaps. 1–16; Ishaan Tharoor, "The long history of the U.S. interfering with elections elsewhere." *Washington Post*, October 13, 2016, https://www.washingtonpost.com/news/worldviews/wp/2016/10/13/the-long-history-of-the-u-s-interfering-with-elections-elsewhere/.

[17] A Program of Covert Action Against the Castro Regime, *Foreign Relations of the United States* [FRUS], 1958–60, vol. 6, *Cuba*, doc. 481, https://history.state.gov/historicaldocuments/frus1958-60v06/d481.

[18] Memorandum of a Conference with the President, White House, Washington, March 17, 1960, 2:30 p.m., FRUS, 1958–60, vol. 6, doc. 486, https://history.state.gov/historicaldocuments/frus1958-60v06/d486 (emphasis added).

[19] Rasenberger, *The Brilliant Disaster*, 143.

[20] Rasenberger, *The Brilliant Disaster*, 143–47.

[21] Rasenberger, *The Brilliant Disaster*, 151–57; Briefing papers used to brief President-elect Kennedy, November 18, 1960, FRUS SUP, 1961–63, vol 10, doc. 232, https://history.state.gov/historicaldocuments/frus1961-63v10-12mSupp/d232.

[22] Memorandum of Discussion on Cuba, Jan. 28, 1961, FRUS, 1961–63, vol. 10, doc. 30, https://history.state.gov/historicaldocuments/frus1961-63v10/d30.

[23] President John F. Kennedy, State of the Union address, January 30, 1961, https://millercenter.org/the-presidency/presidential-speeches/january-30-1961-state-union.

[24] James Monroe, December 2, 1923 State of the Union message, https://www.gutenberg.org/files/5014/5014-h/5014-

h.htm#dec1823 (emphasis added). For the historical
background of the Monroe Doctrine, see part 10 ("The
Monroe Doctrine") of *The Political Writings of James
Monroe*, ed. James P. Lucier (Regnery, 2001).

[25] "Memorandum From the Assistant Secretary of State for
Inter-American Affairs (Mann) to Secretary of State Rusk,"
February 15, 1961, FRUS, vol. 10, doc. 45,
https://history.state.gov/historicaldocuments/frus1961-
63v10/d45.

[26] [Richard Bissell], Paper Prepared in the Central Intelligence
Agency, February 17, 1961, FRUS, vol. 10, doc. 46,
https://history.state.gov/historicaldocuments/frus1961-
63v10/d46.

[27] McGeorge Bundy to President Kennedy, February 18,
1961, FRUS, vol. 10, doc. 46,
https://history.state.gov/historicaldocuments/frus1961-
63v10/d47.

[28] Editorial Note (prepared on May 9, 1961), FRUS, vol. 10,
doc. 48,
https://history.state.gov/historicaldocuments/frus1961-
63v10/d48.

[29] Paper Prepared [by Bissell] in the Central Intelligence
Agency, March 11, 1961, FRUS, vol. 10, doc. 58,
https://history.state.gov/historicaldocuments/frus1961-
63v10/d58.

[30] National Security Action Memorandum No. 31, March 11,
1961, FRUS, vol. 10, doc. 60,
https://history.state.gov/historicaldocuments/frus1961-
63v10/d60.

[31] Paper Prepared [by Bissell] in the Central Intelligence
Agency, March 15, 1961, FRUS, vol. 10, doc. 61,
https://history.state.gov/historicaldocuments/frus1961-
63v10/d61.

[32] Memorandum From the Joint Chiefs of Staff to Secretary of
Defense McNamara, March 15, 1961, FRUS, vol. 10, doc. 62,

https://history.state.gov/historicaldocuments/frus1961-63v10/d62.

[33] Editorial Note, FRUS, vol. 10, doc. 65, https://history.state.gov/historicaldocuments/frus1961-63v10/d65.

[34] Rasenberger, *The Brilliant Disaster*, 311.

[35] Editorial Note, FRUS, vol. 10, doc. 66, https://history.state.gov/historicaldocuments/frus1961-63v10/d66.

[36] Editorial Note, FRUS, vol. 10, doc. 66, https://history.state.gov/historicaldocuments/frus1961-63v10/d66 (emphasis added).

[37] Editorial Note, FRUS, vol. 10, doc. 74, https://history.state.gov/historicaldocuments/frus1961-63v10/d74.

[38] Editorial Note, FRUS, vol. 10, doc. 80, https://history.state.gov/historicaldocuments/frus1961-63v10/d80.

[39] Editorial Note, FRUS, vol. 10, doc. 80, https://history.state.gov/historicaldocuments/frus1961-63v10/d80 (emphasis added).

[40] Adolf A. Berle Jr., recorded interview by Joseph E. O'Connor, July 6, 1967, transcript p. 40, John F. Kennedy Library Oral History Program, https://static.jfklibrary.org/846f7yi2i215jg5800wevu7bho0a17wj.pdf?odc=20231115182642-0500 (emphasis added).

[41] Arthur Schlesinger Jr. to President Kennedy, April 5, 1961, FRUS, vol. 10, doc. 81, https://history.state.gov/historicaldocuments/frus1961-63v10/d81.

[42] Editorial Note, FRUS, vol 10, doc. 84, https://history.state.gov/historicaldocuments/frus1961-63v10/d84.

[43] Editorial Note, FRUS, vol. 10, doc. 92, https://history.state.gov/historicaldocuments/frus1961-

63v10/d92; Rasenberger, *The Brilliant Disaster*, 233–34, 241–60.

[44] Memorandum Prepared in the Central Intelligence Agency to General Maxwell D. Taylor, April 26, 1961, FRUS, vol. 10, doc. 98, https://history.state.gov/historicaldocuments/frus1961-63v10/d98.

[45] Rasenberger, *The Brilliant Disaster*, 286-87, 291.

[46] Arthur M. Schlesinger Jr., *A Thousand Days: John F. Kennedy in the White House* (Mariner Books, 2002), 271–72.

[47] Schlesinger, *A Thousand Days*, 273; cf. Rasenberger, *The Brilliant Disaster*, 306.

[48] Editorial Note, FRUS, vol. 10, doc. 66, https://history.state.gov/historicaldocuments/frus1961-63v10/d66; Rasenberger, *The Brilliant Disaster*, 295.

[49] Schlesinger, *A Thousand Days*, 270.

[50] Editorial Note, FRUS, vol. 10, doc. 66, https://history.state.gov/historicaldocuments/frus1961-63v10/d66; Rasenberger, *The Brilliant Disaster*, 296–98.

[51] Schlesinger, *A Thousand Days*, 270. Schlesinger did not identify any documentary source for these statements, and it is unclear whether he was quoting from memory of a meeting with CIA personnel or whether he was relying on a documentary reference. *A Thousand Days* is notable for its absence of citations to corroborative documentary evidence. Of course, at the time (1965) that *A Thousand Days* was originally published, much of the documentary evidence was classified. Although Schlesinger added a new foreword to the 2002 edition, it does not appear that he changed any of the text that he had originally published in 1965.

[52] Schlesinger, *A Thousand Days*, 273.

[53] Schlesinger, *A Thousand Days*, 274 (quotation and April 17 events); Rasenberger, *The Brilliant Disaster*, chaps. 17–19.

[54] Rasenberger, *The Brilliant Disaster*, 416–17 (quoting Richard M. Nixon, "Cuba, Castro, and John F. Kennedy:

Some Recollections on United States Foreign Policy,"
Reader's Digest, November 1964).

[55] Rasenberger, *The Brilliant Disaster*, 523–24.

[56] Rasenberger, *The Brilliant Disaster*, 525–26.

[57] Rasenberger, *The Brilliant Disaster*, 529.

[58] "C.I.A.: Maker of Policy or Tool?," *New York Times*, April 25, 1966, section on "Kennedy's Bitterness," https://www.cia.gov/readingroom/docs/CIA-RDP82R00025R000700050014-9.pdf; Peter Kornbluh, "JFK wanted to splinter CIA 'into a thousand pieces.' Why didn't he?," Responsible Statecraft, March 27, 2025, https://responsiblestatecraft.org/jfk-files-cia/; Memorandum of CIA Director John McCone regarding his conference with Attorney General Robert F. Kennedy, November 29, 1961, FRUS, vol. 10, doc. 276, https://history.state.gov/historicaldocuments/frus1961-63v10/d276. Cf. Matt Novak, "The Real Story Behind That JFK Quote About Destroying the CIA," Gismodo, March 10, 2017, https://gizmodo.com/the-story-behind-that-jfk-quote-about-destroying-the-ci-1793151211. See also Ted Sorensen, *Kennedy: The Classic Biography* (HarperCollins, 2009; originally published 1965), 294–308, Kindle.

[59] Laurence Chang and Peter Kornbluth, eds., *The Cuban Missile Crisis, 1962: A National Security Archive Documents Reader* (New Press, 1998), 4–7, 362, and referenced documents; Aleksandr Fursenko and Timothy Naftali, *"One Hell of a Gamble": Khrushchev, Castro, and Kennedy, 1958-1964* (Norton, 1997), chaps. 7 and 8; Mark J. White, *Missiles in Cuba: Kennedy, Khrushchev, Castro and the 1962 Crisis* (Ivan R. Dee, 1998), chap. 1.

SELECTED BIBLIOGRAPHY

This selected bibliography does not include all citations of online materials in the endnotes. In each such instance, the endnote includes a URL link to the specific reference.

Not all citations in the endnotes to United States Supreme Court cases include a URL, but US Supreme Court decisions can be accessed and downloaded at https://www.loc.gov/search/?fa=subject:supreme+court by entering the case name and/or citation of the particular case in the "Everything" box. Recent Supreme Court decisions can be accessed and downloaded at https://www.supremecourt.gov/opinions/opinions.aspx.

Adamiak, Richard. "The 'Withering Away' of the State: A Reconsideration." *Journal of Politics* 32, no. 1 (February 1970): 3–18. https://doi.org/10.2307/2128862; https://www.jstor.org/stable/2128862.

Allison, Graham. "The Cuban Missile Crisis at 50: Lessons for U.S. Foreign Policy Today." *Foreign Affairs*, July 1, 2012. https://www.foreignaffairs.com/articles/cuba/2012-07-01/cuban-missile-crisis-50.

Allison, Graham, and Philip Zelikow. *Essence of Decision: Explaining the Cuban Missile Crisis*. 2nd ed. Longman, 1999.

Applebaum, Anne. *Autocracy, Inc.: The Dictators Who Want to Run the World*. Doubleday, 2024. Kindle.

Applebaum, Anne. *Twilight of Democracy: The Seductive Lure of Authoritarianism*. Doubleday, 2020. Kindle.

Aristotle, *Aristotle's "Politics"*. 2nd edition. Translated and edited by Carnes Lord. University of Chicago Press, 2013.

Selected Bibliography

Armstrong, John A. *Ideology, Politics, and Government in the Soviet Union: An Introduction*. 4th ed. University Press of America. 1986

Atwood, Margaret. *The Handmaid's Tale*. Ecco, 1986.

Ben-Ghiat, Ruth. *Strongmen: Mussolini to the Present*. New York: W. W. Norton, 2020. Kindle.

Bird, Danny. "How the 'Red Terror' Exposed the True Turmoil of Soviet Russia 100 Years Ago." *Time*, September 5, 2018. https://time.com/5386789/red-terror-soviet-history/.

Blackmon, Douglas A. *Slavery by Another Name: The Re-Enslavement of Black Americans from the Civil War to World War II*. Anchor Books, 2008. Kindle.

Boyd, Julian P. *The Declaration of Independence: The Evolution of the Text*. Revised edition. Edited by Gerard W. Gewalt. Library of Congress, 1999.

Brennan, Jason. *Against Democracy, with a New Preface*. Princeton University Press, 2017. Kindle.

Castro, Ricardo Neves e. *Global Disorder: The World Adrift*. Published by author, 2024. Kindle.

Chang, Laurence, and Peter Kornbluh, eds. *The Cuban Missile Crisis, 1962: A National Security Archive Documents Reader*. The New Press, 1998.

Chemerinksy, Erwin. *Worse Than Nothing: The Dangerous Fallacy of Originalism*. Yale University Press, 2022. Kindle.

Churchill, Winston S. *The Second World War*. 6 vols. Mariner Books, 1986. Originally published 1948–53 by Houghton Mifflin.

Confucius, *The Analects of Confucius*. Translated and edited by Simon Leys. W. W. Norton, 1997.

Confucius. *The Great Learning*. In *The Chinese Classics*, translated and edited by James Legge. Vol. 1, *The Life and Teachings of Confucius*, 2nd ed. London, 1869.

Cropsey, Joseph. "Karl Marx." In *History of Political Philosophy*, 3rd ed., edited by Leo Strauss and Joseph Cropsey. University of Chicago Press, 1987.

Selected Bibliography

A Declaration of Some Proceedings of Lt. Col. John Lilburne. 1648. In *The Leveller Tracts*, edited by William Haller and Godfrey Davies. Peter Smith, 1944.

Fainsod, Merle. *How Russia Is Ruled*. Revised ed. Harvard University Press, 1964.

Fox, Justin. *The Myth of the Rational Market: A History of Risk, Reward, and Delusion on Wall Street*. HarperCollins, 2009. Kindle.

Frankel, Steven, and John Ray, eds. *Commerce and Character: The Political Economy of the Enlightenment and the American Founding*. University Press of Kansas, 2025. Kindle.

Frantz, Erica. *Authoritarianism: What Everyone Needs to Know*. Oxford University Press, 2018. Kindle.

Friedman, Lawrence M. *A History of American Law*. 4th ed. Oxford University Press, 2019.

Fursenko, Aleksandr and Timothy Naftali. *Khrushchev's Cold War: The Inside Story of an American Adversary*. W. W. Norton, 2006.

Galston, William A. *Anger, Fear, Domination: Dark Passions and the Power of Political Speech*. Yale University Press, 2025. Kindle.

Gessen, Masha. *The Future Is History: How Totalitarianism Reclaimed Russia*. Riverhead Books, 2017. Kindle.

Gessen, Masha. *The Man without a Face: The Unlikely Rise of Vladimir Putin*. Riverhead Books, 2012. Kindle.

Gessen, Masha. *Surviving Autocracy*. Riverhead Books, 2000. Kindle.

Gessen, Masha. *Words Will Break Cement: The Passion of Pussy Riot*. Riverhead Books, 2014. Kindle.

Ginsburg, Tom, and Alberto Simpser, eds. *Constitutions in Authoritarian Regimes*. Cambridge University Press, 2014). Kindle.

Haltern, Ulrich. *The Constitution of the European Union: A Contextual Analysis*. Hart, 2025. Kindle.

Selected Bibliography

Hasen, Richard L. *The Justice of Contradictions: Antonin Scalia and the Politics of Disruption*. Yale University Press, 2018. Kindle.

Hamilton, Alexander, John Jay, and James Madison. *The Federalist*. Gideon edition. Edited by George W. Carey and James McClellan. Liberty Fund, 2001.

Hogue, Arthur R. *Origins of the Common Law*. Liberty Fund, 1986.

Holmes, Oliver Wendell. *The Common Law*. Edited by Mark DeWolfe Howe. Back Bay Books, 1936. Originally published in 1881 by Little, Brown.

Inglehart, Robert. *Cultural Backlash: Trump, Brexit, and Authoritarian Populism*. Cambridge University Press, 2019. Kindle.

Jaqueisse. *The Philosopher Kingdom*. Jabroni, 2024. Kindle.

Johnson, Alan E. "Deism, Unitarianism, and the US Founders." Academia.edu, August 29, 2015. https://www.academia.edu/15269565/Deism_Unitarianism_and_the_US_Founders.

Johnson, Alan E. "Due Process, Procedural." In *Encyclopedia of the U.S. Supreme Court*, edited by Thomas T. Lewis and Richard L. Wilson. Salem Press, 2001.

Johnson, Alan E. *The Electoral College: Failures of Original Intent and Proposed Constitutional and Statutory Changes for Direct Popular Vote*. 2nd ed. Philosophia, 2021.

Johnson, Alan E. *The First American Founder: Roger Williams and Freedom of Conscience*. Philosophia, 2015.

Johnson, Alan E. *Free Will and Human Life*. Philosophia, 2021.

Johnson, Alan E. "From Philosopher Kings to Libertarian Elitists: A Critical Appraisal of Jason Brennan, *Against Democracy*." Academia.edu, October 23, 2023. https://www.academia.edu/106405232/From_Philosopher_Kings_to_Libertarian_Elitists_A_Critical_Appraisal_of_Jason_Brennan_Against_Democracy_With_A_New_2017_Preface_by_the_Author_Princeton_Princeton_University_Press_2017_edited_June_7_2024_.

Selected Bibliography

Johnson, Alan E. "John Locke, Thomas Jefferson, Abraham Lincoln, and the Declaration of Independence." Academia.edu, August 9, 2024. https://www.academia.edu/122721285/John_Locke_Thomas_Jefferson_Abraham_Lincoln_and_the_Declaration_of_Independence.

Johnson, Alan E. "Property Rights." *Encyclopedia of the U.S. Supreme Court*. Edited by Thomas T. Lewis and Richard L. Wilson. Salem Press, 2001.

Johnson, Alan E. *Reason and Human Ethics*. Philosophia, 2022.

Johnson, Alan E. "Review of Jaqueisse's *The Philosopher Kingdom*." Academia.edu, June 12, 2024. https://www.academia.edu/120896197/Review_of_Jaqueisses_The_Philosopher_Kingdom_.

Johnson, Alan E. "The Teaching of Plato's *Seventh Letter*." Master's essay, University of Chicago, 1971. https://www.academia.edu/22999496/The_Teaching_of_Platos_Seventh_Letter.

Kagan, Robert. *Rebellion: How Antiliberalism Is Tearing America Apart—Again*. Knopf Doubleday, 2024. Kindle.

Kennedy, John F. Proclamation 3504 regarding the interdiction of the delivery of offensive weapons to Cuba. October 23, 1962. JFK Library. https://microsites.jfklibrary.org/cmc/oct23/doc4.html.

Kennedy, John F. Statement of President John F. Kennedy. September 4, 1962. *Department of State Bulletin*, 47, no. 1213 (September 24, 1962): 450. https://www.tep-online.info/laku/usa/cuba/jfkstate.htm.

Kennedy, John F. Transcript of President John F. Kennedy's November 22, 1962 address. JFK Library. https://www.jfklibrary.org/node/11861. Video of same at https://www.youtube.com/watch?v=EgdUgzAWcrw.

Kennedy, Robert F. *Thirteen Days: A Memoir of the Cuban Missile Crisis*. W. W. Norton, 2011. Kindle. Originally published in 1969 by W. W. Norton.

Kotkin, Stephen. *Stalin: Paradoxes of Power, 1878–1928*. Penguin Books, 2014. Kindle.

Kotkin, Stephen. *Stalin: Waiting for Hitler, 1929-41*. Penguin Books, 2018. Kindle.

Khrushchev, Nikita. *Memoirs of Nikita Khrushchev*. Vol. 1, *Commissar (1918–1945)*; Vol. 2, *Reformer (1945–64)*; Vol. 3, *Statesman, 1953–64*. Edited by Sergei Khrushchev. Translated by George Shriver and Stephen Shenfield. Pennsylvania State University Press, 2004–7.

Khrushcheva, Nina. "Russia's Descent Into Tyranny: How Four Years of War Have Remade Society." *Foreign Affairs*, December 30, 2025. https://www.foreignaffairs.com/russia/russias-descent-tyranny.

Khrushchev, Sergei. *Nikita Khrushchev and the Creation of a Superpower*. Translated by Shirley Benson. Pennsylvania State University Press, 2000. Kindle.

Lenin, Vladimir. *The State and Revolution: The Marxist Theory of the State and the Tasks of the Proletariat in the Revolution*. 2nd ed. 2018. In *Communism: Selections from Marx, Engels, Kropotkin, Lenin, Stalin, Trotsky*. Andrii Ponomarenko, 2023. Kindle.

Lerner, Ralph. "Prologue: Commerce and Character: The Anglo-American as New-Model Man" (1979). In *Commerce and Character: The Political Economy of the Enlightenment and the American Founding*, edited by Steven Frankel and John Ray. University Press of Kansas, 2025. Kindle.

Levitsky, Stephen et al., Lucan A. Way, and Daniel Ziblatt. "The Price of American Authoritarianism: What Can Reverse Democratic Decline?" *Foreign Affairs*, December 11, 2025. https://www.foreignaffairs.com/united-states/american-authoritarianism-levitsky-way-ziblatt.

Leyland, Peter. *The Constitution of the United Kingdom: A Contextual Analysis*. 4th ed. Hart, 2021. Kindle.

Lewis, Thomas T. and Richard L. Wilson, eds. *Encyclopedia of the U.S. Supreme Court*. 3 vols. Salem Press, 2001.

Lincoln, Abraham. "The Perpetuation of Our Political Institutions." Address Before the Young Men's Lyceum of Springfield, Illinois. January 27, 1838.

http://www.abrahamlincolnonline.org/lincoln/speeches/lyceu
m.htm.

Lindsay, James M. "TWE Remembers: Adlai Stevenson Dresses
Down the Soviet Ambassador to the UN (Cuban Missile
Crisis, Day Ten)." Council on Foreign Relations. October 25,
2012. https://www.cfr.org/blog/twe-remembers-adlai-
stevenson-dresses-down-soviet-ambassador-un-cuban-
missile-crisis-day-ten.

Locke, John. *An Essay Concerning Human Understanding*.
Edited by Peter H. Nidditch. Oxford University Press, 1975.

Locke, John. *Two Treatises of Government*. Edited by Peter
Laslett. Cambridge University Press, 1988. Kindle.

Lowry, Annie. "How the Richest People in America Avoid
Paying Taxes." *The Atlantic*, August 25, 2025.
https://www.theatlantic.com/economy/archive/2025/08/billio
naire-tax-
study/683987/?gift=jvRXZia7Ag6tGK6Imt0JSx7BaigEIQH
VDEbcbO1mVx0.

Madison, James. *Federalist No. 10*. November 22, 1788.
Founders Online, National Archives.
https://founders.archives.gov/documents/Madison/01-10-02-
0178.

Madison, James. Speech in the Virginia Ratifying Convention.
June 20, 1788. In *Documentary History of the Ratification of
the Constitution,* digital edition, edited by John P. Kaminski
and Gaspare J. Saladino. Charlottesville: University of
Virginia Press, 2009.
http://rotunda.upress.virginia.edu/founders/RNCN-02-10-02-
0002-0009.

McCormick, John, Rod Hague, and Martin Harrop. *Comparative
Government and Politics*, 13th ed. Bloomsbury Academic,
2025. Kindle.

McFaul, Michael. *Autocrats vs. Democrats: China, Russia,
America, and the New Global Disorder*. Mariner Books,
2025. Kindle.

McGranahan, Lucas. "Delicate Dance: Two Faculty Projects
Examine the Awkward Partnership Between Democracy and
Capitalism." *University of Chicago Magazine* 117, no. 1 (Fall

2024): 27–31. https://mag.uchicago.edu/law-policy-society/delicate-dance.

McLean, Bethany, and Joe Nocera. *All the Devils Are Here: The Hidden History of the Financial Crisis*. Portfolio, 2010. Kindle.

Marx, Karl. *Critique of the Gotha Program*. Translated by anonymous. Grapevine, 2023. Kindle.

Marx, Karl, and Friedrich Engels. *The Marx Reader: Manifesto of the Communist Party; Wage Labour & Capital; and Value, Price & Profit*. Edited by Juliette Rogers. Mockingbird, 2020. Kindle.

Mikoyan, Sergo. *The Soviet Cuban Missile Crisis: Castro, Mikoyan, Kennedy, Khrushchev, and the Missiles of November*. Edited by Svetlana Savranskaya. Translated by National Security Archive. Stanford University Press, 2014.

Monroe, James. *The Political Writings of James Monroe*. Edited by James P. Lucier. Regnery, 2001.

Morgenthau, Hans J. *Politics Among Nations: The Struggle for Power and Peace*. 3rd ed. Alfred A. Knopf, 1961.

Nowak, John E., and Donald D. Rotunda. *Constitutional Law*. 8th ed. West, 2010. Kindle.

Oliver, J. Michael. *The New Libertarianism: Anarcho-Capitalism*. Published by the author, 2013.

Orwell, George. *1984*. Mariner Books, 1949.

Pipes, Richard, ed. *The Unknown Lenin: From the Secret Archive*. Yale University Press, 1995.

Plato. *Republic. The Republic of Plato*. 2nd ed. Translated and edited by Allan Bloom. Basic Books, 1991.

Plato. *Republic*. Translated and edited by Joe Sachs. Focus, 2007.

Rakove, Jack N. *Original Meanings: Politics and Ideas in the Making of the Constitution*. Vintage Books, 1997.

Rand, Ayn. *The Virtue of Selfishness: A New Concept of Egoism*. Signet Books, 1964.

Rasenberger, Jim. *The Brilliant Disaster: JFK, Castro, and America's Doomed Invasion of Cuba's Bay of Pigs*. Scribner, 2011. Kindle.

Ravitch, Diane. *An Education: How I Changed My Mind about Schools and Almost Everything Else*. Columbia University Press, 2025.

Reich, Robert B. *The Common Good*. Alfred A. Knopf, 2018. Kindle.

Roberts, David D. *Totalitarianism*. Polity, 2020. Kindle.

Rothbard, Murray N. *The Ethics of Liberty*. New York University Press, 2002), Kindle. Originally published in 1982 by Humanities Press.

Rothbard, Murray N. *For a New Liberty: A Libertarian Manifesto*. 2nd ed. Ludwig von Mises Institute, 2006. Kindle. First edition published in 1972 by Macmillan. Second edition initially published in 1978 by Collier Books.

Rothbard, Murray N. *Power and Market: Government and the Economy*. 4th ed. Ludwig von Mises Institute, 2006. Kindle. First edition published in 1970 by the Institute for Humane Studies.

Sanger, Matthew. "Anarchic Theory and the Study of Hunter-Gatherers." *The SAA Archaeological Record* 17, no. 1 (2017): 39–44. https://theanarchistlibrary.org/library/matthew-sanger-anarchic-theory-and-the-study-of-hunter-gatherers.

Schlesinger, Arthur M. *A Thousand Days: John F. Kennedy in the White House*. Mariner Books, 1993. Originally published in 1965 by Houghton Mifflin.

Service, Robert. *Lenin: A Biography*, Belknap Press of Harvard University Press, 2000.

Service, Robert. *Stalin: A Biography*, Cambridge, MA: Belknap Press of Harvard University Press, 2005.

Shiller, Robert J. *Irrational Exuberance*. Revised and expanded 3rd ed. Princeton University Press, 2015. Kindle.

Smith, Adam. *An Inquiry into the Nature and Causes of the Wealth of Nations*. Edited by Edwin Cannan, with an introduction by Max Lerner. Modern Library, 1937.

Snyder, Timothy. *On Tyranny: Twenty Lessons from the Twentieth Century*. Tim Duggan Books, 2017. Kindle.

Snyder, Timothy. *The Road to Unfreedom: Russia, Europe, America*. Tim Duggan Books, 2018. Kindle.

Snyder, Timothy. "We Should Say It. Russia Is Fascist." *New York Times*. May 19, 2022. https://www.nytimes.com/2022/05/19/opinion/russia-fascism-ukraine-putin.html.

Sorensen, Ted. *Counselor: A Life at the Edge of History*. HarperCollins, 2008. Kindle.

Sorensen, Ted. *Kennedy: The Classic Biography*. Harper Perennial, 2009. Kindle. Originally published in 1965 by Harper. 2005.

Sorensen, Theodore C. *Decision-Making in the White House: The Olive Branch or the Arrows*. Columbia University Press, 2005. With a foreword by John F. Kennedy. Originally published in 1963 by Columbia University Press.

Stewart, Katherine. *Money, Lies, and God: Inside the Movement to Destroy American Democracy*. Bloomsbury, 2025. Kindle.

Stiglitz, Joseph E. *The Road to Freedom: Economics and the Good Society*. W. W. Norton, 2024. Kindle.

Storing, Herbert J, ed. *The Complete Anti-Federalist*. University of Chicago Press, 1981).

Storing, Herbert J. *What the Anti-Federalists Were For: The Political Thought of the Opponents of the Constitution*. University of Chicago Press, 1981.

Storing, Herbert J. and Murray Dry, eds. *The Anti-Federalist: Writings by the Opponents of the Constitution*. University of Chicago Press, 1985. Abridgement of *The Complete Anti-Federalist*.

Strauss, David A. *The Living Constitution*. Oxford University Press, 2010. Kindle.

Strauss, Leo. *The Argument and the Action of Plato's "Laws"*. University of Chicago Press, 1975.

Strauss, Leo. *The City and Man*. Rand McNally, 1964.

Strauss, Leo. *Natural Right and History*. Chicago: University of Chicago Press, 1953.

Strauss, Leo. "Plato." In *History of Political Philosophy*, 3rd ed., edited by Leo Strauss and Joseph Cropsey. University of Chicago Press, 1987.

Strauss, Leo. *What Is Political Philosophy? and Other Studies*. Free Press, 1959.

Taubman, William. *Khrushchev: The Man and His Era*. W. W. Norton, 2003.

Taylor, Matthew D. *The Violent Take It by Force: The Christian Movement That Is Threatening Our Democracy*. Broadleaf Books, 2024. Kindle.

Thaler, Richard H. *Misbehaving: The Making of Behavioral Economics*. W. W. Norton, 2015. Kindle.

Tharoor, Ishaan. "The long history of the U.S. interfering with elections elsewhere." *Washington Post*, October 13, 2016. https://www.washingtonpost.com/news/worldviews/wp/2016/10/13/the-long-history-of-the-u-s-interfering-with-elections-elsewhere/.

Torres-Spelliscy, Ciara. "The History of Corporate Personhood." Brennan Center for Justice, April 8, 2014. https://www.brennancenter.org/our-work/analysis-opinion/history-corporate-personhood.

U.S. Department of State. *Foreign Relations of the United States*, 1958–1960. Vol. 6, *Cuba*. Washington, DC: Government Printing Office, 1991. https://history.state.gov/historicaldocuments/frus1958-60v06.

U.S. Department of State. *Foreign Relations of the United States*, 1961–1962. Vol. 10, *Cuba*. Washington, DC: Government Printing Office, 1997. https://history.state.gov/historicaldocuments/frus1961-63v10.

U.S. Department of State. *Foreign Relations of the United States*, 1961–1963. Vol. 11, *Cuban Missile Crisis and Aftermath*. Washington, DC: Government Printing Office, 1996. https://history.state.gov/historicaldocuments/frus1961-63v11.

Weber, Max. "Politics as a Vocation." In Max Weber, *The Vocation Lectures*, edited by David Owen and Tracy B. Strong, translated by Rodney Livingstone. Hackett, 2004. Kindle.

Weiner, Tim. *Legacy of Ashes: The History of the CIA*. Doubleday, 2007.

Selected Bibliography

White, Mark J. *Missiles in Cuba: Kennedy, Khrushchev, Castro and the 1962 Crisis.* Ivan R. Dee, 1998. Kindle.

Wilson, Richard L. "Judicial Review." In *Encyclopedia of the U.S. Supreme Court*, edited by Thomas T. Lewis and Richard L. Wilson. Salem Press, 2001.

Zane, Maxcy. *The Story of Law.* 2nd ed. Liberty Fund, 1998. Originally published in 1927 by Ives Washburn.

Zelikow, Philip, and Earnest May, eds. *The Presidential Recordings: John F. Kennedy; The Great Crises*, 3 vols. W. W. Norton, 2001.

Zelikow, Philip, and Earnest May, eds. *The Presidential Recordings: John F. Kennedy; The Great Crises.* Vol. 1, *July 30–August 1962*, edited by Timothy Naftali. W. W. Norton, 2001.

Zelikow, Philip, and Earnest May, eds. *The Presidential Recordings: John F. Kennedy; The Great Crises.* Vol. 2, *September–October 21, 1962*, edited by Timothy Naftali and Philip Zelikow. W. W. Norton, 2001.

Zelikow, Philip, and Earnest May, eds. *The Presidential Recordings: John F. Kennedy; The Great Crises.* Vol. 3, *October 22–28, 1962*, edited by Philip Zelikow and Earnest May. W. W. Norton, 2001.

INDEX

Note: The discussions in this book of the Cuban Missile Crisis (chapter 5) and the Bay of Pigs invasion (appendix) name a very large number of officials in the governments of the United States, the United Kingdom, continental Europe, the Soviet Union, and Cuba. An index naming each of these officials would be excessively long. Accordingly, this index lists, with respect to these crises, only those officials who were key figures in them.

abortion, 28–30, 45, 65

Adams, John, 26

anarchism, 4–5, 7–22, 47, 50, 72, 109, 178, 179, 186

anarchocapitalism. *See* anarchism

Aristotle, 230n25 (chap. 4)

authoritarianism, 2, 6, 21, 67, 69–70, 91, 95–97, 116, 121–22, 124, 182–89, 191, 197–200, 231n32 (chap. 4), 235n16 (chap. 5)

Batista, Fulgencio, 111, 116, 191, 195

Bolshevik revolution in Russia, 1, 6, 186–88, 234n13 (chap. 5)

Brennan, Jason, 93–94

Bush, George W., 39

Castro, Fidel, 6, 108, 111–75, 191–217

Churchill, Winston, 108, 234n4 (chap. 5)

Communism, 1, 108, 123–71, 182–217

constitutional democracy. *See* democratic republic

Index

courage, 177

COVID-19. *See* disease prevention

critical thinking, ix, 67, 104, 124. *See also* reason

Deism, 25–26

demagoguery, 63, 67, 91, 95, 103

democratic republics, 3, 4, 5, 12, 13, 37, 49, 50, 57, 73, 79–89, 97–105, 180

direct democracies, 3, 4, 81, 83, 89–91, 103, 104

disease prevention, 63–64

Eisenhower, Dwight D., 6, 111, 113, 145, 149, 173, 192–96, 214, 216, 217

Engels, Friedrich, 6, 108–9, 182–86

epistocracy, 91–94, 103

Erastianism, 95, 96

ethics, vii, ix, 1, 4–5, 22, 25, 51, 61, 65, 72, 74, 78–79, 91, 92, 93, 101, 103–4, 105, 176–81

fallacies, 13. *See also* reason

fascism, 96, 182

forms of government, 74–105

Franklin, Benjamin, 25–26

Galston, William A., 244n2 (epilogue)

Hamilton, Alexander, 40–42, 48, 86

Hitler, Adolph, 20, 21, 67, 68

Hobbes, Thomas, 96, 118

ideology, 37, 77, 95, 103, 105, 123, 124, 172, 186, 191

January 6, 2021 insurrection, 38

Jaquiesse, 93

Jay, John, 40

Jefferson, Thomas, 25, 33–34, 80–81, 86, 228n9 (chap. 4)

Kennedy, John F., 5, 6, 106-8, 125–75, 195–217, 234n4 (chap. 5)

Index

Kennedy, Robert F., 129, 137, 144, 145, 148, 156, 168, 170, 209, 237n45 (chap. 5)

Khrushchev, Nikita, 5, 106–7, 110–75, 189–217

Lenin, Vladimir, 6, 109–10, 186–89

Lincoln, Abraham, iv

Locke, John, 34, 51–53, 55, 185

Madison, James, iv, 40, 43, 74, 82–83

Marx, Karl, 6, 108–9, 183–86

McNamara, Robert, 106–75, 195–217

meritocracy. *See* epistocracy

Mikoyan, Anastas, 118, 119, 121

minarchism, 5, 10, 72–73

Montesquieu, Charles Secondat, Baron de, 78–79

Mussolini, Benito, 67

Nazism, 2, 21, 28, 68, 96, 176

oligarchy, 94–95

pandemics. *See* disease prevention

Plato, 92–93, 177, 230nn24–25 (chap. 4)

Putin, Vladimir, 21, 69–70, 182, 189

Rand, Ayn, 5, 10, 72–73

rationality. *See* reason

reason, iii, iv, viii, ix, 4, 5, 22, 24, 25, 26, 51, 52, 57, 60, 61, 62, 63, 65, 67, 69, 71, 74, 75, 91, 102, 104, 105, 107, 108, 121, 123, 124, 125, 172–81, 234n4 (chap. 5)

religion, 1, 24, 33, 36–37, 45, 64, 66, 76–79, 85, 89–90, 96–97, 123

representative democracy. *See* democratic republic

rights, individual, 23–40

Roosevelt, Franklin D., 108, 234n4 (chap. 5)

Rusk, Dean, 106–75, 195–217

Shakespeare, William, 177

Index

Smith, Adam, 77–78

Social Darwinism, 86

Socrates, 48, 74, 89–90, 92, 97

Stalin, Joseph, 67, 93, 96, 110, 120, 189

Strauss, Leo, 230nn24–25 (chap. 4)

theocracy, 78, 79, 95, 96

totalitarianism, 2, 6, 37, 60, 67, 93, 95–96, 110, 121, 124, 172, 181, 182, 189, 197

Trump, Donald J., 63, 68, 70, 71, 95, 99–100, 102

Virtue. *See* ethics

Weber, Max, 7, 179

ABOUT THE AUTHOR

Alan E. Johnson is an independent philosopher, historian, political scientist, and legal scholar. He is the author of *Free Will and Human Life*; *Reason and Human Ethics*; *Reason and Human Government*; *The First American Founder: Roger Williams and Freedom of Conscience*; *The Electoral College: Failures of Original Intent and Proposed Constitutional and Statutory Changes for Direct Popular Vote*, second edition; and other publications in the fields of philosophy, history, law, and political science.

He holds an AB (political science) and an AM (humanities—philosophy and history) from the University of Chicago and a JD from Cleveland State University College of Law. He retired in 2012 from a long career as an attorney in which he focused primarily, though not exclusively, on constitutional and public law litigation.